The Koine Conversation
A Grammar and Exegetical Guide to the New Testament

Paul Kenneth Hubbard

The Koine Conversation

Contents

Preface

In the preface of the first edition of James Hewett's very valuable Greek grammar, *New Testament Greek*, he sets forth his strategy: "Forms and vocabulary are introduced at a rate such that by the end of two semesters, the student will have covered all the grammar and vocabulary necessary to enter basic exegesis courses." This grammar for Koine Greek, *The Koine Conversation*, is designed to get the student more quickly immersed in the text. Thus, we begin doing translation work after two *weeks*. Our methodology was inspired by C. S. Lewis' encounter with learning Greek under his tutor, "The Great Knock" (W.T. Kirkpatrick). Kirkpatrick gave Lewis a manuscript of the Iliad and a Greek dictionary and simply began reading.

In Hewett's second edition, he adds a much-needed discussion about meaning.[1] And he clearly specifies that "some of the meaning contained in an utterance is grammatical meaning."[2] Secondly, there is "lexical meaning," Hewett says. These are general meanings which have become attached to a particular word in a particular language.[3] But he goes no further. The premise of this grammar is that meaning is not locked up in individual words and it is definitely not locked up in the nuances of grammar. Meaning resides *in the sentence*.

In truth, meaning begins in the mind of the writer as a sentence, not isolated word fragments. The written or spoken sentence is his attempt to express that meaning. Even if he were writing or speaking in *broken* English, we could still make allowances for this. Thus, even though the sentence might be crude, and even grammatically faulty, the intended meaning could still be crystal clear. And of course, we must go still further and say that the sentence derives much of its meaning from the larger conversation, the genre and the sitz im leben ("situation in life") in which it is embedded – whether it is a short Gospel pericope[4] or an extended theological argument in Romans or Hebrews.

The New Testament is itself a conversation – an apostolic conversation. And this implies that the conversation is not just between these authors and their readers, but also between *themselves*. This means that if we know that one author influenced another, we will better understand what he is saying to us and perhaps even why he is saying it. For example, the Synoptic Gospel is essentially a genre of writing, to which at least three authors, Matthew, Mark and Luke conform, and the material is

---

[1] Hewett, Chapter 2.
[2] Ibid., 13.
[3] Ibid., 14.
[4] Formed from "cut" and "around", "pericope" has become a formal term of biblical criticism which designates a short vignette which seems to stand alone as a literary unit.

so similar in construction that it is certain that there is literary interaction between these three men. Thus, wherever possible, this grammar will present comparisons between authors – how is their expression the same? How is it different?

Each author is, indeed, different. He not only has his own place in the apostolic conversation – influencing others, perhaps, perhaps being influenced by others – but he also has his own theological and philosophical agenda, he has his own spirituality and psychology and he has his own personality, which together also results in his own *style*. These factors must all be taken into account as we see them, in order to more fully understand what each author is trying to say.[5]

Language is inherently ambiguous and imprecise. A sentence is not like a mathematical formula which denotes a discreet and precise mathematical form. A sentence is something between math and music; although its medium and mode is intrinsically ambiguous and ambivalent, it can convey complex meaning to the mind with considerable precision. Just as complex words are made up of many overlapping denotations and connotations, connected with strange etymological bonds, forming a molecule of potential meaning (see Figure 1 below), so a sentence achieves a significantly higher level of sophistication by forming distinct and actual syntactical, compound substances with these 'meaning molecules.' If a picture is worth of thousand words, a sentence brings that picture to life.

Language is much more like chemistry than it is math. In chemistry, most of the elements of the periodic table are very open to reconfiguration at a very low level and thus an astonishing number of molecular configurations are possible. And in many cases, the slightest variation at even the most fundamental levels – say between H^2O and H^2O^2, yields startling differences in physical behavior. And so it is with words and the sentences they form.

This recombinant potential of words is the reason why it so important to think about how each author uses each word in each configuration. Because a molecule will behave much differently as it is combined with other molecules to form compounds – many of which are very sophisticated. We must constantly be searching for the linguistic chemistry of each author and the linguistic chemistry of the New Testament corpus itself.

As in music, if we know the author of a work, we will also have some idea of how the work is to be performed on our instruments. Likewise, if we pay attention to matters of genre, editorial agenda and style, we will have a much better idea of what

---

[5] Some conservative/fundamentalist Evangelicals believe that the special inspiration of the Holy Spirit has washed out all these factors, making them irrelevant. This is not true. There is simply no evidence of this in these materials.

each author is attempting to say. In all cases, we will be asking ourselves – not 'what does this sentence mean?' - but what does the author *mean to say* in this sentence? The sentence cannot be divorced from the author. We must always try to understand: what is the *intent* of the author? And in time, we begin to know what is being said, why it is being said, how it is being said and by whom it is being said. It might even become possible to say: I *know* this author.

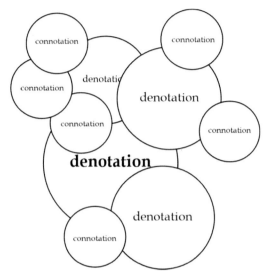

Figure 1. The Word Meaning Molecular Structure

In this grammar we will not spend too much time on how words are pronounced. As Hewett says, we do not know exactly how Greek words were pronounced in New Testament times.[6] Thus, we will merely put forth the standard *theory* of how they might have been pronounced. Since pronunciation will only be used during classroom translation exercises and within our own minds as we read, this should not greatly concern us.

So this grammar, technically, is not so much a grammar as it is a study guide of the Koine conversation that we call the New Testament. The objective is not to speak or write Koine. The objective is to translate the Koine New Testament. Just this one document; nothing more, nothing less. This corpus contains only a little less than 140,000 words – which is comparable to a medium sized, modern novel. But much of this material is repetitive. The vocabulary of the three Synoptic Gospels is necessarily redundant, and though John is much different in style, he also necessarily uses many of the same words to tell the Gospel story. Likewise, the Johannine corpus uses simple, repetitive language and his vocabulary remains essentially stable, even when he switches genres in his epistles and in his Revelation.

---

[6] Hewett, 1.

This is also true of the Pauline corpus. Paul writes simply and fairly repetitively since he is essentially explaining the same theology to different churches. The simplicity of these writings can be seen by analyzing the "significant word vocabulary;" that is, words that are used 35 times or less. Many of the rest are common, easily remembered words, like conjunctions, pronouns and articles. Matthew, for example, uses 18,382 words, but only 1,325 are used 35 times or less. This is about 7% of Matthew's vocabulary. Luke's more sophisticated Greek is not much more complicated, at 8%. Romans, which employs more technical words to express theological ideas, is not much more - 13%. Hebrews' more sophisticated argument tops the list at almost 20%.

When all is said, the New Testament writers only use less than 6000 words to accomplish their literary mission. English has 259,000 words. Therefore, a mere high school fluency with Greek is all that is required to begin making good sense out of the sentences that we see.

Most grammars of most language courses begin by dwelling exclusively upon grammar constructs – declensions, conjugations, parsing, linguistic theory, etc. This is predicated upon the assumption that the student will be encountering a wide range of literature in his new language. But the Greek New Testament[7] is fixed. The manuscript has been stabilized by generations of scholars and many scholarly committees have already produced fine translations of what has been said in this material. Thus, in this grammar, the student of the New Testament will be learning how other translators have translated this manuscript, and they will be introduced to the possibility and the opportunity of making their own. And this is a relevant and necessary project because the modern translator has a distinct advantage over past translational scholarship.

There are now computer programs that allow the student to search the Koine manuscript by Strong's number.[8] This changes everything. These programs have been developed only a decade and a half ago, and the student can now formulate his own "internal lexicon;" that is, instead of consulting lexicons which have indexes of generalized, static meanings from a great variety of sources, the student can search for every occurrence of a word in the *author's* corpus in order to see, from context, what the author means when *he* uses a word. Furthermore, this can be compared or contrasted to the way other authors in the New Testament materials use the word. Thus an "internal lexicon" can be generated that more precisely defines what it is that the author is saying.

---

[7] Hereafter abbreviated: GNT. (Stuttgart : Deutsche Bibelgesellschaft, American Bible Society, United Bible Societies, 2014).

[8] Various programs enable searches by word root and even searches into the LXX manuscripts.

In the final analysis, the Greek New Testament is an "open book test," concerning the making of our own translation. And with the resources that are now easily accessible to every student, it is simply a matter of time before a superior translation can be produced. Indeed, the tools that we will discuss in this guide put an intelligent and hardworking student in the scholar/translator class. The only difference is that the student cannot arrive at conclusions as fast as conventional scholars.

To this must be added the sheer *perspicuity* of the apostolic conversation with which we have to deal. The New Testament claims for itself an unusual clarity and directness; it is a body of literature that has been specifically developed for the *oi polloi* – the man on the street. The ordinary man. Not the elitist. Not the scholar. Not the gnostic seer that must break a secret code to elicit meaning. In his gospel, the Apostle John claims that the truth and understandability of the witness of Christ is as direct and plain and, in fact, inescapable as light itself. Indeed, a primary audience for the kingdom of the New Testament is children.[9]

Yet the modern religious establishment speaks much about "interpretation" by theological technicians as if this were a completely different step taken *after* mere, mechanistic translation occurs. But in fact, "interpretation" is part of the translation of *every* word. Translation cannot happen unless we know, or suspect, what it is that the author is trying to say – whether he is writing ordinary dialogue or making a theological point. The proper sense of every word is always subject to the contextual clues that the author himself includes to guide the reader in understanding the sense that he intends. This is particularly true on the low level of irony, for example. If translation were merely the mathematical substitution of words with absolute meanings from one language to another, there would never be such a literary phenomenon. This is why it is nearly impossible to write an artificial intelligence program that can recognize irony.[10]

If an author intends irony, he will give sufficient contextual clues to enable a reader to understand what is going on. Paul says: "forgive me this wrong." But he is not asking for forgiveness.[11] Consider too the meeting between Jesus and Martha just before Lazarus is raised. The atmosphere is truly super-charged with emotional

---

[9] Matthew 18:2-4; 21:16.

[10] You can often see this too when a layman, who is unfamiliar with the text, reads a passage in a public service of worship. Unless the text is very simplistic, the *sense* of what is being said will be almost unintelligible; that is, if the author has laid anything - even if it be the slightest bit of sophistication - "between the lines," the reader will miss it. He will read every word correctly, but he will not understand – and the audience will not understand what he has read.

[11] *For what is it wherein ye were inferior to other churches, except it be that I myself was not burdensome to you? forgive me this wrong.* 2nd Corinthians 12:13. (KJV) Unless specified, all quotations will be from the KJV; all quotations from the Greek will use the text of the *OnLineBible* program.

drama. To miss this is an act of bad translation; it is an act of simply not listening to what John is doing. It is John, as the editor, who is creating this dramatic catharsis. The more mechanistically we approach the text, the less likely we will be to understand this and to give a proper literary rendering.

There are, essentially, no words in this Koine conversation which mean "interpret." There are only words for "translate." There is a place where Phillip helps the Ethiopian Eunuch to *understand* what Isaiah is saying. And there is a place where Peter says that there are some things in Paul's writings that are hard to understand. But these situations have nothing to do with our modern concept of "interpreting." It is one thing to miss an irony that Paul intends. But then, we must try to understand why he is using irony. After we have understood the proper literary sense of what he is saying, we ask ourselves: what is the proper philosophical and theological sense of what he is saying?

When modern exegetes speak of "interpreting," they imply that they are *brokering* meaning to us which would otherwise be obscure. They say that unless we adopt a particular religious, existential mindset, that the literary, philosophical and theological sense of what is being said will be completely insensible to the ordinary reader.[12] This runs completely counter to the mindset of the authors of the New Testament. Both Jesus and John very directly assert that beyond the internal witness of the Holy Spirit within the soul, their words need no human interpreter.

Consider Luke's matter-of-fact comments concerning the perspicuity of what he writes:

Forasmuch as many have taken in hand to set forth in order a declaration of those things which are most surely believed among us, Even as they delivered them unto us, which from the beginning were eyewitnesses, and ministers of the word; It seemed good to me also, having had perfect understanding of all things from the very first, to write unto thee in order, most excellent Theophilus, That thou mightest know the certainty of those things, wherein thou hast been instructed.

Thus, Luke is not interpreting history; he is making a confession. The truth is that the historical and theological material that these authors are presenting to us is so

---

[12] Some even claim that the philosophical and theological sense of what these men are saying is illogical – illogical in the ordinary sense of the word. And to buttress this position, Paul's first letter to the Corinthian Church is quoted: *Now we have received, not the spirit of the world, but the spirit which is of God; that we might know the things that are freely given to us of God. Which things also we speak, not in the words which man's wisdom teacheth, but which the Holy Ghost teacheth; comparing spiritual things with spiritual. But the natural man receiveth not the things of the Spirit of God: for they are foolishness unto him: neither can he know them, because they are spiritually discerned.* Therefore, it is maintained, a special class of religious existentialists must be consulted to obtain even the most rudimentary "interpretation" of what is being said.

straitforward, we could do the same in broken English, without any emphasis on scholarly precision - and achieve the same results. This is what perspicuity means.

This Koine Conversation, part grammar, part study guide, is designed to forge an enduring relationship between the student of the Word and the Koine Greek of the New Testament materials. Because Koine is the language in which the Holy Spirit has engaged the world in conversation with God – and His only begotten Son. It could have been any language. But it was Koine. This textbook will cover the basics of working with Koine – its syntax and its figures of speech, and how these elements apply to the practical work of understanding the apostolic conversation of the New Testament materials. This textbook will also give examples of some of the tools that are available to facilitate working with the Koine, and some suggested methodologies of applying those tools as an essential part of a Church leader's personal life of prayer, study, teaching or preaching of the word of God to the modern, multi-lingual world.

Introduction

In olden days, when peoples were conquered, they were not only dispossessed of their land – they were dispossessed of their language. The peasant's connection with the land was visceral and spiritual, independent of the tax rate or the government in power. But the peasant's connection with all of reality was mediated by his language. Change that, and everything else changed. Sometimes the required transition to the conquering language was effected by massive resettlements of the people deep into the bowels of the host nation, as in the case of the deportation of Judah to Babylon. Sometimes massive numbers of people from the host nation were brought in, as in the case of the resettlement of Samaria. Conquerors understood that complete subjugation meant replacing the indigenous language. And this is because the very ethos of a civilization is bound up in its language.

In the case of the New Testament materials, we have a complex language situation. The lingua franca is Koine Greek. The language of the ruling elite, essentially ignored in these materials, is Latin. Aramaic and also Hebrew are still important to the Jews. But when all the discussions about what language Jesus spoke are done, the fact remains that all four gospellers, two of which were intimate associates with Jesus, wrote their documents in Koine Greek. And they are filled with the dialogues of Jesus. Additionally, all Old Testament quotations appear to be coming from the Greek translations, which are collectively referred to as the Septuagint.

Paul's revelation from Jesus,[1] and his first sermons,[2] begin in the "Hebrew tongue," but all his letters are nevertheless written in Koine. John's apocalyptic dialogue with Jesus is also recorded in Koine. At first, Matthew probably wrote his presentation of Christ in Aramaic, but then, apparently, thought better of this and rewrote his Gospel in Koine.[3] Since the Greek Matthew shows no sign of being a translation of the Aramaic, there is a strong presumption that at some point Matthew becomes convinced that the conversation of Christ is not a parochial dialogue within an idiomatic culture, but a conversation intended for both the Jew and for all the nations (παντα τα εθνη[4]). The New Testament materials are written in the universal language of the current empire. Their intended audience, therefore, is the world.

For us, as pastors and teachers, the benefit of working with Koine is this commonality. But there is yet another benefit. Because, as we have said, Koine represents a "vulgar tongue," having descended to the people from the Attic Greek, it is a relatively "fresh" language, vibrant, earthy and unsophisticated. For example,

---

[1] Acts 26:14.

[2] Acts 21:20.

[3] See the discussion in Paul Kenneth Hubbard, *The Jonas Genre* (St Andrew's Publishing, 2009), 23ff.

[4] As in the "great commission" verbiage of Matthew 28:19.

9

though Luke's style is quite artistic, generally speaking, the Koine as employed by the New Testament men carries relatively little cultural baggage. Because of its relative freshness, there are very few problems with "dead" or dying metaphors. Because of its commonality, there is very little jargon, cliché, colloquialism or conceit that the translator must deal with. The language is full of the simple life and energy of the market place, the fields - the docks. Many amateur attempts at biblical criticism confuse the *style* of Mark with this very vulgarity of the language itself.

Generally, Koine's editorial and narrative language is no more sophisticated than a high school geography book. Sometimes the language becomes difficult to follow, but the difficulty is very often caused not by the language, which remains simple, but by the ideas, and sometimes the psychology that we are not familiar with. For example, John says that Jesus wept. Why? The answer must be derived almost entirely from context. The supporting editorial words εμβριμαομαι and ταρασσω do not easily resolve the issue. We must understand the characters and the dialogue before we can understand why Jesus wept. In 2nd Corinthians 12:16 Paul says: *But be it so, I did not burden you: nevertheless, being crafty, I caught you with guile* (δολος). All other uses of this word in the New Testament give it a very strong connotation of wickedness, including Paul's, so it is likely that a rare connotation is here being employed. Or else, this is mere irony. But irony is uncharacteristic of Paul's expression. Nevertheless: we must explain: what is he talking about?

Yes, Koine is common and simple. And yes, there are things that are hard to understand (δυσνοητα[5]), but for those things, we have the doctors of the church to help us. And we have Paul's promise that if in our understanding we be "otherwise minded," God himself will reveal these things to us.[6] John is emphatic about this point. He says that our "anointing" in the spirit of Christ will preserve us from the seductions of worldly religion because it will teach us concerning all things (χρισμα διδασκει υμας περι παντων[7]).

The writers of the New Testament materials very strongly imply that our central problem in receiving their words will not lie in the language. The central problem in receiving the incarnate word will lie within us. Paul says: *For now we see through a glass, darkly; but then face to face.*[8] But if we closely examine why this is so, we will find that this refers not to any intrinsic weakness in the incarnation of the word into the language of men. It refers to <u>our</u> weakness. Jesus says: *The light of the body is the eye: if therefore thine eye be single, thy whole body shall be full of light. But if thine eye be evil, thy whole body shall be full of darkness.*[9] The problem is not with the light. The

---

[5] 2nd Peter 3:16.
[6] Philippians 3:15.
[7] 1st John 2:27.
[8] 1st Corinthians 13:12.
[9] Matthew 6:22-23.

problem is with the eye through which it must pass. The central, Synoptic parable of the Sower says that the seed sown is the very word of God - without sin. There is nothing wrong with this seed. It is the soil of our souls, the very womb of the mind - that is the problem. At best we are an "at risk" pregnancy. And worse, we might be infertile.

In one sense, because of the fall of our Father Adam, we have all been born blind. But in another sense, we are morally complicit in our own blindness. In Romans, Paul reasons that even though God himself illuminates the eternal verities within men's souls, even as men begin to see God's eternal power and Godhead, they refuse to glorify God as God. They are not thankful for the light, but *return* to their vain imaginations, and their foolish heart is darkened.[10] John makes an almost identical argument. John does not allow the basic culpability of man to come to rest upon the universal blindness that has descended upon the human race. He says that the light comes to every man that opens the womb.[11] Yet some men nevertheless *choose* blindness: *And this is the condemnation, that light is come into the world, and men loved darkness rather than light, because their deeds were evil. For every one that doeth evil hateth the light, neither cometh to the light, lest his deeds should be reproved. But he that doeth truth cometh to the light, that his deeds may be made manifest, that they are wrought in God.*[12]

Jesus asked the infirm man at the pool of Bethesda: θελεις υγιης γενεσθαι (do you *want* to become whole?) There is here evidence that this man was, in some deep psychological sense, still embracing his infirmity. Mark adroitly brings out this very idea in the epileptic boy pericope. Mark makes it clear that the problem is not with Jesus' power. The problem is with the father's *belief* in Jesus' power. Mark has Jesus cutting to the heart of the real problem. Suddenly the man blurts out the fact that Jesus has hit his mark: *Lord, I believe; help thou mine unbelief!*

Mark therefore completes the argument that Paul has begun. Though the initial "conversion" to the Gospel can be seen as the falling away of scales from the eyes, the reality of complete conversion, as illustrated by the career of Peter, is that it takes a lifetime before the fullest possible sight is restored. Mark's unique pericope about the blind man of Bethesda illustrates this very thing – a gradual healing of blindness. Even after Jesus anoints the blind man with his own spit, there is still a problem: *And he took the blind man by the hand, and led him out of the town; and when he had spit on his eyes, and put his hands upon him, he asked him if he saw ought. And he looked up, and said, I see men as trees, walking.*[13]

---

[10] Romans 1:18-25.
[11] John 1:9 *That was the true Light, which lighteth every man that cometh into the world.*
[12] John 3:19-21.
[13] Mark 8:23-24.

Even Paul admits that his own conversion is not complete: *Not as though I had already attained, either were already perfect: but I follow after, if that I may apprehend that for which also I am apprehended of Christ Jesus* (διωκω δε ει και καταλαβω εφ ω και κατεληφθην υπο του χριστου ιησου[14]). In this sense, Paul is completing an unfinished conversation of the Song of Solomon: *I opened to my beloved; but my beloved had withdrawn himself.*[15] Paul is saying that however much it might seem to *us* that we are diligently searching for the mind of Christ in the Church and in her founding documents, we are merely playing into the hands of the Beloved. John is also very clear about this. He says that we do not come to the light, the light comes to us.[16] If we but labor to enter into that rest (σπουδασωμεν ουν εισελθειν εις εκεινην την καταπαυσιν[17]) and adopt the typological submissiveness of Mary: *let it be to me according to your* word (γενοιτο μοι κατα το ρημα σου[18]), the daystar will, of its own, rise in our hearts.[19]

The Koine Conversation, then, cannot be merely an academic exercise. How could it be? Just as the apostles found themselves in the presence of the Son of the living God, so we find ourselves in the presence of the living word. What we believe about language in general will determine how we approach the Koine. For example, the modern world, in which we must live and move and have our being, is not so much "post-Christian" as it is *post-language*. The language theories of Bertrand Russell, Ludwig Wittgenstein and B.F. Skinner are very insistent that language is an invention of man. But the men of the New Testament are equally insistent that human language, like the ear, tongue, voice box and the entire dental apparatus, is the creation of God. He is not learning to speak in our language, we are learning to speak in his.[20] We have no language apart from him.

The Psalmist claims that the created order pours forth language about God's glory.[21] The New Testament authors make it clear that this is not a hyperbolic figure of speech. The Apostle Paul strongly reiterates the language theory of the psalmist: *For the invisible things of him from the creation of the world are clearly seen, being understood by the things that are made, even his eternal power and Godhead.*[22] The categories and differentiations of creation were formed by God himself; they are not projected upon the face of chaos by human existentialism. We do not cobble together fragile, faulty

---

[14] Philippians 3:12.

[15] Song of Solomon 5:6.

[16] John 1:5,9.

[17] Hebrews 4:11.

[18] Luke 1:38.

[19] φωσφορος ανατειλη εν ταις καρδιαις υμων (2nd Peter 1:19).

[20] A significant modern departure from humanistic language theories is the work of Jean Piaget. His studies very strongly suggest that the child gives evidence of having pre-positioned language categories, even before he learns to speak in a human dialect.

[21] Psalm 19:1-3.

[22] Romans 1:20.

analogies to speak of God. He has already spoken to us by pressing down the very image of his character[23] upon the clay of creation.[24]

But more than this is the stunning claim by the New Testament writers, especially in Colossians, John and Hebrews, that Christ is the <u>intersection</u> between God and man in <u>every area of creation</u>. And this is because it was *by him … all things* [were] *created, that are in heaven, and that are in earth, visible and invisible, whether they be thrones, or dominions, or principalities, or powers: all things were created by him, and for him: And he is before all things, and by him all things consist.*[25] Hebrews says that creation was *spoken* into existence by the word of God.[26]

John places the keystone in this line of argumentation: <u>Christ</u> is that word. Once this idea is in place, we have the key to the language theory of the apostles. In Luke, Christ tells Satan that *man shall not live by bread alone, but by every word of God.*[27] John makes it clear that that Christ is that bread: *I am that bread of life.*[28] Note closely this construction. John here is not primarily making a metaphor between physical bread and spiritual words. How could it be? Physical bread itself is spoken by God into existence. We will soon learn in John that the real contrast between ordinary bread and Christ is that one is perishable; the other is imperishable.

Some claim that God can speak - but in a sacred language which only Church officials can understand. Some claim that God can speak, but "lisping" a sacred language, which only systematic theologians can understand. Some claim that God can speak, but in religious myths which only liberally-minded scholars can understand.[29] But when the ordinary man reads the New Testament materials he sees that there is nothing in them about what God cannot communicate. He sees that everywhere there is a flush of what God *can* communicate. And that communication is Christ. Because Christ is the word of God. If there is merely the appearance of communication between God and man, then we have a species of linguistic docetism.[30]

---

[23] The essence of this expression; "pressing down his image of his character" is perfectly captured in *Hebrews*, in which it said that Jesus is the very stamp of his character: χαρακτηρ της υποστασεως αυτου.

[24] κτισις.

[25] Colossians 1:16-17.

[26] Hebrews 11:3 *Through faith we understand that the worlds were framed by the word of God.*

[27] Luke 4:4.

[28] John 6:48.

[29] The list can go on and on; for example, God can speak, but only in an irrational language that the anti-intellectual, "born again" fundamentalist can understand. God can speak, but only with a circular, inaccessible logic that only the "elect" can understand.

[30] This is the belief that Christ only *seemed* to take upon himself human form – that this was mere illusion.

Just as Jesus was united to ordinary flesh, so it is has been claimed that the New Testament materials are the incarnation of the Holy Spirit. As such, their form is inseparable from their spirit. This is to claim no more than that this incarnation is of the same *kind* (γενος) as the incarnation of Christ - his human form is, since the incarnation, inseparable from his spirit. As a corollary, the New Testament materials are the conjugation of human minds and the spirit of Christ, yet without sin. But just as the body of Christ is a complex organism, so too are the New Testament documents. Pieces cannot be severed from the body which gives them life.[31] As Christ's body is hierarchically arranged, so too are the New Testament documents hierarchically arranged. As Christ came in the weakness of human flesh, so God fully employs the weaknesses of human ordinariness in order to achieve extraordinary precision in expression of his word. God says *precisely* what he intends through human imprecision.

We have said that though Koine is common and simple, the central problem in understanding Koine lies deep within souls that have become habituated to darkness. And though we could say more, we are here saying nothing more than what Plato had said about men in a darkened cave who begin to turn to the light behind the shadows. We are here saying nothing more than the fact that this is not just a purely academic matter. Bright light hurts. The apostles do say more. They tell us *why* the light hurts. They tell us why repentance hurts, and they tell us why conversion is sometimes such a slow process.

Mark elaborates at least three ideas: the cares of this world, the deceitfulness of riches, and the lusts of other things.[32] The Synoptics give a specific example: we love the praise of men more than the praise of God. And this does not just apply to "those other guys" to which John refers: *For they loved the praise of men more than the praise of God.*[33] The Synoptics insist that <u>all</u> men are guilty of this by making Peter's equivocating loyalty typological of everyman, who is especially guilty of this very

---

[31] We normally encounter this idea under the rubric of not taking a "verse" out of context. But as it embodies Paul's metaphor of the indivisible nature of the body in 1st Corinthians 12, this would include all attempts to isolate theological truth from the body in which it is placed. For example, this applies perhaps by calling a "book" "canonical" (or uncanonical) without sufficient reference to the "canonical" (if such a word must be used) *corpus* in which it resides. In our study of the New Testament corpus, we shall see why this is so important, especially in consideration of a book like James, which Martin Luther once called an "epistle of straw." (Luther had a similarly low view of Esther, Hebrews, Jude, and Revelation.) Our role as ministers and educators is not to make pontifical statements about which books are "canonical" and which are not. God has already spoken through the catholic church about this. Our role is to understand how each part of the canon is related to the canonical corpus in which it resides.

[32] Mark 4:19.

[33] John 12:43.

thing.[34] John summarizes the situation: men love the cloak of darkness, because it is a congenial covering for the sweetness of sin.[35]

Again, although this language study is an academic exercise, it can never be *merely* an academic exercise. Not just because the very act of language is itself to enter into the very presence of Christ - but because the *specific* words of Christ have become incarnated into a *specific* language. When we enter into the presence of the Koine that the apostles employ, we enter into the very presence of the historical Christ.

This is why what we believe about language in general will determine how we approach the apostolic words of Christ which have become incarnate in the Koine. When we come into contact with this Koine conversation, we come into direct contact with Christ. What we believe about the nature of that contact will directly determine what is possible by means of that contact. Will we merely foist our own subconscious philosophical and religious presuppositions upon this *mere* academic exercise? We dare not. Concerning the incarnation, we have the intersection of God and man; therefore, our *contact* with that which has been incarnate is both physical and spiritual. If we believe that Christ was merely a physical phenomenon – an ordinary reed shaken by the winds of historical cause and effect, we are merely materialists, no matter how magical we insist was his super-sensory contact with the divine. If we believe that Christ was purely spiritual and did not really conjoin himself with our flesh and our blood and our literature, we become docetists,[36] no matter how clever we insist the illusion might have been.

We believe that just as Christ became fully physical in the person of Jesus, so the New Testament materials are a fully physical manifestation of the Spirit of Christ. Modern theological liberals believe that the connection between the spiritual and the materials themselves is purely accidental; that is, our contact with God is as tangential here as our contact through any other "inspired," human literature. Modern Fundamentalists believe that the New Testament materials are so holy in their inspiration that they never really come into contact with any physical aspect of *mere* literature at all. Stripped of all physical landmarks, the ordinary *propositional content* of these documents is lost in a sea of fundamentalist existentialism. And in both cases, the liberal and the fundamentalist hermeneutic - the Jesus which emerges has no contact with history, and looks very much like a folksy presuppositional projection which these interpretive communities have brought to these materials in the first place.

---

[34] Matthew 16:23. But especially Peter's betrayal in the courtyard.
[35] John 3:19.
[36] Again, Docetism, from the Greek word δοκειν, which means "to seem," was an early Christian heresy that maintained that Christ did not truly incarnate himself into human flesh, but merely took on the appearance of human flesh. He was a kind of phantasm that did not tire, did not suffer, and did not die. These phenomena too were only appearances.

If we believe these things, all the proficiency in Koine in all Christendom will not help us to understand what the men of the New Testament materials are saying. But if we become as ordinary children, that is, if we drop our super-sophisticated theories about how "inspiration" works and approach this Koine conversation by considering, in progressive order, the physical, literary processes by which it is constructed, we will, almost effortlessly - with the simplicity of a child - find ourselves in the very presence of the Jesus of history, the holy grail of modern biblical criticism. This is essential. We must first discover the physical literary forms - the physical words, the basics of epistemology and presuppositions, genre, authorship, sitz im leben, etc. And this we will do, if God permit.

Koine is a dead language; therefore, this language text will be different from most Greek grammar books. And this is because most Greek grammars proceed as if the global objective were to make the student proficient in expressing himself in Koine Greek – creating new literature in Koine or reading extra-Biblical literature that has been written in Koine. This is not our objective. It is sometimes said that Latin is a "dead" language, and is thus compared with the Koine. But this is not true. Latin dwarfs Koine in its universality and in the very breadth of material that has been written in it.

And even if it could be said that Latin is dead - it has died such a recent death in our civilization that we half expect that it might sit up in some academic morgue and ask; "where have I been?" So much of the life of our own civilization has been bound up in Latin that it can never really be said that it is completely dead, so long as our civilization endures. But the Koine is in the pluperfect tense. It is an action that has been completed once for all in the past. We will thus not be asking questions like: "how would I express myself in Koine?" Or: "how would Josephus express himself in Koine?" Rather, we will confine ourselves almost entirely[37] to the question: "how did the men of the New Testament materials express *themselves* in Koine?"

The study of Koine is also different from the study of other languages in another important respect. Although you will find the secular lexicons to support it, and you will find a significant body of illuminating literature; albeit cognates derived from a polyglot of patristic, Septuagint or other Greek literature - for all practical purposes, the New Testament corpus stands as a singular obelisk;[38] <u>therefore, much of the longitudinal scope of its words must be determined mostly from cues that are carried in its own internal lexicon.</u>

---

[37] Ultimately we should be able to enter this corpus with our own theological jargon, to see if it is consistent or not consistent with its language.

[38] See especially Walter Bauer's discussion, which begins on pg. ix of *A Greek-English Lexicon of the New Testament and other early Christian Literature*, 2ⁿᵈ edition, University of Chicago, © 1979.

From time to time, we will make reference to the external Greek lexicons, especially for words that are used only once or twice in our corpus, but a book of meanings derived from hundreds of years of use of several literary stages of the Greek, will resolve only the most basic etymological questions. Therefore, this grammar will concentrate almost exclusively on the internal, contextual clues as to how each author uses a particular word.

Philologically and philosophically, this text will also depart from conventional grammars in its basic approach to learning language. You will often hear, in the conventional grammars, that the chief impediment to learning the Greek is that the student does not know English. We believe that this is an impediment only if the goal is, first, to dynamically sift the Greek through the semantic categories of English. But this is not the goal. The goal is not to learn how to make a "dynamic equivalent" translation of the Greek into the language categories of English "on the fly" so to speak, in our own minds.

Take music, for example. When we learn an instrument, we first see the notes on the staff. Then we think (if we are English speaking) "this is an E♭." Then we think, "this is the fingering for an E♭." The goal of this course is to eliminate the intermediate step of rearranging what we see on the page into our parochial language categories before we admit what we see into our minds. The goal is to see the note on the page and then to immediately play that note <u>without any mental reference to what it might be called in our own language</u> (whether that language be English or Chinese). The goal is to think and understand, as much as it is possible, in the language categories of Koine (as employed by the men of the New Testament).[39]

We already know _the_ language categories (according to Piaget[40]) of thought itself. Socrates said the same thing. He said that you don't teach a man an eternal verity like geometry; you merely catalyze a man's ability to articulate in his own mind, and to others, what he already knows. However beautiful (or ugly) Koine and English may be, they are transient conventions. But the dialogue of the spirit of Christ with every soul is eternal. As we progress through this language grammar, something familiar should emerge from our process. And that familiarity will have very little to do with how English teachers teach English. Or German teachers teach German. But it will have a great deal to do with how our mothers taught us her language.

Here is another example of what we mean by thinking primarily in the language categories of Koine. In conventional grammars, when we first encounter the Greek

---

[39] Of course, this is an impossible goal. But it was necessary to be categorical in order to make the point that we must at least _try_ to think in Greek.

[40] See for example his: _The Child's Conception of the World_ (London: Routledge and Kegan Paul, Ltd., 1929).

sentence, we immediately proceed to rearrange the words in our own minds into their "proper" place. In one sense, this is essential, since the English is not inflected; that is, since it has no case endings, we cannot tell what is the subject and what is the direct object in the sentence except by internal clues, word arrangement - and a little intuition. Since the Greek, like so many other languages, is inflected, it is often immediately apparent what is the indirect object in a sentence and what mood[41] the verb is in.

Theoretically, then, you could jumble up all the Greek words, helter-skelter, and spill them out on the page and still be able to understand the gist of the sentence. But the Koine is not spilled out helter-skelter upon the page. The order of the Koine words, although not nearly as functional in determining syntax as in the English, is nevertheless an important semantic witness. Stated another way: <u>the order of the Koine sentence is the order that these semantic ideas occurred in the mind of the author who wrote it.</u> Word order in the Koine is therefore not meaningless, as many conventional translation techniques imply. If we are going to think in Greek, this is the first place to begin. We must say the sentence in our minds in the exact sequence that it occurred in the mind of its author, however awkward our English translation might sound. We must remember this. Our primary purpose here is not to make a translation into the English. Our primary purpose is to learn to think in the language categories of Apostolic Koine, so that we might listen more attentively to what is being said. Our first translation of the Koine is not for everyone else. It is for our own minds.

If we want to learn language like a child, we begin at the level of the individual word. Specifically, we must begin with the noun. And this is because Christ is the ultimate noun. But Christ is not just a word. Christ is *the* word. Christ is the intersection of the noun and the verb, which is briefly comprehended in the statement; "I am." John certainly does not shrink from this in his Gospel. Yet at the first two times this construction occurs in John, translators balk. For example, in Jesus' encounter with the woman at the well, John records Jesus as saying: λεγει αυτη ο ιησους εγω ειμι ο λαλων σοι[42] which is: *Jesus says to her: I am the one speaking to you.* The KJV and the NKJV both insert a pronoun and split the subject/verb (εγω ειμι) with the participial construction (ο λαλων) to relieve the pressure of John's wordplay: *Jesus saith unto her, I that speak unto thee am <u>he</u>.*

Likewise, when Jesus comes to the disciples, walking on the sea in the middle of the storm, John follows Matthew and writes: ο δε λεγει αυτοις εγω ειμι μη φοβεισθε (*But*

---

[41] For example, the "indicative" mood simply states the action of the verb. But by looking closely at the endings attached to the verb, we can also tell if the verb is in the "subjunctive" mood, which has an element of uncertainty (I *may* go) or the "imperative" mood; for example, the crowd calls out to Pilate <u>*crucify*</u> him!

[42] John 4:26.

he says to them: "I am. Fear not."), yet the KJV and the NKJV both insert a pronoun: *But he saith unto them, "it is I; be not afraid."* But when we come to the eighth chapter, John's confession is unavoidable. He has Jesus toying with the religious establishment. The Jews retort by ridiculing Jesus: *Thou art not yet fifty years old, and hast thou seen Abraham?* Jesus responds: αμην αμην λεγω υμιν πριν αβρααμ γενεσθαι εγω ειμι. (*Amen, Amen, I say to you: before Abraham began to be, I am*). Consistently, the Jews immediately take up stones to stone Jesus. Why do they do this? Whether Jesus was, at this point, speaking Aramaic or Greek, Jesus has come very close to appropriating the tetragrammaton (YHWH) for himself. And this is blasphemy.

Only Mark picks up on this. And he does it in a highly visible break from Matthew. When Jesus comes before the high priest, he is asked: *Art thou the Christ, the Son of the Blessed?* Matthew has Jesus respond with a cryptic: συ ειπας[43] (*thou sayest*). But then, what blasphemy has caused the high priest to tear his robes? Just because he quotes Daniel?[44] Mark explains. Instead of συ ειπας, Jesus says: εγω ειμι. This is why the high priest tears his robe. He tears his robe in Mark for the same reason that they seek to stone him in John – for blasphemy – for making himself equal with God.

John believes that it is through Christ that all human verb tenses descend. Christ is the *Alpha and Omega, the beginning and the ending, says the Lord, which is, and which was, and which is to come, the Almighty.*[45] And this is to be contrasted with the false Christ – *he that that was, and is not, and yet is.*[46] All the Apostolic confessions are emphatic – God is not a dead, immovable philosophical abstraction of Greek philosophy.[47] Nor is it "beneath him" to have contact with his creation.[48] God is a *living* God. And Christ is the Son of this living God.

God is both a righteous judge and a merciful father. Righteousness (δικαιοσυνη) and mercy (ελεος) are nouns; that is, eternal attributes of God, but bound up in them are all sorts of verbal ideas. The noun is inseparable from the verb. Hence, they descend

---

[43] Which is the same cryptic response Jesus gives to Judas when Judas asks: Is it me? Imagine if Jesus had said: Yes, Judas, it **is** you. But the Gospel writers make it clear that the Apostles were not following this cryptic conversation between Jesus and Judas.

[44] Matthew 26:64b *Hereafter shall ye see the Son of man sitting on the right hand of power, and coming in the clouds of heaven.* Daniel 7:13 *I saw in the night visions, and, behold, one like the Son of man came with the clouds of heaven, and came to the Ancient of days, and they brought him near before him.*

[45] Revelation 1:8.

[46] Revelation 17:8b.

[47] For example, in Parmenides, Plato seems to have Socrates scratching his head on this one. The reader knows that Socrates is right about the one and the many; nevertheless, Socrates can't prove it against Parmenides. The whole dialogue is an enigma in the Socratic corpus. But it begs for the answer that the Church now has – which is the Trinity.

[48] As so many of the Gnostics had maintained – positing a veritable phalanx of intermediary æons which shielded God from the contamination of finiteness, until we come to Marcion, who more logically maintained that YHWH himself was evil and that the physical creation itself was a bungled mess.

(καταβαινω) into creation in the person of Christ. As we embrace the eternal word, we ourselves become eternal. Jesus ascends and draws all things to himself.[49] Part of *Hebrews'* argument is to contrast the once for all nature of Jesus sacrifice with the constantly repeating sacrifices of Judaism: *For then must he often have suffered since the foundation of the world: but now once in the end of the world hath he appeared to put away sin by the sacrifice of himself. And as it is appointed unto men once to die, but after this the judgment: So Christ was once offered to bear the sins of many.*[50] Nevertheless, since Christ is the α and the ω, his sacrifice in space and time is an incarnation of an eternal sacrifice: ... *the Lamb slain from the foundation of the world.*[51]

Jesus tells us that his Father is eternally consistent; that is, he never changes his mind. He never lies. He never breaks his promise. The languages of the world will all pass away, but the word of God will never pass away.[52] As the languages of the world began to be hopelessly confused at Babel by human pride, so they began to be permanently united at Pentecost by Apostles humbly speaking the eternal Gospel in the languages of men: *And how hear we every man in our own tongue, wherein we were born? Parthians, and Medes, and Elamites, and the dwellers in Mesopotamia, and in Judaea, and Cappadocia, in Pontus, and Asia, Phrygia, and Pamphylia, in Egypt, and in the parts of Libya about Cyrene, and strangers of Rome, Jews and proselytes, Cretes and Arabians, we do hear them speak in our tongues the wonderful works of God.*[53]

And thus we listen and thus we speak. We attempt to listen in the original language of the Apostles because English is not on this list. And like any other vulgar tongue, the English that we speak is different from even that which our own fathers have spoken. Not only that, the mind-set of a "post-language" world is also not on this list. As "servants of the word" we must stand in the gap, created not only by the relatively neutral vicissitudes of an evolving language, but that which is created by an ever-devolving worldly rebellion against God and against his word, which is Christ. And we must translate that which was first spoken unto us in Koine. As the language of men attempts to flee from Christ into the darkness of Bertrand Russell's "linguistic analysis," Ludwig Wittgenstein's "language games," and B.F. Skinner's "verbal behavior," we must pursue them with translations of the unchanging Gospel into their inhospitable idioms. The world will not come to us. We must go to them.

But before we cast down anyone else's proud imaginations and every high thing that exalts itself against the knowledge of God, and bring anyone else's thoughts

---

[49] John 12:32 *And I, if I be lifted up from the earth, will draw all things unto me. The KJV inserts "men" but the Greek clearly says* παντα *(all things).*

[50] Hebrews 9:26-28b Also Hebrews 7:27 Who *needeth not daily, as those high priests, to offer up sacrifice, first for his own sins, and then for the people's: for this he did once when he offered up himself.*

[51] Revelation 13:8b.

[52] Matthew 24:35 *Heaven and earth shall pass away, but my words shall not pass away.*

[53] Acts 2: 8-11.

into captivity and obedience to Christ,[54] we must first begin with our own. Koine may be a "dead language" but it is no more dead than history itself. And since Christ is the α and the ω, history is just as alive to him as the present and the future. Since he gives life to all things. Before we come to any theory about "inspiration" or "canon" or "bible" or "word of God" or any other theological notion like that, we must first come to the historical *documents* of the New Testament community.

The New Testament materials begin as literature. The believing community which grew up about Jesus of Nazareth begins as sociology. This literature and this sociology is embedded in ordinary history. Much of the problem with the "critical" literature with which we must deal is primarily its *historiography*, not its theology. Therefore, in the "critical" literature, much of which is written by a hostile audience, unconcerned about the witness of history, you will find many discussions which cast doubt upon the *authorship* of almost every manuscript in the New Testament corpus. But this doubt is as spurious as the pseudographic material itself.[55] And this is because the doubt flows from a spurious historiography. But to the ordinary historian, the prima facie witness of history easily draws an immense gulf between the pseudographic material, much of which is an obvious Gnostic imposition, and the New Testament corpus.

We say again: before we make any theories about the religious authority of this corpus, we must first accept the witness of ordinary history. The ordinary witness of history is this: with the exception of some preliminary doubts about a few manuscripts, the New Testament documents were universally believed to have descended directly from the core of the apostolic community which surrounded the historical Christ. And we are here not speaking of something like the Donation of Constantine, which was also universally believed to have descended from a specific historical source, but was false. We are here talking about multiple, independent, unvested witnesses to the historical source and pedigree of these documents. And upon the mere, ordinary witness of history, the integrity of these documents, as having descended to us directly from the historic, apostolic community of Jesus of Nazareth, is established beyond reasonable doubt.

This does not say anything about whether the Apostles who wrote these documents were telling the truth. They may have been lying. Or perhaps they may have been projecting a vast mythological overlay upon the ordinary facts of history.[56] Or they may have been attempting, in the most primary literary sense possible, to put their audience in contact with the phenomena of what they saw and what they heard. We will test these theories. The language itself will tell us. If a man is lying, it will

---

[54] 2nd Corinthians 10:5.
[55] Materials written in or near the first century, falsely claiming to be authored by an apostle.
[56] See especially Appendix 3: "Ten Reasons Why The New Testament Is Not Presenting Myth"

eventually show up in his story, if we pay close attention. And if a man is mythologizing, his literature will eventually evince the telltale signs of a mythological genre.

For convenience and brevity and as a working hypothesis, this book will assume that the apostles may be taken at face value; that is, that they were attempting to put their audience into ordinary experiential contact with the phenomena of what they saw and what they heard. They were not lying. We will presume them innocent unless proven guilty in our own research. This is, after all, a language book. This book is not primarily about the truth of what the Apostles say. This book is about _what_ the Apostles have said by means of the Koine. And this is a purely technical matter. What is not so technical is that we must first do what we expect our audience to do. We must _listen_ to what the historic, apostolic community of the historical Jesus of Nazareth has to say. Then we must judge. No one can do this for us. But this thing is sure: once we have come into contact with the truth, there is nothing upon the face of the earth that will make us relinquish that truth.

In conventional grammar books on Greek, there will sometimes be arguments that such and such a piece of grammatical minutiae has caused "great controversy" or is of some enormous theological import. This kind of gnostic scholasticism, again, gives the student the impression that only the expert language technician can understand what is being said. But this is contrary to the whole tenor of the New Testament documents. They purport to be ordinary, common, simple, straight forward. Generally, they remonstrate with us: "why do you not understand my speech?"[57] And this is because they purport to be so plain as to be understood by a child. The most difficult parts are not unlocked by worldly language technicians, but by spiritual wisdom that is acquired over time – as the child matures as a man in Christ. It is not the extraordinary, supernatural wisdom of this world, to be sure. It is just ordinary maturity.

Maturity will tell us that technical skill in language is of considerable importance. But the technical skill required is easily obtained. All it takes is time. And it is of the same _kind_ of thing as that a sharp ax is the most important thing in chopping down trees. A believer can, over the years, chop away at the text with the blunt ax of a language once removed from the original. Or he can spend some quality time sharpening his ax. And the acquisition of significant language navigational skills is no more difficult than properly sharpening an ax. It takes some quality time. And it takes some patience and discipline. But once the sharp ax is acquired, a man will marvel at how simple it all now seems. So simple, a child could do it. There is

---

[57] John 8:43.

absolutely no substitute for a sharp ax to a wise woodsman. Once he sees this, he will never go back to a blunt one.[58]

And this is especially true in that there are so many language helps now available – the interlinearies and lexicons and concordances and computer programs all conspire to make a man an expert. But as in the case of the scholar, there is a danger here. If a man is given a world-class education on the "principles of carpentry," he will study tool mechanics, jargon, wood physics, geometry, etc. etc. Then he will enter into a wood shop with every conceivable tool at his disposal. But if he has not learned the simple <u>finesse</u> of *working* with wood, every piece of furniture he turns out will be junk. Now go to the woodshop of an old boat builder. He has not received a world class education in boat-building. The tools he uses are primitive. Yet his very fingers have conformed to the shape of them. He follows no blue-print, and yet *everything* he turns out seems almost magical in quality, durability and sheer beauty. This is the boat that the prudent man takes into a storm.

With all these technical helps now at the disposal of the ordinary man for learning Koine, the only difference between him and a scholar is that he is much less likely to be beguiled by a sense of accomplishment and pride. There is no academic peer group to which to kowtow in order to preserve membership. And since membership in the establishment "scholars guild" includes remuneration, he does not stand upon the sand of vested interest. His translation will not be constantly booby-trapped by warning voices that one's livelihood or reputation are on the line, or other irrelevant ulterior motives.

The ordinary man, in the quiet of his own study, makes his translation in the presence of Christ alone – not worrying what any other man might think of it. So do not be discouraged by claims that only the scholar can know. And do not be negligent to accept the challenge of developing the finesse of translating the Koine into the language of your congregation. You are not attempting to apply the word to their souls, you are helping them to apply their souls to the word. When Jesus fed the 5000 and the 4000, he distributed the bread first to the apostles; then the apostles distributed to the people. Jesus makes the bread; you *serve* that bread.

This grammar will make many departures from conventional grammars. We want you to have confidence in these departures and it is therefore necessary to say a word about the state of the art in lexical and grammatical studies. If we consult the introduction to one of the most popular lexicons – *A Greek English Lexicon of the New*

---

[58] The mere fact that almost all theological students who are charged with feeding wood to the fires of their congregations rarely go back to the discipline of sharpening the ax of proficiency in Greek is indicative of a major problem. And that problem is that their schools have never given them the power to sharpen their own axes. Their schools have never given them a love for a sharp ax. Learning Greek should not be a pointless rite of passage - a fraternity exercise. It is essential.

Testament and Other Early Christian Literature by Walter Bauer, we there find that the history of dictionaries specifically intended for the Greek New Testament is a relatively new phenomenon.

This history opens with a Geek-Latin glossary of seventy-five unnumbered pages in the first volume of the Complutensian Polyglot of 1522.[59] Then we come to the *Lexicon Graeco-Latinum in Novum Testamentum* by Georg Pasor, published at Herborn in Nassau. Ludovicus Lucius put out his *Dictionarium Novi Testamenti* at Basel in 1640 with its words arranged for the first time in strict alphabetical order instead of by word roots. Then we come to C.A. Wahl's Greek-Latin Lexicon of 1822. The first dictionary to appear after the epoch-making discoveries of papyri, etc., beginning about 1890, was Erwin Preuschen's Greek-German lexicon of 1910, but unfortunately, he did not make much use of this new material. The revision of his lexicon to this end was completed by Walter Bauer of Gottingen. Subsequent revision of Bauer's enormously comprehensive work was undertaken by W. F. Arndt and F. W. Gingrich and was first published in 1979. From the first letters of these three names, we arrive at the anachronym that many students have come to refer to as the "BAG" – until the invention of the computer – the state-of-the-art lexicon for our literature.

But since the time of the publication of the "BAG" there has been a revolution in linguistic technology – not only with the introduction of the personal computer, but also with the introduction of many basic computer programs that give the user instant contact with a host of lexical resources that were unavailable to previous editors. We owe an enormous debt of gratitude to the men who dedicated their lives to the production of printed lexicons, concordances, grammars and Greek texts. From time to time we will refer to these texts. But for the most part, this grammar will focus on the current state of lexical studies, which has been enormously effected by the power and speed of computer assisted study. Because of the power and speed of computer assisted study of the New Testament literature, we are no longer confined to the lexicons based on the *assumed* grammars of the period, and to indices of translator's words used to convey our literature. Thanks to computer assisted technology, accessible to the non-scholar everywhere, we have a technology which puts us into direct contact with the internal grammar of our literature - of the writers themselves. Thanks to Gutenberg, resources like the "BAG", the United Bible Societies' *Greek New Testament* and *Strong's Concordance* became available to the ordinary pastor. We did not begrudge technology then. Nor should we begrudge technology now.

---

[59] This discussion is a paraphrase from the forward of the first addition to *A Greek English Lexicon of the New Testament and Other Early Christian Literature* by Walter Bauer, pg. v, © 1979, The University of Chicago Press.

One thing is clear. The current state of Koine instruction is at a very low ebb. We have only to judge by the fruits of such instruction. Students come out of Greek classes remembering very little. Frankly, they hate Greek. Except for an occasional dip into the technical literature when preparing a sermon or a lesson, pastors and teachers do not remain (μενω) in a continuing relationship with the Koine. Greek instructors may vehemently object to this analysis, but the state of Biblical criticism also tells the same story. Despite all the technological improvements in materials and instruction, the world is no closer to finding the historical Jesus as it was when Albert Schweitzer first wrote his book – *The Quest for the Historical Jesus.* We are no closer to solving the Synoptic Problem than were the Church Fathers. We are no closer to solving the authorship of *Hebrews* than the guess work of Erasmus and Luther. We are no closer to dating John than the earliest controversies doubting his Apocalypse. And the academic chairs of the science of Biblical criticism are dominated by scholars hostile to the very ethos of their source material.

During the course of this introduction, you saw that in some cases, Greek words and phrases have made their appearance in our discussion for no apparent reason except to imply that these Greek constructions are a fair equivalent to what is being said in the text. This indeed is their purpose. We have already begun the project of learning the language. A good, preliminary test of a private theological idea is to see if there is a phraseological equivalent in the Greek New Testament. If there is not, then this is very strong prima facie evidence that this may be a problematic theological idea. If every thought is to be brought into captivity to Christ, then we should test our every thought to see if can be expressed in the language of the GNT. This is perhaps the best and quickest way to discover that some familiar phrase you might be using is mere theological jargon which has become decoupled from its original meaning – or perhaps never really had a clear meaning in the first place. This is not to say that the GNT is an exhaustive repository of the *word*. It is to say that it is an inexhaustible template which all ideas may be tested (δοκιμαζω[60]).

Take for example, the popular religious phrase "born again." This phrase does not occur in the GNT. You'll find it *translated* thusly three times. John twice puts two words together: γενναω and ανωθεν. γενναω means "to beget." But ανωθεν means "above" or "top" - not "again." If we take our "On Line Bible" program[61] and search the Strong's number for ανωθεν, you will find that of all of its 18 occurrences, not one of them has the connotation of "again." Matthew says that the temple veil was rent from top to bottom; i.e., απο ανωθεν εως κατω. Here our inquiry is greatly facilitated by the fact that the word is paired with its own antonym.[62] Luke expresses

---

[60] A good example of this connotation is 1st John 4:1 *Beloved, believe not every spirit, but try* (δοκιμαζω) *the spirits whether they are of God: because many false prophets are gone out into the world.*
[61] Which may be obtained at http://www.onlinebible.net/.
[62] Whenever we find these "antonymical" constructions we will try to include them, since this is a direct witness to what a particular author, standing within the Koine, *believes* to be antonymical.

a slight variant of the word when he tells Theophilus that since he has followed all since the beginning (ανωθεν) … One could easily insert "from the top" and not be far from what Luke is intending to say - just as when we say in music rehearsal: "let's take it from the top." From the top of what? From the top of the page. John says that Jesus' clothes were divided among the soldiers, but when they came to his tunic (χιτων), they decided to cast lots for it since it was sewn from the top (εκ των ανωθεν) without seam throughout. James says that *Every good gift and every perfect gift is from above* (ανωθεν)*, and comes down from the Father of lights…*

Then where did this construction "born again" originate? Primarily, it originates with Nicodemus himself. It is Nicodemus that redirects Jesus argumentation and makes <u>ανωθεν</u> refer to *number* - not kind: *How can a man be born when he is old? can he enter the <u>second</u> time into his mother's womb, and be born?* But Jesus' argues that the birth of which he speaks has nothing to do with number. It has everything to do with its *place of origin.*

Perhaps, in the course of your career, you may one day find yourself writing theological papers which only the initiated academia understand. Or perhaps you may find yourself writing papers that only the initiated academia reject. In either case, a good calibrator for whether or not you, yourself, understand what it is that you are saying, if not its very truth, is to apply this test. See if you can translate what you are saying into the Koine of the New Testament men. You will find this test oft repeated during the course of this book, in both passive appearances of words and phrases and in active discussions.

This applies also in the case of attitude. Perhaps you find yourself at wit's end with your congregation or with your superior, and you find yourself becoming a little satirical. If your conscience demands, you must ask yourself: "is this attitude on the menu of acceptable spiritual behaviors?" Expressed in the language of the New Testament: 'does this attitude conform to the image of Christ being formed in my soul?'[63] Specifically, do I find evidence of this sort of thing in the New Testament documents?

As we mentioned before, in 2nd Corinthians, Paul says: χαρισασθε μοι την αδικιαν ταυτην (forgive me this wrong). What wrong? If we look into the context just previous to this, we find that the "wrong" is that Paul is not taking payment from the Corinthian Church.[64] There is obvious irony here. But how much? Here again we find a tepid translation. Translators use the word "wrong" only 11 times. But only once do they use it to translate αδικια. Why do they do this? Most probably their reasoning is that αδικια is a very serious Pauline theological word. It means

---

[63] Galatians 4:19 *My little children, of whom I travail in birth again until Christ be formed in you…*
[64] 2nd Corinthians 12:13.

"unrighteousness" – "iniquity." Yet here Paul appears to be casually pressing it into the service of irony. This offends our Puritan sensibilities of literary decorum. Why would Paul appear to trifle with a key word which plays such a crucial role in the Pauline apocalypse? We may attempt to relieve some of the pressure of this dilemma by noting that the style of 2ⁿᵈ Corinthians is strangely *un-Pauline*.[65] This may be so, but the inescapable catholic position on the authorship of this book is that however much it might have been the result of composite authorship, Paul has placed his imprimatur upon it. The pressure remains.

You can see this kind of proving, or rather the evidence of this kind of proving, in the sermonizing of the Church Fathers. With them, there is not the kind of proof-texting and meticulous footnoting that occurs in modern exegetical writing. In the sermons of the Church fathers, primary, New Testament expressions seem to rise unbidden to the surface of their thinking. This kind of interleaving of language and ideas betrays the fact that these Church Fathers are so immersed in the New Testament materials that they do not attempt to make fine distinctions - between what they are saying and what the Apostles have said.

While we are on the subject of testing our thought forms - the most elementary building blocks of our expression, we should treat of yet another problematical idea that has a direct bearing on the translational procedures used in this book. An extremely popular idea in literary analysis is the idea of the *literal*. There is a presumption in our culture that scientific descriptions of things use "literal" language and religious descriptions of things use *non-literal* language. There is no support for such a distinction in the New Testament materials. And there is no clear distinction even in our own culture as to what such a dualism might mean.[66]

The Apostles argue that because of Christ, there are no hopeless dualisms with which we must deal. Thus to distinguish between that which is literal (real) and that which is a "figure of speech" (unreal) is a false dualism. There is no such discussion in the New Testament. The Gospels and the Epistles claim that there is a physical connection between the word and the figure of speech, the absolute and the relative, the permanent and the temporary - in the person of Christ. Over and over again in the Gospels it is said that the relationship between that which is of this world[67] and that which is eternal in the heavens is that they are *parabolic* to one another. Christ unequivocally claims that his words are eternal, even though they have been spoken in the temporary, ordinary languages of Aramaic and Greek culture.

---

[65] This is the second time that we have noted this about 2ⁿᵈ Corinthians.
[66] For an excellent treatment of this problem see Owen Barfield's *Poetic Diction*, (Wesleyan University Press) c 1973.
[67] Paul says in 1ˢᵗ Corinthians 7:31b …*for the fashion of this world* (του κοσμου τουτου) *passeth away.*

In the New Testament, if we start with something temporary - say, a man's hand - and we draw a line from the temporary side of the parabola to the permanent side, we find that it connects with something real and proportional and true: *If you then be risen with Christ, seek those things which are above, where Christ sits on the right <u>hand</u> of God.*[68] What we have in the New Testament is not dualism, or a denial of one thing or another.

Though Plato comes very close in establishing the relationship between the temporary and the permanent, there was a weakness in his argument. And that weakness is that if the temporal and the eternal are not somehow *physically* connected, there can be no true relationship between them - at least not one that we can be sure of. The relationship can be shadowy imitation, faulty art, mystical emblem, or analogous allegory. But these relationships, ultimately, will be defective.

The New Testament claims that the two lines of the parable - the temporal and the eternal - come together *physically* in Christ. He is the intersection between God and man, between spirit and flesh, between the infinite and the finite, between the creator and what has been created. Christ is bread. He is not a metaphor for bread. He is the true bread. The bread that we make with wheat and oil is the metaphor.

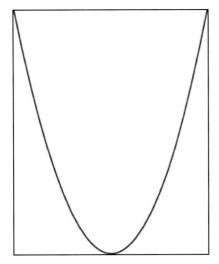

Figure 2. The Parabola

But as we noted, there is a physical connection between the temporary wheat and oil substance which God has spoken into existence and the eternal bread of heaven, which is Christ.

Earthly bread is not <u>just</u> a Platonic shadow (σκια).[69] It is real. It is temporary. But it is no less real. If we say that figures of speech are inventions of human language, we are completely shut up to ultimately meaningless anthropomorphisms. But figures of speech are not human inventions. All things have been made according to heavenly patterns (τυπος).[70] Let us repeat again: *The categories and differentiations of creation were formed by God himself, they are not projected upon the face of chaos by human existentialism. We do not cobble together fragile, faulty analogies to speak of God. He has already spoken to us by pressing down the very image of his character upon the clay of creation.* <u>All</u> things in the created order are therefore figures of speech. They are figures of the speech of God.

---

[68] Colossians 3:1.

[69] Colossians 2:17a *Which are a **<u>shadow</u>** of things to come…*

[70] τυπος. Specifically, Hebrews 8:5 *Who serve unto the example and shadow of heavenly things, as Moses was admonished of God when he was about to make the tabernacle: for, See, saith he, that thou make all things according to the **<u>pattern</u>** showed to thee in the mount.*

If you have come to this grammar with vague expectations about reading Greek or becoming fluent in Greek, you will soon be disoriented, disillusioned, and disappointed. And this disappointment will be particularly exacerbated by the conventional grammars. After a year of studying charts, tables, vocabulary and linguistic categories, the student cannot confidently translate a single sentence. And this is because many of the conventional grammars are really *linguistic* studies by means of the Koine. This grammar attempts a reversal of these priorities. This grammar attempts a study of the Koine of the New Testament materials which, when necessary, makes reference to linguistics. At the end of this book you will have already translated *many* sentences. But more importantly, you will have acquired some essential navigational skills for a voyage into the very ethos of New Testament Koine. At the end of this book you will be able to read Koine. We make no promises about how fast and how much. Nor are such promises necessary. We have a lifetime of commitment before us.

Chapter 1: John 1:1 – 1:3

Letters

We will begin our study of the Koine without recourse to any punctuation marks except word spacing and the traditional system of versification.[1] Our text will look simple, if not spartan. We do this for two reasons: 1) as far as we can tell, the original documents were written without them and 2) this greatly simplifies the inflectional forms that we must learn. It is true that we thus introduce some ambiguity into our study, but our text will be no more ambiguous than that which the authors themselves first presented to the world. It is one thing to rely upon translations by today's Greek scholars, and upon the current state of the original manuscripts, which are provided, for example, by the United Bible Societies *Greek New Testament*, to help resolve ambiguity. But we must remember that every added mark of punctuation, accent, breathing mark or any other enclitic is a *translator's* notation which probably does not descend from any of the autographs of our literature.

The Greek alphabet has 24 letters, most of which are pronounced like their English equivalents:[2]

α	**a**lpha	
β	beta	
γ	gamma	
δ	delta	
ε	**epsilon**	
ζ	zeta	
η	**eta**	long sound of *a* - as in Hades
θ	theta	
ι	**iota**	mostly, a short *i*[3]
κ	kappa	
λ	lamda	
μ	mu	
ν	nu	
ξ	xi	
ο	**omicron**	always short
π	pi	
ρ	rho	
σ	sigma	(at the end of the word s is written as an ς)

---

[1] Although technically, these are not verses – as in a poem. They are sentences, being prose.

[2] Vowels marked in bold.

[3] At the beginning of the word, iota carries the sound of Y (as in yellow) – for example Ιησους (Jesus) or Ιακωβ (Jacob).

τ	<u>t</u>au	
υ	**upsilon**	as <u>oo</u>, but with more pursing of the lips
φ	phi	as <u>f</u> in <u>ph</u>ysician
χ	chi	as <u>ch</u> in lo<u>ch</u>, but more guttural than kappa
ψ	psi	as <u>ps</u> in shi<u>ps</u>
ω	**omega**	always long

Diphthongs are combinations of vowels that often occur together.

<u>Diphthong</u>	<u>Pronunciation</u>
αι	<u>ai</u>sle
ει	fr<u>ei</u>ght
οι	b<u>oi</u>l
υι	qu<u>ee</u>n
αυ	n<u>ow</u>
ευ	f<u>eu</u>d
ου	s<u>ou</u>p

Translation Exercises in John 1:1

We begin with John because John begins at the beginning. Grammar notes from a conventional grammar, Hewett's, *A Beginning and Intermediate Grammar*, will be footnoted for further study.[4] You should use any other of the many fine reference sources available to argue your own translation case. Many words have a considerable range of denotation and connotation. We will therefore primarily examine how John uses each word in his Gospel. Say the sentence aloud and write each sentence.

εν   αρχη   ην   ο   λογος
In the beginning was   the   word

εν	a preposition which means "in." But it also means the numerical "one." Context will easily settle this. We will see an example in John's 3rd sentence.
αρχη	John uses this word eight times, twice here in this thought, but also in another construction: *this beginning of miracles Jesus did in Galilee.* And another: *For Jesus knew from the beginning who they were that believed not.* Jesus says that the devil was a *murderer from the beginning.* John, therefore, consistently employs the simple denotation of "beginning." Matthew and Mark use this word a total of eight times and also exclusively employ this denotation. Even though Luke also employs this meaning, he also shows that the word has other uses: Luke 12:11 *And when they bring you unto the synagogues, and unto magistrates and powers, take ye no thought how or what thing ye shall answer, or what ye shall say...*[5]

In Acts, Luke shows another use: *I was in the city of Joppa praying: and in a trance I saw a vision, A certain vessel descend, as it had been a great sheet, let down from heaven by four corners; and it came even to me...*[6] Hebrews adds yet another connotation: *Therefore leaving the principles of the*

---

[4] This is the 2nd corrected printing of 2011. These references will be abbreviated "Hewett" and the page number or section number at which more information can be found.

[5] Paul uses this word once in Romans with this very connotation: Romans 8:38 *For I am persuaded, that neither death, nor life, nor angels, nor principalities, nor powers, nor things present, nor things to come;* Likewise, once in 1st Corinthians 15:24 *Then cometh the end, when he shall have delivered up the kingdom to God, even the Father; when he shall have put down all rule and all authority and power.* We call the wife of our president the "first" Lady in the same sense. This is Paul's primary use of the word, though he does use it sparingly with its ordinary connotation of "beginning": Philippians 4:15 *Now ye Philippians know also, that in the beginning of the gospel.*

[6] 11:5

doctrine of Christ, let us go on unto perfection.[7] John gives us an excellent anchor for this word and for two others by using it antonymically – that is, with its opposite form:

Revelation 22:13 εγω ειμι |το α και το ω| |αρχη και τελος| |ο πρωτος και ο εσχατος|

εγω ειμι	= I am
το α και το ω	= the <u>alpha</u> and the <u>omega</u>[8]
αρχη και τελος	= <u>beginning</u> and <u>ending</u>
ο πρωτος και ο εσχατος	= the <u>first</u> and the <u>last</u>

ην   this is the imperfect indicative form of the verb ειμι[9] ("to be"), meaning simply: "(he, she, or it) was." See discussion below on the tense and person of λυω.

ο   this is the definite article "the." As in other languages, it will assume many forms throughout the text as it changes gender, number and case along with its noun.

λογος   John uses λογος just a few times more than the Synoptic average. And he uses it consistently as "word." But it can have a high theological use as it does in John's first idea, or it can simply be the ordinary "word" (even though it is used in an extraordinary and powerful way), for example: *Verily, verily, I say unto you, If a man keep*[10] *my **word** he shall never see death.*[11] Matthew also uses λογος as "word," but Matthew too pushes the word towards a more generalized use. For example: *But I say unto you, That every idle word that men shall speak, they shall give <u>account</u> thereof in the day of judgment.*[12] For every idle "word," Matthew uses ρημα, which is the ordinary "word." You may translate it as "word" here too, but remember: Matthew uses two different words, indicating that we should make some distinction too. "Account" is a very good choice. Luke begins Acts with this connotation: *The first <u>word</u> I have made…* which is nicely rendered by the KJV: *The former*

---

[7] 6:1.

[8] Notice that John does not spell out α and ω.

[9] Hewett, 44. At this point, just look at the various forms. Note the use of the "moveable" ν at the end of the 3rd person singular and plural. This is used only for euphony but it can be confusing when encountered in the text.

[10] This phrase: "keep…word" phraseologically links John's Gospel with both 1st John and Revelation. Only John combines these words in this sense – 7 times in his Gospel, once in 1st John, 5 times in Revelation.

[11] John 8:51.

[12] Matthew 12:36.

treatise I have made... But generally, when λογος appears, translate "word" unless some generalized sense is unavoidable. This is particularly true in John.

In Koine, each verb is identified by tense, (present, past, future, etc.); and the person; that is, <u>who</u> is doing the verbal action. Is it "I," "you," "we," "they?" Here is a beginning paradigm which displays the different endings of person affixed to the verb λυω ("to loosen or to make free"[13]) in the present tense."[14]

λυω	I free
λυεις	You free (singular)
λυει	He, she or it frees
λυομεν	We free
λυετε	You (plural) free
λυουσι	They free

<u>Exegetical Considerations</u> Usually, when αρχη is used, there is elaboration. Whether we speak of the "beginning of sorrows" or the "beginning corner of a sheet," there is usually a clear statement or clear implication of what we are beginning. Is it the beginning of creation? Is it the beginning of the Gospel? To what beginning does John refer in this sentence? Beginning of what? He is intentionally ambiguous. Therefore, there is the strong presumption that John is making a kind of parallel to the Genesis account, which begins: εν αρχη εποιησεν ο θεος τον ουρανον και την γην.[15] And this presumption is strengthened by the fact that Matthew's Gospel begins with Abraham; Luke's with Adam. We maintain that this is our first bit of evidence that John is looking both at Matthew and Luke as a source. But John pushes the Synoptic prologue to the *very* beginning.

---

[13] For example: John 1:27 *He it is, who coming after me is preferred before me, whose shoe's latchet I am not worthy to **unloose**. And John 11:44 And he that was dead came forth, bound hand and foot with graveclothes: and his face was bound about with a napkin. Jesus saith unto them, **Loose** him, and let him go.*

[14] You can study much more about the different tenses, moods, and voices of Greek verbs in Hewett, Appendix 6; pg 311-312.

[15] *In the beginning God made the heaven and the earth.* (From the *On Line Bible*, LXX manuscript).

και ο λογος ην προς τον θεον
and the word was with   God

και	και is a workhorse in our documents, meaning "and." Sometimes it means "also." Sometimes it expresses the idea of "but." Its appearance can help break up sentences into smaller parts.
προς	προς is a preposition which almost invariably means "to" or "towards," indicating motion. Yet here there is no apparent motion – simply relation. For example, John says that Peter stood _at_ the door (προς τη θυρα) without.[16] Yet the KJV and the NKJV here both translate προς as "with." The ordinary preposition for "with" is μετα. John could have used μετα, as he does in 13:33: Little children, yet a little while I am _with_ (μετα) you. But he doesn't.
τον	Here is the article again agreeing with the masculine noun "God" as a direct object, yet not required in the conventions of English syntax.
θεον	Simply: "God." In all grammar books, nouns are introduced in the nominative case; that is, the form of the word as it would appear as the subject of a sentence. The nominative form for God is θεος as in the next phrase. Here we see John's first use of God - in the accusative case; i.e., as a direct object.

Exegetical Considerations An important point to remember is that while Gabriel stands in the presence of God, this is not to say that Gabriel knows this fully. John is later to have Jesus say: _No man hath seen God at any time; the only begotten Son, which is in the bosom of the Father, he hath declared him._ John repeats this two more times: _Not that any man hath seen the Father, save he which is of God, he hath seen the Father._[17] _No man hath seen God at any time._[18] Paul agrees: _Who only hath immortality, dwelling in the light which no man can approach unto; whom no man hath seen, nor can see: to whom be honour and power everlasting._[19]

---

[16] John 18:16.
[17] John 6:46.
[18] 1st John 4:12.
[19] 1st Timothy 6:16.

και θεος ην ο λογος
And God was the word

<u>Exegetical Considerations</u> Since there are no new words in this construction, we have only to note that θεος and ο λογος is in the "nominative case." But which is the subject of the sentence and which the "predicate nominative"? Read the discussion of the function of ειμι in Hewett, 5.8 for more information about this.[20] But first translate as written: "and God was the word." If it is read the way Yoda[21] speaks, the difficulty disappears. John was not a Gnostic. The Johannine corpus stands firmly against Gnostic thinking. John would never prove a major doctrine or place a major doctrine in confusion by the use or misuse of an iron-clad grammatical rule. The subject of this entire sentence is λογος.

---

[20] Hewett concludes that the "nominative [noun] with the article is the subject." But is it always the subject?
[21] The sage, Jedi Master in *Star Wars*.

ουτος ην εν   αρχη   προς τον θεον
This one was in the beginning with   God

ουτος   ουτος is one of the "demonstrative pronouns." It can be used as an
             adjective or as a substantive. There are many different forms for this
             word, based on how it is used in the sentence. Here is a chart with all
             the forms for this word. John uses most of them.[22]

ουτος, αυτη, τουτο: this, these						
	Singular			*Plural*		
	Masculine	**Feminine**	**Neuter**	**Masculine**	**Feminine**	**Neuter**
N[23]	ουτος	αυτη	τουτο	ουτοι	αυται	ταυτα
G[24]	τουτου	ταυτης	τουτου	τουτων	τουτων	τουτων
D[25]	τουτω	ταυτη	τουτω	τουτοις	τουταις	τουτοις
A[26]	τουτον	ταυτην	τουτο	τουτους	τουτας	ταυτα

---

[22] See Hewett 8.2 for a fuller discussion.
[23] Nominative – the subject in the sentence, for example.
[24] Genitive - used generally to designate something which belongs to a set of things.
[25] Dative – the indirect object of a sentence, for example.
[26] Accusative – generally, the direct object.

παντα   δι   αυτου εγενετο
all things through him   began

παντα παντα is an adjective[27] that means "all things." There are many different forms for this word, based on how it is used in the sentence. Here is a chart with all the forms for this word. Marked in bold are the forms that John uses in his Gospel.[28] You can see that John uses only 10 of the possible 24 variations. And only three of these (marked with an asterisk) are used with any great frequency: the masculine singular and plural nominative - and the form in our phrase, which is almost always translated "all things." Concentrate on these.

πας, πασα, παν: all, every, whole						
	Singular			*Plural*		
	Masculine	Feminine	Neuter	Masculine	Feminine	Neuter
N	**πας***[29]	πασα	**παν**[30]	**παντες***[31]	πασαι	**παντα***[32]
G	παντος	**πασης**[33]	παντος	**παντων**[34]	πασων	παντων
D	παντι	παση	παντι	πασι(ν)	πασαις	πασι(ν)
A	παντα	**πασαν**[35]	παν	**παντας**[36]	πασας	**παντα**

δι   An abbreviated form of δια, this word is used a few hundred times in the New Testament materials. John uses it 52 times. It means "by" (the thought here is "by means of" or "through"). It may simply mean "because" or "therefore." For example, John often couples δια with τουτο.[37] A typical construction occurs in John 12:27: *Now is my soul troubled; and what shall I say? Father, save me from this hour? but for this cause came I unto this hour.* The last part of this phrase is: αλλα ("but")

---

[27] It would be very helpful to consider Hewett's discussion – 16.5.2.
[28] Did John write Revelation and the epistles alleged to be by his hand? Comparing the usage ratios of words like παντα is an excellent way to test such a theory. If the distribution of forms is the same in these books, then this is excellent, direct evidence that the same author wrote them all. This is a tell-tale linguistic characteristic which would be very difficult for a false author to consciously emulate.
[29] 15x. (that is, 15 times).
[30] 5x.
[31] 14x.
[32] 21x. This combines the frequency for the use of the nominative and the accusative.
[33] 1x.
[34] 4x.
[35] 2x. John uses this form to agree with feminine nouns – "truth" and "judgment."
[36] 3x.
[37] 15x.

δια τουτο (for this cause) ηλθον ('I came') εις ("to") την ωραν ("the hour") ταυτην (this). Note the two (underlined) uses of the demonstrative pronoun in the above paragraph. "Hour" is a feminine noun. It occurs singularly and in the "accusative" case. Check the chart above and you will see that ταυτην agrees with "hour." But in the δια τουτο construction, the demonstrative pronoun changes to neuter. Therefore we know that Jesus is not saying merely 'because of <u>this hour</u> I came.' He is saying something more generalized, which is here unspecified by John – hence the switch away from the feminine case and to the neuter use.

αυτου   αυτου is a personal pronoun[38] which means "he" "she" or "it." It is "declined" like the "demonstrative pronoun." Note below that in both the singular and the plural, the genitive and dative forms of the personal pronoun, respectively, are the same for both the neuter "it" and the masculine "he." How can we tell which is which when used in the text? So far, we do not know if John is talking about a personal word or an impersonal word. So far, we <u>could</u> translate: *All things were made by it; and without it was not any thing made that was made. In it was life; and the life was the light of men.* But suddenly in the 10th sentence, John tips his hand with the unequivocal use of the masculine, accusative singular: και ο κοσμος αυτον ουκ εγνω. *And the world did not know **him**.*

αυτος, αυτη, αυτο: he, she, it							
	Singular				*Plural*		
	Masculine	Feminine	Neuter		Masculine	Feminine	Neuter
N	αυτος	αυτη	αυτο		αυτοι	αυται	αυτα
G	αυτου	αυτης	αυτου		αυτων	αυτων	αυτων
D	αυτω	αυτη	αυτω		αυτοις	αυταις	αυτοις
A	αυτον	αυτην	αυτο		αυτους	αυτας	αυτα

εγενετο   εγενετο is the aorist[39] form (3rd person,[40] past tense) of a verb which in the present tense is spelled γινομαι. Of the 600 or so sentences that

---

[38] Hewett, 1.2.1.

[39] For now, "aorist" designates the past tense.

[40] For now, note that this verb does not agree in number with "all things." This sometimes happens in the Greek. But in this sentence, note that the verbal action seems split between "him" and "all things." Because this is not an unambiguous statement. Though we have tentatively translated "were made by him" we must note that εγενετω is not just a simple past tense; its "voice" is "middle deponent," which means that it is half passive and half active. Note too that αυτου is genitive. The genitive is used much more expansively in the Greek than in English. All things began through him. This is not just preposition and object. The beginning of things so thoroughly pertains to him, that the genitive is very appropriate. Have confidence in ordinary, sometimes ambiguous expressions.

γινομαι is used in our literature, it assumes this form (εγενετο) almost a third of the time; i.e., 3rd person, aorist, indicative. It is very often translated correctly "and it came to pass." Luke uses it 40 times as an editorial stitching device.[41] In contrast, John uses this construction 16 times. But he never uses it as Luke does. The KJV translators, therefore correctly avoid this translation. For John, εγενετο simply means "began to be," or "began," or "happened," or just "was." And this simplicity allows him to here say something immense. *All things through him began.* It is therefore an unnecessary imposition to say, as the KJV and the NKJV, that all things were *made* by him. There are words for "make," such as ποιεω, which John uses 97 times for "do" or "make," but not here. Remember, you are the translator. Be reluctant to wander from the primary connotation of a word unless the context seems to demand it. And beware of inserting words if they are not necessary.

Remember, grammar technicalities do not bear gnostic secrets. Paul will, in passing, reiterate the same idea in Romans 11:16 οτι εξ αυτου και δι αυτου και εις αυτον τα παντα. ("For of him, and through him, and to him, *are* all things.") It is clear that in this sentence, it doesn't matter what prepositional idea one uses with Christ – they are all valid. And here, you must supply the *verb* (a situation which occurs frequently). The AV translators therefore submit "*are*" (they italicize words that are not in the text), which agrees in number with τα παντα. And a phrase in Colossians confirms that depending on the preposition one uses, the object of the preposition can be in the objective case, of course, or the dative case. There are no enigmas here: τα παντα δι αυτου και εις αυτον εκτισται ("all things were created by him, and for him"). And in John we see that depending on how the preposition is used, the case will change: John 7:43 σχισμα ουν εν τω οχλω εγενετο δι αυτον (So there was a division among the people because of him).

[41] This compares with Matthew's "behold" (ιδου) and Mark's "immediately" (ευθεως).

κα χωρις αυτου εγενετο   ουδε εν   ο γεγονεν
and without him   began   not one thing which has become.

χωρις   χωρις means "without" or "apart from," an adverb which always appears in this form. John uses this word twice more in his Gospel. He has Jesus say: *apart from me, you can do nothing.* Also, when John looked into the tomb, he saw the *face cloth not lying with the linen clothes but <u>by itself</u> folded up...* For Paul, χωρις is a pivotal word in his Roman's argument: *but now the righteousness of God <u>apart from</u> the law has appeared.*[42]

ουδε   ουδε is a conjunction which means "but not" "neither," "nor," "not even." Combined here with εν ("one") it becomes "not one (thing[43])." This construction occurs only once more – in Matthew. Matthew says that Jesus responded to Pilate: ουδε εν ρημα ("not one word").

o   This is the "relative pronoun." In the genitive it usually means "of whom." In the dative it usually means "to whom." In the accusative, simply: "whom." Here it more logically means "which." Note that without the various accent marks, added by translators and grammarians, this nominative, singular, neuter use of the relative pronoun in this sentence is indistinguishable from the nominative, singular, masculine form of the *definite article.* Let's display them both together.

Relative Pronoun ος, η, o: who, what, which						
Singular				*Plural*		
	Masculine	**Feminine**	**Neuter**	**Masculine**	**Feminine**	**Neuter**
N	ος	η	o	οι	αι	α
G	ου	ης	ου	ων	ων	ων
D	ω	η	ω	οις	αις	οις
A	ον	ην	o	ους	ας	α

Definite Article o, η, το,: "the"[44]						
Singular				*Plural*		
	Masculine	**Feminine**	**Neuter**	**Masculine**	**Feminine**	**Neuter**
N	o	η	το	οι	αι	τα
G	του	της	του	των	των	των
D	τω	τη	τω	τοις	ταις	τοις
A	τον	την	το	τους	τας	τα

---

[42] Romans 3:21.

[43] Though there is no "thing" in the sentence, the construction "not one..." is incomplete. "Not one ...what?" Thus, we supply "thing."

[44] There is no Greek equivalent for our "indefinite article": i.e., "a" or "an" For example, our **an** apple **a** day keeps the doctor away" would be said in the Koine: "**the** apple **every** day keeps the doctor away."

γεγονεν   Here we see another form of γινομαι (which means "to become") – the perfect. For us, for now, this is merely a more specific form of the past tense.

Exegetical Considerations Don't be too restrictive about applying language rules. Though we are calling χωρις an adverb, it also functions, in this sentence (and many others), adverbially (the *how* or *why* of the verb "become") *and* prepositionally (in what relation to "him"). And in the Greek, the *object* of a preposition can be in the dative or the genitive or the accusative, depending on the function of that object in the idea of the sentence. In our first two sentences, we even see a rare case in which the object, αρχη, of the preposition εν, is in the *nominative* (εν αρχη). This appears to be due to a convention when using εν with αρχη,[45] because whenever αρχη appears in the dative (αρχης), it carries the preposition απο ("from"). In the case of χωρις, as it is used prepositionally, its object will be in the genitive.

Let's put the above two phrases together: παντα δι αυτου **εγενετο** και χωρις αυτου **εγενετο** ουδε εν ο **γεγονεν** - *all things through him **began** and without him **began** not one thing which **has become**.* John is not being redundant – he is being very specific. Through Christ all things that have a beginning have come into being through his agency. Yet Christ himself, begotten by the Father. For example, it is John, and only John that uses the title μονογενης for the Son, [46] which is a compound word formed from μονος and γινομαι (or perhaps γενναω).

---

[45] For example, Luke uses it once this way (Acts 11:15); Paul once (Philippians 4:15).
[46] The use of μονογενες is an important thematic linkage between John's Gospel and his first epistle, which, in turn, is important evidence for the unity of authorship of these two books.

Chapter 1 Review

The Relative Pronoun

<table>
<tr><td colspan="7" align="center">ος, η, ο: who, what, which</td></tr>
<tr><td></td><td colspan="3" align="center">Singular</td><td colspan="3" align="center">Plural</td></tr>
<tr><td></td><td>Masculine</td><td>Feminine</td><td>Neuter</td><td>Masculine</td><td>Feminine</td><td>Neuter</td></tr>
<tr><td>N</td><td>ος</td><td>η</td><td>ο</td><td>οι</td><td>αι</td><td>α</td></tr>
<tr><td>G</td><td>ου</td><td>ης</td><td>ου</td><td>ων</td><td>ων</td><td>ων</td></tr>
<tr><td>D</td><td>ω</td><td>η</td><td>ω</td><td>οις</td><td>αις</td><td>οις</td></tr>
<tr><td>A</td><td>ον</td><td>ην</td><td>ο</td><td>ους</td><td>ας</td><td>α</td></tr>
</table>

The Article

<table>
<tr><td colspan="7" align="center">ο, η, το,: the</td></tr>
<tr><td></td><td colspan="3" align="center">Singular</td><td colspan="3" align="center">Plural</td></tr>
<tr><td></td><td>Masculine</td><td>Feminine</td><td>Neuter</td><td>Masculine</td><td>Feminine</td><td>Neuter</td></tr>
<tr><td>N</td><td>ο</td><td>η</td><td>το</td><td>οι</td><td>αι</td><td>τα</td></tr>
<tr><td>G</td><td>του</td><td>της</td><td>του</td><td>των</td><td>των</td><td>των</td></tr>
<tr><td>D</td><td>τω</td><td>τη</td><td>τω</td><td>τοις</td><td>ταις</td><td>τοις</td></tr>
<tr><td>A</td><td>τον</td><td>την</td><td>το</td><td>τους</td><td>τας</td><td>τα</td></tr>
</table>

The Demonstrative Pronoun

<table>
<tr><td colspan="7" align="center">ουτος, αυτη, τουτο: this, these</td></tr>
<tr><td></td><td colspan="3" align="center">Singular</td><td colspan="3" align="center">Plural</td></tr>
<tr><td></td><td>Masculine</td><td>Feminine</td><td>Neuter</td><td>Masculine</td><td>Feminine</td><td>Neuter</td></tr>
<tr><td>N</td><td>ουτος</td><td>αυτη</td><td>τουτο</td><td>ουτοι</td><td>αυται</td><td>ταυτα</td></tr>
<tr><td>G</td><td>τουτου</td><td>ταυτης</td><td>τουτου</td><td>τουτων</td><td>τουτων</td><td>τουτων</td></tr>
<tr><td>D</td><td>τουτω</td><td>ταυτη</td><td>τουτω</td><td>τουτοις</td><td>τουταις</td><td>τουτοις</td></tr>
<tr><td>A</td><td>τουτον</td><td>ταυτην</td><td>τουτο</td><td>τουτους</td><td>τουτας</td><td>ταυτα</td></tr>
</table>

The Personal Pronoun

<table>
<tr><td colspan="7" align="center">αυτος, αυτη, αυτο: he, she, it</td></tr>
<tr><td></td><td colspan="3" align="center">Singular</td><td colspan="3" align="center">Plural</td></tr>
<tr><td></td><td>Masculine</td><td>Feminine</td><td>Neuter</td><td>Masculine</td><td>Feminine</td><td>Neuter</td></tr>
<tr><td>N</td><td>αυτος</td><td>αυτη</td><td>αυτο</td><td>αυτοι</td><td>αυται</td><td>αυτα</td></tr>
<tr><td>G</td><td>αυτου</td><td>αυτης</td><td>αυτου</td><td>αυτων</td><td>αυτων</td><td>αυτων</td></tr>
<tr><td>D</td><td>αυτω</td><td>αυτη</td><td>αυτω</td><td>αυτοις</td><td>αυταις</td><td>αυτοις</td></tr>
<tr><td>A</td><td>αυτον</td><td>αυτην</td><td>αυτο</td><td>αυτους</td><td>αυτας</td><td>αυτα</td></tr>
</table>

Chapter 2: John 1:4 – 1:8

εν αυτω ζωη ην και η ζωη ην το φως των ανθρωπων
In him   life was and the life was the light of   men

ζωη   ζωη is our first feminine noun, meaning "life." It is declined just like the feminine article and feminine pronouns as shown in *Chapter 1 Review*. John uses this word twice as much as the Synoptics combined.[1] A little more than half that time, John couples this word with "eternal" to form "eternal life." In all but one of these cases, "life" comes first, then the adjective "eternal" (αιωνιον). This is standard practice. But the phrase itself is primarily Johannine.

<u>Exegetical Considerations</u>: Matthew, Mark and Luke effectively treat of eternal life only once, in the Rich Young Man pericope. And there the subject is not eternal life. It is that righteousness is not about doing good, but repudiating the world, taking up the cross, and following Christ. Luke adds the additional pericope about the Good Samaritan, which opens with a certain lawyer asking Jesus: *what shall I do to inherit eternal life?* But here again the emphasis is about Jesus' answer to 'what shall I do?' not 'what shall I get?' The good Samaritan pericope, in which this term appears in passing, is also about true righteousness, not eternal life.

Eternal life is mentioned only five times in the entire Pauline corpus, and he does not develop this phrase. Much more colorful is Paul's statement: *For our light affliction, which is but for a moment, worketh for us a far more exceeding and <u>eternal weight of glory</u>* (αιωνιον βαρος δοξης). Jude also uses the phrase once in passing. But John's first epistle, by contrast, makes two very pointed, Johannine statements about eternal life: *Whosoever hateth his brother is a murderer: and ye know that no murderer[2] hath eternal life abiding in him.*[3] John's second epistolary mention seems to be a direct summary of this Gospel prologue: *And this is the record, that God hath given to us eternal life, and this life is in his Son.*[4]

Paul often speaks in a teleological mode; that is, what we do now is in preparation and in expectation of some future event, for example, the redemption of the body, the return of Christ in judgment, the inheritance of glory – and he places eternal life at the end of a process: *But now being made free from sin, and become servants to God, ye*

---

[1] 32x.

[2] Yet another distinct linkage between John and 1st John is this word, ανθρωποκτονος (murderer), which is used only here and in John 8:44. Throughout this book, this will be called a "monohit." A monohit, then, refers to a word that two – and only two - authors share.

[3] 1st John 3:15.

[4] 1st John 5:11.

have your fruit unto holiness, and the end everlasting life.[5] But John strongly affirms that for us, eternal life has already begun. Only John (five times in his Gospel and twice in 1st John[6]) combines the present, active indicative of "to have" (εχω) with "eternal life." Here is a representative statement: *Verily, verily, I say unto you, He that hears my word, and believes on him that sent me, has everlasting life, and shall not come into condemnation; but has passed[7] from death unto life.*[8] This explains the Johannine modulation of this Synoptic cognate: *Verily I say unto you, There be some standing here, which shall not taste of death, till they see the Son of man coming in his kingdom.*[9] John modulates to an unequivocal: *Verily, verily, I say unto you, If a man keep my saying, he shall never see death.*[10] He elaborates his rationale for this alteration in Revelation. There he makes it clear that Jesus is not talking about ordinary biological death, which is part of the warp and weft of the ecosphere. He is talking about *spiritual* death - a second death. A death that comes from below: *Blessed and holy is he that hath part in the first resurrection: on such the second death hath no power… But the fearful, and unbelieving, and the abominable, and murderers, and whoremongers, and sorcerers, and idolaters, and all liars, shall have their part in the lake which burneth with fire and brimstone: which is the second death.*[11]

φως   Φως is a 3rd declension neuter noun[12] which means light. John uses this word about 20 times and in a highly theological sense. Most of the time it occurs as you see it here - φως. In John, we will see this somewhat unusual noun only thrice in the genitive φωτος (one will appear in three more sentences) and once in the dative – φωτι.

Exegetical Considerations: In the popular, modern mind, light is a cold fact of photons impinging upon the retina. But in the mind of John, light not only illuminates what is covered by darkness – light is the very fire of life. Mark, too, says: *And Peter followed him afar off, even into the palace of the high priest: and he sat with the servants, and warmed himself at the fire.*[13] The word that Mark uses for fire is φως. But the word for fire is πυρ, not φως. Yet if we follow modern physics far enough, it comes to the same place. Light is frequency. Frequency is motion. Motion is so proportional to heat that we may even say that motion *is* heat. Eventually we must

---

[5] Romans 6:29.

[6] If 1st John is a pseudograph, it is beginning to look as if this forgerer is paying very close attention to the phraseological characteristics, if not the essential doctrine, of John. The forgerer will soon begin to look so like John, that we must conclude that he *is* John.

[7] John here uses the perfect tense; it is a specific, past event.

[8] John 5:24. Here again is a phraseological monohit with 1st John: μεταβεβηκαμεν εκ του θανατου εις την ζωην – "has passed from death to life."

[9] This is Matthew's rendition. Luke and Mark modify this slightly.

[10] John 8:51.

[11] Revelation 20:6; 21:8.

[12] See Hewett, 137.

[13] Mark 14:54.

conclude that at 0 degrees Kelvin, there can be no life and no light – what cosmologists now call "heat death."[14]

Light without heat is a false light. Consistently, the Johannine contrast is not, finally, between light and dark. The contrast in the Johannine corpus is between "truth" and "lie." There are simply no alternatives to truth. There are only lies. Likewise, there is no alternative to Christ, there is only "antichrist" *For many deceivers are entered into the world, who confess not that Jesus Christ is come in the flesh. This is a deceiver and an antichrist.*[15] He looks like a lamb, but has the voice of the dragon.[16] The closest theological cognate to this Johannine idea is again, Paul: *And no marvel; for Satan himself is transformed into an angel of light.*[17]

ανθρωπων

> ανθρωπως means "man." Here we see it in the genitive plural, hence "of men" This masculine noun is declined just like the masculine article and masculine pronoun, and since John uses all forms, we will present them here.

	Singular		*Plural*
N	ανθρωπος		ανθρωποι
G	ανθρωπου		ανθρωπων
D	ανθρωπω		ανθρωποις
A	ανθρωπον		ανθρωπους

> Most of the genitive singular constructions in John occur in the phrase "son of man." And yet this title occurs only once outside of the Gospels and in Stephen's confession, as he is being stoned: *Behold, I see the heavens opened, and the son of man standing on the right hand of God.*[18]

Exegetical Considerations: In just two sentences, we have encountered something very strangely new. Though John is phraseologically and structurally very strongly related to the Synoptic literary template, his prologue breaks out upon an immense Christology.

---

[14] This may explain the somewhat strange idea in Dante's Inferno that Satan is trapped in the center of Hell, *in ice.*

[15] 2nd John 1:7.

[16] Revelation 13:11 *And I beheld another beast coming up out of the earth; and he had two horns like a lamb, and he spake as a dragon.*

[17] 2nd Corinthians 11:14.

[18] Acts 7:56.

και το φως εν τη σκοτια φαινει και η σκοτια αυτο ου κατελαβεν[19]
and the light in the darkness shines and the darkness does not apprehend it.

σκοτια   σκοτια is a feminine noun, hence the associated feminine article (τη),
              just before it (just as the neuter noun φως is accompanied with a neuter
              article το[20]). Except for one use by Matthew and one use by Luke,
              σκοτια is used only by John, both in his Gospel and in his first epistle.
              All four uses in 1st John contrast light with darkness. So do four of
              John's uses in his Gospel. But beware, this is not just a simple contrast.

              Popular agnosticism draws a parallel between John's use of light and
              dark and the Essene dualism. But the moment we begin to examine
              John, we see that there is no dualism. Dualism is the default position of
              a lazy mind. John is attempting to tell us something here in this
              sentence which is much more sophisticated. Yes, there is the basic
              contrast between light and darkness, but it is not "reversible." As St.
              Augustine has said, there is no substance, per se, to darkness, therefore
              it cannot be in an *absolute*, dualistic relationship with light. Light can
              disperse darkness but darkness cannot disperse light.

              There is either the presence of light or the absence of light. The
              darkness can take pleasure in its absence, but it can do nothing but
              passively receive its *presence* in abject submission. This is perhaps why
              John has chosen the feminine form of darkness instead of the neuter
              form σκοτος, which is much more frequently used by Matthew and
              Luke. Because *all* things are feminine in relation to God. John does use
              this neuter form once in 3:19, and here also in contrast with light.
              Though we come now to the doors of conjecture. Why do you think
              that John makes this change?

---

[19] Compare this with οτι η σκοτια παραγεται και το φως το αληθινον ηδη φαινει (*because the darkness
has past and the light true now shines.* 1st John 2:8)
[20] If you are not sure of this, refer back to the chart on Chapter 1 Review and confirm this. When an
English sentence is filled with pronouns, it is sometimes difficult to sort out who is who, but in the
Greek, because of the gender distinctions, we have a much clearer idea. And this sentence is a very
good place to develop the discipline of keeping track of the article.

φαινει   φαινει is the third person ("he", "she" or "it") singular of φαινω. It means "shine." It is in the present tense. Since φως is neuter, and John has not yet clearly identified light with Christ, we more naturally will say: "it shines."

<u>Exegetical Considerations</u>: We already have strong prima facie evidence that John is following the contours of the Genesis opening. There we find, before any figures of speech become attached to the word, that darkness possesses a neutral quality such

that the Psalmist may say: *Yea, the darkness hideth not from thee; but the night shineth as the day: the darkness and the light are both alike.*[21] God says: "let there be φως." Suddenly, there is contrast – the day and the night. And this contrast belongs to the same set of neutral contrasts which follow: heaven and earth and the sea and dry land. In David's song in celebration over his enemies,[22] which is repeated in the psalms, we see

God himself *employing* darkness to manifest his glory: *He made darkness his secret place; his pavilion round about him were dark waters and thick clouds of the skies.*[23] In the picture above, we see Rembrandt employing neutral contrast between light and dark. There is no dualism here. Contrast reveals the world. Observe also the contrast between light and darkness in the Ansel Adams photograph (right). For John, darkness is relational. In this sentence, darkness is feminine, into which light shines. We must therefore pay close attention to the Johannine argument. As it develops, we will indeed see darkness become a figure of speech for both ignorance and wickedness. But it is only when men turn from the light to darkness that it loses its neutrality. And in this sense, there is no darkness in God *himself*: *God is light, and in him is no darkness at all.*[24]

κατελαβεν   κατελαβεν is the 3rd person singular, aorist tense of καταλαμβανω. You can see that it has gone through considerable permutation from the present tense. Much like irregular verbs in English, there are internal modifications as the verb changes into the past.[25] An internal μ

---

[21] Psalm 139:12.
[22] 2nd Samuel 22. Especially v 10.
[23] Ps 18:11.
[24] 1st John 1:5b.
[25] For example, "swim" changes to "swam" instead of "swimmed."

has dropped out and κατα has changed to κατε. καταλαμβανω is formed with the preposition kata which can mean "according to," "after," "against," etc., and the verb λαμβανω, which means either "to receive" or "to take." John uses it three more times – twice in reference to the woman "taken" in adultery and once in a very similar form as we see in our sample sentence: *Walk while ye have the light, lest darkness "come upon" you.* Yet the KJV translates καταλαμβανω as "comprehend." It is true that Luke uses this word in this ordinary sense three times in Acts, but that is not the sense of the word as John is using it here. In the epileptic boy pericope, Mark has the father say, *Master, I have brought unto thee my son, which hath a dumb spirit; And wheresoever he taketh him, he teareth him.*[26] One might easily substitute "overcome" or "apprehend." Perhaps the closest parallel to John's usage is Paul's confession in Philippians: *…but I follow after, if that I may apprehend that for which also I am apprehended of Christ Jesus.*[27]

ου   is the negative particle, just like our "no" or "not." Above we saw it combined with δε to form ουδε, a stronger negative than just ου, most often found in multiple negatives - most of the time translated as "neither" or "nor." Here it simply means "not." When ου precedes a word which begins with a vowel, a κ (or, often, a χ) is added, for ease of pronunciation. Yet ου also spells the relative pronoun "which" in the genitive, masculine and neuter singular.[28] How can you tell them apart? The relative pronoun does not "acquire" a κ when preceding a word beginning with a vowel - which occurs very often. Additionally, "which" does not fit the context of the sentence. So it will be easy to determine which ου is "which" and which is "not."

Before we move on, let's take another look, then, at our translation:

και το φως εν τη σκοτια φαινει και η   σκοτια **αυτο** ου **κατελαβεν**
and the light in the darkness shines and the darkness **does**   not apprehend **it**

We have broken from our word order at the end of the sentence for good reason. If we leave it as it is we have: …"and the darkness it does not apprehend," we do not have closure. Does not apprehend what? In this case, the sentence requires an object for this verb. The object is "it" – that is, light. Observe closely the pronoun, αυτο. Referring quickly to our charts in *Chapter 1 Review*, we see that αυτο is neuter. It must therefore go with "light," which is neuter, not σκοτια, which is feminine. This

---

[26] Mark 9: 17-18a.
[27] Philippians 3:12b.
[28] See Chapter 1 Review.

is probably yet another reason why John chooses the feminine form of "darkness" instead of the more common neuter form – σκοτος – to avoid confusion.

εγενετο ανθρωπος[29] απεσταλμενος παρα θεου ονομα αυτω ιωαννης

There was a man   having been sent from   God - name   to him John

απεσταλμενος   απεσταλμενος is the perfect passive participle of αποστελλω, which means "send." It is perfect because its past action has particular relevance to the present;[30] it is passive because the subject is passively *receiving* the action instead of initiating it; it is a participle because it is a verb that has become an adjective.[31] As such, the participle, even though it begins as a verb, will take on endings as if it were a noun, and will thus agree in case, person and number with the noun that it is defining.

In passing, let us note how αποστελλω has taken on the form that we see in this sentence. Since it is a participle, and it is defining "man" (ανθρωπος), which is the subject of this sentence, it takes on the nominative, first person singular, masculine ending "ος." There is nothing new here. The μεν is an indicator that the participle is passive. And just as we saw with κατελαβεν, the structural changes in the word itself are indicators that the verb has changed to the past tense (the **o** has changed to **e**, the τελ has changed to τ<u>α</u>λ, and an λ has dropped out.

The most notable use of "sent" in John is to construct sentences that tell us that Jesus has been sent by the father into the world and, in turn, Jesus has sent the apostles on a continuing mission into the world.

παρα   παρα is a preposition that has multiple uses. It can mean "of" or "by" or "alongside" or "from" or "with." One good way to get at the conventional, central way a writer will use a preposition is to find a sentence which contains it own antonym. For example Jesus says: *I came forth from* (παρα) *the Father, and am come into the world: again, I leave the world, and go to* (προς) *the Father.*[32] Since προς indicates motion toward, or perhaps a relationship which stands towards, παρα is a relation which moves or stands *apart* from an object.

---

[29] Here is "man" in the nominative.

[30] And in the case of this verb, never occurs in the aorist passive participle form. You will see this often – it is not so much that the author is making such fine textual gradations as he is repeating a convention. In the case of "sent" and its continuing relevance to the present – the pool of "Siloam" (Aramaic) - John translates for us with the same word: απεσταλμενος.

[31] See Hewett, 19.2.

[32] John 16:28.

Take for an example, παραβολη, which is used only in the Synoptics and twice in Hebrews, which John does not use. It is a compound word formed from παρα and βαλλω, which means "to throw out." In the case of a mathematical parabola, one line is thrown out _from_ another in exact proportion - but displaced oppositely from a shared axis.

John uses this preposition (παρα) 31 times in his Gospel in various ways, so be flexible in your translation, but do not wander too far from the core idea of "from." The object of this preposition will often be in the genitive case, as in this example, but sometimes it will be in the dative case. When παρα precedes a word beginning with a vowel, it will drop the final **a** (for euphony).

ονομα

In John, we will always find ονομα occurring in this form (nominative singular) except for its use in the genitive construction; for example, "in the name of" (εν τω ονοματι). Its occurrence in the sentence is abrupt, hence the dash in our translation. To understand what John is saying we must look at the words with which it is associated. Our first clue is the <u>dative</u> pronoun αυτω. Then we see "John" (ιωαννης) in the nominative. Therefore, _name_ and _John_ "agree" together. αυτω must then tell us the relationship between these two nouns and the relationship between this group of words and the sentence itself. Without αυτω we have merely "name, John." We would of course say: "by the name of John," or "who was named John." Let's define the dative and see if we are on track:

"The dative case is …generally used to indicate the noun to whom something is given. The name is derived from the Latin dativus, meaning "appropriate to giving." The thing being given may be a tangible object — such as "a book" or "a pen" — or it may be an intangible abstraction, such as "an answer" or "help." The dative generally marks the indirect object of a verb, although in some instances, the dative is used for the direct object of a verb pertaining directly to an act of giving something. In certain languages, the dative case has assimilated the functions of other now-extinct cases. Dative also marks possession in Classical Greek, which has lost the locative and instrumental cases."[33]

---

[33] Wikipedia.

Although this syntax seems idiomatic to John, it is not without a tradition or "convention." We remember the elaborate story in Luke about how John's name was <u>given</u> to him. It is quite logical and permissible, therefore, to understand αυτω as embracing the whole idea of "by the given name of John." The convention that John is here following also appears in the LXX. For example, we have και ονομα αυτω μανωε (whose name was Manoah).[34]

John does repeat this convention three times more – once in 3:1 ην δε ανθρωπος εκ των φαρισαιων νικοδημος <u>**ονομα αυτω**</u> (There was a man of the Pharisees, named Nicodemus…) and twice in Revelation: και ειδον και ιδου ιππος χλωρος και ο καθημενος επανω αυτου <u>**ονομα αυτω**</u> ο θανατος (6:8 *And I looked, and behold a pale horse: and his name that sat on him was Death*) and και εχουσιν εφ αυτων βασιλεα τον αγγελον της αβυσσου <u>**ονομα αυτω**</u> εβραιστι αβαδδων (9:11 *And they had a king over them, which is the angel of the bottomless pit, whose name in the Hebrew tongue is Abaddon*).

It might even be John's own idiom. This will happen again and again in your translation – you must take an idiom which sounds awkward and has no exact rule for translation – but translate it nevertheless. We do the same thing in ordinary conversation with others in our own language. Do not hesitate to do it here. One more example of an unusual idiom – this time from Mark. και ηρξατο αυτους αποστελλειν δυο δυο, which is: *and he began them to send two two*.[35] Here there is not even a dative indicator, yet the phrase demands the insertion of "by" – two *by* two. Here again we find this convention in the LXX: And they went in unto Noah into the ark, two and two of all flesh, wherein is the breath of life…[36]

---

[34] Judges 13:2 and elsewhere.
[35] Mark 6:7.
[36] Genesis 7:15.

ουτος ηλθεν εις μαρτυριαν
this one came in witness

ινα	μαρτυρηση	περι	του	φωτος
in order that	he might witness	concerning	the	light

ινα	παντες	πιστευσωσιν	δι	αυτου
in order that	all	might believe	through	him

ουτος   We have seen this demonstrative pronoun[37] before in chapter 1 when John said *this one was in the beginning with God*.

ηλθεν   Believe it or not, the present tense, first person form of this verb is ερχομαι. It is therefore a highly irregular verb. You will see this form, ηλθεν, - the third person, aorist version of ερχομαι, 16 more times in John. The verb means "come." You will see this verb in all its other forms many times in John (~142x). We must come to savor the various forms of the words we see. We must become familiar with them just as we are familiar with our own wives, who also permutate into various forms: mother, lover, friend, advisor, craftswoman, gardener and many other rare and unusual forms. The list below shows a sampling of the forms that John uses in his Gospel (with various, random personal endings). If you discard the endings, you can see definite patterns in the verb stem (underlined).

ερχεται	51	Present
ερχομενον	14	Present Participle
ερχηται	2	Present Subjunctive
ερχεσθω	2	Present Imperative
ερχεσθαι	1	Present Infinitive[38]
ηρχοντο	4	Imperfect
ηλθεν	17	Aorist
ελθων	9	Aorist Participle
ελθειν	8	Aorist Infinitive
ελθε	1	Aorist Imperative[39]
ελθη	7	Aorist Subjunctive
ελευσονται	3	Future
εληλυθεν	12	Perfect
εληλθει	5	Pluperfect

---

[37] You may want to review the different types of pronouns (Hewett, 1.2.1).

[38] John 6:15 *When Jesus therefore perceived that they would come and take him by force, to make him a king, he departed again into a mountain himself alone.*

[39] John 4:16 *Jesus saith unto her, Go, call thy husband, and come hither.*

εις is a common preposition which means "into," "in," ""unto," "to," "towards," etc. μαρτυριαν is a word which John alone has adapted from its ordinary legal use to a special theological sense; that is, what Jesus was sent to tell us - is his "testimony." This implies that if the world is a stage, the drama can be described in terms of the courtroom. Therefore, we have translated: "in witness." God has placed himself in the dock; Christ is on the witness stand giving testimony. We are the judges. John therefore concludes: *He that hath received his underline{witness} hath set to his seal that God is true.*[40]

Exegetical Considerations: Of the 33 times this word, μαρτυριαν, is used in our literature, John uses it 27 times, distributed proportionally throughout his Gospel, his first and third epistle, and his Revelation. This also is evidence for unity of authorship of these manuscripts. More importantly, of these 6 non-Johannine uses, only one occurs in the sense that John is using it – consistently, this occurs in Jesus' dialogue to Paul while he was in a trance.[41]

Although we do not find μαρτυρια used in Paul in the Johannine sense, it is only in Paul that we find a theology inflected with ideas from the courtroom – especially in his pre-imprisonment theology, which reaches its full development in Romans. If we were to take the Romans argument alone, it would seem that the whole purpose of Jesus' death was to achieve a forensic rehabilitation of our legal/moral status with God. It is in this argument that we find not only the forensic basis of our justification – but the forensic basis of *God's* justification. Paul labors to dismiss the charges against the righteousness of God himself *...to declare, I say, at this time his righteousness: that he might be just, and the justifier of him which believeth in Jesus.*[42]

The language in John is different, but the argument is parallel. In John, Jesus is on trial from the very beginning. However damning the circumstantial evidence against Jesus – that he is guilty of blasphemy – his witness is nevertheless true. Except for one non-theological occurrence in Titus, the combination of these two words μαρτυρια (witness) and αληθης (true) occurs only in John.[43]

---

[40] John 3:33.

[41] Acts 22:18 *And saw him saying unto me, Make haste, and get thee quickly out of Jerusalem: for they will not receive thy testimony concerning me.*

[42] Romans 3:26.

[43] Eight times in his Gospel and also once in 3rd John.

ινα   ινα almost invariably means "in order that." And it is almost
             invariably followed by a verb which is in the subjunctive mood. In
             the Greek, the subjunctive mood is used to express the element of
             contingency. The action of the verb following may happen or it may
             not happen. In the case of our sample sentence: John came in witness
             that he _might_ witness to the light ... There is no intrinsic commentary
             about whether John succeeded in his mission. The sentence merely
             states that he came in order that...

Exegetical Considerations: In English, the subjunctive mood is not often
intentionally employed – probably because it has been unintentionally obviated by a
widespread philosophical orientation that is constantly making a distinction
between that which is "real" or "actual" and that which is possible, or likely, or
probable.[44] For example, notice how many times people use "really," "actually" -
and their philosophical cognates, in ordinary conversation. In modern English
parlance, we live and move and have our being in the subjunctive mood, so there is
no longer any point in making a special effort to distinguish it.

But in the Greek, the subjunctive mood lies very visibly on the surface of the
language because life is full of uncertainty and contingency. One must be careful not
to read back into the Greek subjunctive the modern philosophical orientation of
chaos, chance and parallel universes. For example, when Jesus comes walking on the
water the disciples make no effort to decide whether or not what they see is "real" or
illusory hallucination or a mirage. These words are not in the Greek mind. The
disciples immediately take fright because they believe that what they are seeing is a
φαντασμα - that is, a ghost.[45] The subjunctive mood is used many, many times in
our literature - and that very un-philosophically; therefore, we must make a
determined effort to keep the modern mindset from wandering into our analysis of
the authors with whom we must deal. Whether we are talking about Jesus'
resurrectional appearances, the Damascus road epiphany, a vision, or an
apocalypse, we must understand that these things are simply not subject to the
modern question: 'did this "really" happen?'

μαρτυρηση   And here we have the aorist _subjunctive_ of "witness." It may seem to
             us that John is being redundant. For example, a rhetorician might
             attempt to streamline this sentence by saying "He came in order to
             witness..." But John _knows_ he is being redundant. He is repeating for

---

[44] Modern science sees the possibility of multiple realities, in which the principle of probability within
chaos predominates. See discussions concerning Schrodinger's Cat, for example. (See particularly the
"Copenhagen interpretation" of this idea.)
[45] Matthew 14:26.

emphasis and clarity. One of the literary characteristics of John that we will see as his Gospel unfolds is this repetitiveness.

When we come to a word that is being deformed from its normal use for the purpose of achieving a metaphorical construction, we call it "poetic diction." Therefore, when we come to a deformed syntax we must, as our default position, assume that we have come to an intentional piece of *editorial* diction. If we see no editorial motive for this deformation, we may then mark it up to editorial style or unknown convention, as in the case of Mark's duo duo. But in our sample sentence, we must notice that because "witness" is used as a noun and as a verb, much less notice comes to rest upon the idea of "he came," John is not concerned with the narrative detail as much as he is concerned to clarify the <u>role</u> of John the Baptist. John came in witness in order to witness. But what is the substance of his witness?

περι του φωτος

John's testimony is about light. περι is a very common preposition which means "the things concerning which" or "about which." Whenever περι is used, it is almost always conjoined with the genitive. Since the genitive implies possession, it is only natural that this should be so. Underlying this construction, then, is the idea that the substance of John's testimony is about the things which *pertain* to the light. Things which "belong" to such a discussion.

Another way to grasp the idea behind a primary word is to watch how it is taken up into the formation of compound words. From an analysis of how περι contributes its idea to these compound words[46] we will see that it contributes the idea of "around." περιαγω means "go around."[47] περιαστραπτω means to "shine around."[48] When we construct a Venn diagram of meaning, we begin by drawing a <u>circle</u> around a word. Mark clearly illustrates the sense of this:

και περιβλεψαμενος κυκλω τους   περι αυτον καθημενους...[49]
and   looking around   the circle of those   around him   sitting ...

---

[46] You may conduct such a survey by looking at the dictionary included in your GNT. Begin with περι and observe how it is used in its various compounds which alphabetically follow.
[47] αγω means "go." Matthew 4:23 *And Jesus <u>went around</u> all Galilee.*
[48] αστραπτω means "shine" Ac 9:3 *And as he journeyed, he came near Damascus: and suddenly there <u>shined round</u> about him a light from heaven.*
[49] Mark 3:34.

58

Exegetical Considerations: John says that John the Baptist was sent to give testimony about the Son *himself*, the very light of men. The role of John the Baptist was to draw a circle and put Christ in the middle of it. We shall soon see why.

ινα παντες πιστευσωσιν δι αυτου

> The new word in the final part of our selected sentence is πιστευω, which means "believe." First, let's take the word apart. πιστευ is the stem. the third person plural ending would have normally been ουσι, but changes to ωσι to indicate the subjunctive. The ν at the end of the word has nothing to do with the personal ending – it is added, as in the case of ουκ and αλλα above, merely to make it sound smoother in the sentence, just as we add a<u>n</u> "n" to the article when it precedes a word beginning with a vowel or vowel sound.

Exegetical Considerations: John uses this word, πιστευω, very distinctively. Of 26 times that "believe" is used in the subjunctive mood in the New Testament materials, John accounts for nearly two thirds of them. He uses this verb almost as many times as all three Synoptics combined. Yet John never uses it as a noun; that is, πιστιν ("belief")! This kind of linguistic data should not be dismissed as a literary anomaly, unknown convention or authorial style. Especially when such uses are directly related to a major thematic element in John. This is John's prologue. We are reading editorial commentary here. While the Synoptics end their Gospels on a note of doubt, misunderstanding, incompleteness or fear, John writes a book with one hotly pursued objective: to encourage Christians to *believe* God's testimony in Christ.

The Synoptics do not tell us *what* to believe about Christ. They present empirical data within a literary template which places the reader more fully in the place of apostolic bewilderment, confronting the phenomena of Christ. Without the epistles, it is not altogether clear what we should believe. Not so with John. He is constantly telling us *what* to believe. And why we should believe it - from the beginning to the end: *For God so loved the world, that he gave his only begotten Son, that whosoever believeth in him should not perish, but have everlasting life.*[50] *... But these are written, that ye might believe that Jesus is the Christ, the Son of God; and that believing ye might have life through his name.*[51] John's editorial motive is clearly pastoral.

And there is one more thing to notice about this verb, "believe." John uses the

---

[50] John 3:16.
[51] John 20:31.

preposition δια; that is, we must believe *through* him.[52] In modern parlance, "to believe" means to believe <u>in</u> something. In popular religion, we get a reward of salvation because we *choose* to "subscribe," or even "assent" to a list of propositions. But this does not touch what John (or Paul) mean by "believe." For John and also for Paul, it is an oxymoron to say that we "choose to believe." And no author says that we must believe, passively, "in" (εν) something. John often does couple the more fuller preposition εις with "believe", but εις carries stronger connotations of *motion* - of "unto" and "into" and "upon" which εν does not carry.[53] For example, consider Romans 10:10 *For with the heart man believeth unto* (εις) *righteousness; and with the mouth confession is made unto* (εις) *salvation,* where it is clear that to translate εις as "in" would change the whole thrust of the Paul's meaning. εις, therefore, has been chosen to convey the <u>transitive</u>[54] nature of the act of believing that εν does not.

The process of distinguishing the object of belief is important to John and Paul not only because of what one believes, but <u>who</u> one believes. And if we follow the verb "believe" in its usage in the second sense (who), we will observe the use of the dative case. And this is the primary sense of "believing" that we see in the New Testament materials. We believe Christ, we believe the word, and we believe God. That's <u>who</u> we believe. In terms of <u>what</u> we believe - we believe everything. That is, everything that is true. We do not believe a lie, we believe all things that are true. It is the only rational response.

Therefore Paul says: "love believes all things."[55] The demons do not believe all things. They only believe some things.[56] They even believe the first commandment: *And Jesus answered him, The first of all the commandments is, Hear, O Israel; The Lord our God is one Lord...*[57] *You believe that God is one; you do well: the devils also believe...*[58] But that, in itself, won't help them. The author of Hebrews explains why Paul's 'belief apart from works' justified Abraham but not the demons. Because Abraham believed that God was worthy of trust: *By faith Abraham, when he was tried, offered up Isaac: and he that had received the promises offered up his only begotten son, Of whom it was said, That in Isaac shall thy seed be called: accounting that God was able to raise him up, even from the dead...*[59]

---

[52] Note too that the "him" in question is in the genitive case, αυτου. The genitive here helps to resolve the ambiguity of who the pronoun refers to – John the Baptist or Jesus. Later, John writes (12:11): οτι πολλοι δι αυτον ... επιστευον (because many *through him* believed), using the accusative case (αυτον).
[53] And the combination of εις and "believe" occurs rarely in other authors. For example; once in Matthew: *But whoso shall offend one of these little ones which believe in* (εις) *me...* (18:6)
[54] That is, the verbal <u>action</u> which requires an object.
[55] 1st Corinthians 13:7.
[56] That is, they are not consistently rational.
[57] Mark 12:29.
[58] James 2:19.
[59] Hebrews 11:17-19b.

οὐκ ἠν ἐκεινος το φως αλλ ινα μαρτυρηση περι του φωτος
not was that (one) the light, but that he might witness concerning the light

οὐκ, again, is the negative particle, just like our "no" or "not." When it precedes a word which begins with a consonant, the κ is dropped, again, for ease of pronunciation. αλλ is a conjunction which sets up a contrast – and corresponds most closely to our use of "but." Here again, changes occur merely for euphony; that is, when αλλ precedes a word that begins with a consonant, it becomes αλλ<u>α</u>, adding an "α."

Here again we must emphasize that word order is significant. The word that begins this sentence – that first emerges from the mind of John - is "not." The most important idea is the "notness" (so to speak) of what is to follow. ἐκεινος[60] is a demonstrative pronoun meaning "that" or "those" and takes the same endings as οὐτος. The next question in our minds should be: *that*…what? Since John does not immediately specify that which εκεινος refers, we must supply one from context.

Our first clue is that εκεινος is the nominative singular form. Therefore John's referent is the man who he has been talking about – namely, John the Baptist. We then have "not was that *man* (or that *one*) the light." John could have said: οὐκ ην αυτος το φως (that is, "he was not that light") But he didn't.[61] We may say that in John's choice of εκεινος, he may be attempting to embrace not only John the Baptist, but the *act* of coming as a witness. We might also then translate: 'The purpose of that *coming* was not as light, but to witness concerning the light.' John is not splitting hairs here. He is, again, being repetitive.

Exegetical Considerations: If we read ahead in the account, we see that John is, early on, loosely following the Synoptic account. But he is greatly amplifying the Synoptic theme which differentiates John the Baptist from Christ. Matthew applies a heralding role to John by quoting Isaiah 40:3. But there is ambiguity here. Is this the heralding of Christ? Shortly (in Matthew), John the Baptist differentiates himself from someone else who has a different baptism, whose sandals he is "not worthy to bear." Then John, at the baptism of Christ, says: *"I have need to be baptized of you – and you are coming to me?"*[62]

---

[60] Hewett, 8.2.2

[61] Likewise, John could have said earlier: "And the word was God" (και ο λογος ην θεος). But he didn't. By deforming this word order, John brings more emphasis upon his subject – the logos; the light.

[62] Matthew 3:14.

Further on, Matthew has Jesus apply Malachi 3:1a[63] to John. And by various Synoptic dialogues we may infer that John the Baptist is the greatest of Old Testament prophets. But there is still ambiguity here. If John is the greatest prophet, who is Jesus? We are learning about the role of John the Baptist, but we are not necessarily clarifying the role of Christ. John is doing precisely this. John – and only John – specifically applies the Aramaic title of μεσσιας (Messiah) to Jesus. And in many instances that we shall soon seen in John's prologue, he belabors the categorical distinction between John and Jesus. Why is John belaboring this relatively brief Synoptic distinction between John the Baptist and Jesus? And this question is particularly vexing if we accept the idea that the Gospel of John was written towards the end of the century, when the role of John the Baptist and the identity of Christ have long since become doctrinally fixed.

Is there anything internal to our literature that might help us to understand what the Apostle John is doing? Yes, there is something. Far into Acts we find that there is still considerable confusion about "the way." We see Apollos making his evangelistic rounds a stop or two ahead of Paul. First Apollos preaches in Ephesus, then he leaves for Corinth.[64] Then Paul arrives in Ephesus behind Apollos and finds that he has preached merely an embryonic form of the Gospel, which centers upon the baptism of John. And even though Aquila and Priscilla take Apollos aside and lay out the "way of God" more perfectly, Luke does not specify what it is that they said to Apollos – nor Apollos' response. Whatever it was that they told Apollos, he nevertheless left the church of Ephesus without the baptism of the Holy Ghost.

Paul follows and sees the problem of a Gospel centering upon the baptism of John with a vague theological concession that Jesus is somehow the Christ of God. Paul remonstrates and attempts to differentiate the baptism of John with a new baptism – the baptism of Christ. Those who accept this and who are baptized are immediately beset with ecstatic utterances and prophecy. But there are only a dozen men who accept Paul's position.[65] When Paul writes his first letter to the church of Corinth in the mid to late fifties there is still considerable controversy and confusion about the role of John the Baptist and the role of Christ: *For it hath been declared unto me of you, my brethren, by them which are of the house of Chloe, that there are contentions among you. Now this I say, that every one of you saith, I am of Paul; and I of Apollos; and I of Cephas; and I of Christ.*[66]

We may safely conclude that the Synoptic material is coming into general circulation during Paul's imprisonment (around 60AD) from comments in Luke, secretary to Paul during this imprisonment. And since this material makes a specific effort to

---

[63] *Behold, I will send my messenger, and he shall prepare the way before me.*
[64] Acts 18:24 – 19:1.
[65] Acts 19:7.
[66] 1st Corinthians 1:11-12.

distinguish the baptism of Christ from the baptism of John, this confirms our suspicion that the cult of John the Baptist is still a concern even at this late date. If the Gospel of John elaborates upon this editorial concern, then the dating of John is driven much closer to 60AD, especially since sources external to our literature place him firmly at Ephesus. John had come to reside at Paul's vacated diocesan seat – Ephesus. Is there anything in our literature that connects John with Ephesus? Yes, there is. John receives his apocalypse at Patmos, and island in the Aegean, a short journey from Ephesus. And Ephesus is the first addressed of the seven churches of Asia in the Johannine Apocalypse.

In summary: John's editorial concern to distinguish the role of Jesus from John the Baptist drives the date of his Gospel in the direction of 60AD. But more importantly, John's *physical* connection with Ephesus gives us a potential rationale for such a concern. Style, thematic emphasis, setting – these meta-literary considerations must inform our perception of the context from which we must make our translations. Because there will be many instances where we must resolve translational ambiguity from within the context of these meta-literary considerations alone.

Chapter 2 Review

Let us review what we have translated:

εν αρχη ην ο λογος και ο λογος ην προς τον θεον και θεος ην ο λογος
ουτος ην εν αρχη προς τον θεον παντα δι αυτου εγενετο και χωρις
αυτου εγενετο ουδε εν ο γεγονεν εν αυτω ζωη ην και η ζωη ην το φως
των ανθρωπων και το φως εν τη σκοτια φαινει και η σκοτια αυτο ου
κατελαβεν εγενετο ανθρωπος απεσταλμενος παρα θεου ονομα αυτω
ιωαννης ουτος ηλθεν εις μαρτυριαν ινα μαρτυρηση περι του φωτος ινα
παντες πιστευσωσιν δι αυτου ουκ ην εκεινος το φως αλλ ινα
μαρτυρηση περι του φωτος

Make a handwritten transcription of this passage. As you form each word, think about what it means. Think about its place in the sentence. Allow each sentence to speak for itself. Enunciate each word. And do not worry about accent. Whether you are from Macedonia or Achaia, God is no respecter of accent. Give each word the attention that it needs. You are not in a hurry. And do not worry about what you might be missing. You will be taking this walk several times throughout the course of your life. Concentrate on what you are *not* missing. Just as the naturalist is a sensory sponge as he walks through the woods, allow yourself to be passively open to your linguistic environment.

Chapter 3: John 1:9 – 1:12

ην το φως το αληθινον ο   φωτιζει παντα ανθρωπον ερχομενον εις τον
was the light   the true   which lights   all   men   coming   into   the

κοσμον
world

αληθινος   Of the 25 times this word is used, 20 of these are Johannine. And they are equally distributed throughout John, 1ˢᵗ John and Revelation. It is an adjective which means "true." Here John is defining "light." The "true light" is a phrase which occurs only once more – in 1ˢᵗ John 2:8b … *the darkness is past, and the <u>true light</u> now shineth.* Based on our preliminary linguistic discoveries, let us assume, as a working hypothesis, that 1ˢᵗ John is indeed written by John. 1ˢᵗ John may then be used to help illuminate John. For example, in our sample sentence, John combines the ideas of "light," "true" and a verbal form of "light." In our 1ˢᵗ John reference, there is the same combination, except that John uses a different verbal form of light: φαινω.[1] This 1ˢᵗ John reference also resonates in another way. The combination of light, true and darkness (σκοτια) has occurred just four sentences ago in the Gospel: και το φως εν τη σκοτια φαινει.

<u>Exegetical Considerations</u>: The question then emerges: 'why the switch?' Why doesn't John consistently say that the light shines (φαινω)? There may not be enough information to answer this question, because the answer might be that this is merely a negligible idiomatic quirk. But we should ask the question. If something catches the eye of a naturalist walking in the woods, he pauses to investigate. It may be nothing. It may be something. It may be something wonderful. But the habit of stopping to study that which catches the eye - for whatever the reason - is an important characteristic of the naturalist. And it should be an important characteristic of our studied, exegetical walk through our translational woods. It may be that you don't have the time to stop and properly examine that which catches your eye. But why don't you have time? The naturalist is not in a hurry. Why should you be? In the private dialogue of which we speak, speed with which you translate is functionally irrelevant. And if you do not have the time now, when will you? The Lord does not care about speed or quantity. Only men care about these things. The Lord cares for intimacy, truth and quality.

John uses φαινω once more in his Gospel. And that is in reference to John the Baptist. The Apostle John is still summing up his argument which distinguishes

---

[1] This combination of "light" and "shine" is used only by John (2x); 1ˢᵗ John (1x) and Revelation (1x).

John the Baptist from Christ. Here Jesus says that the witness of John the Baptist is, in one sense, superfluous. Christ does not need the witness of John – it is we who need it. Christ needs no herald. He will suddenly come to his temple. Ready or not, here he comes. John the Baptist was given so that *men* might prepare themselves for the visitation: *Ye sent unto John, and he bare witness unto the truth. But I receive not testimony from man: but these things I say, that ye might be saved. He was a burning and a shining **light**: and ye were willing for a season to rejoice in his light. But I have greater witness than that of John…*[2] The word (bolded and underlined) that John here uses is λυχνος, which is the common word for candle.

The light of John the Baptist is temporary and derivative in nature. The light of Christ is eternal: *And the city had no need of the sun, neither of the moon, to shine in it: for the glory of God did lighten it, and the Lamb is the light (*λυχνος*) thereof.* The light of the moon helps men to navigate in the darkness. But it is reflected light. When day itself comes, the *true* source of light makes the light of the moon superfluous. John repeats this idea again in Revelation 22:5 *And there shall be no night there; and they need no candle, neither light of the sun; for the Lord God giveth them light and they shall reign for ever and ever.* This is the only place outside our sample sentence in which φως and φωτιζω are combined in the same sentence. From a linguistic perspective, John is consistent.

Although John is structurally similar to Matthew, one of the key differences between John and Matthew is that John is constantly putting in explanatory dialogue. He is having a much more direct conversation with his reader. The editorial dialogue in Matthew is much cooler.[3] As we have noted before, John is explicit: *But these are written, that ye might believe that Jesus is the Christ, the Son of God; and that believing ye might have life through his name.*[4]

Examine this clear statement of editorial intent for a moment. John is saying three things about his purpose, which comes under the umbrella of his subjunctive use of "believe" (πιστευω). Remember that for John, a belief is not something that we possess – as if it were an object – like a sock that can be moved around inside a drawer. A belief always lives as a verb in John. He writes in order that his witness might provoke us to believe three things: 1) that Jesus is the Christ of God 2) that Jesus is the Son of God. 3) and that the nature of our belief be such as to produce life in us. John is therefore setting out an argument for our own good. Again here is the

---

[2] John 5:33-36a.
[3] In *Understanding Media*, Marshall McLuhan differentiates the *kind* of communication with temperature; i.e., "hot" communication is explicit, direct, propositional – such as a written argument specifying reasons that such and such a policy should be adopted by the government. "Cool" communication is implicit, perhaps even subliminal – like much of today's advertising, in which the media itself becomes the message.
[4] John 20:31.

pastoral motive. We will see this pastoral motive very clearly in John's epistles. John's position is that the act of belief in these things produces life in us. He will soon be explicit about this too. He has already become explicit about what we are to believe.

When John says that Jesus is the "true light" he is not setting up Jesus in opposition to a light that is false. He is setting him up in contrast with a light that is derivative. God gave Israel bread from heaven. But whoever ate of that bread died, because that bread was temporary bread for a temporary life. Jesus is the true bread αρτον…αληθινον[5] in the same sense that John is saying that Jesus is the true light. The manna in the wilderness was not false bread. It was simply *temporary* bread.[6]

Hostile worldliness stares uncomprehending at the surface tension of John and finds it impenetrable. The world therefore generates two equal but opposite theories about what John is doing. On the one hand, (it is said) John is merely dressing up a Gnostic theology that has come (it is said) from his prior indoctrination as an Essene. On the other hand, John is an inscrutable mystic, who is attempting to grasp metaphysical realities that are so beyond human comprehension that his writing is almost incomprehensible. But the moment we *listen* to what John is saying, we see that neither of these two theories could possibly be true. John is a very tactile person: *That which was from the beginning, which we have heard, which we have seen with our eyes, which we have looked upon, and our hands have handled, of the Word of life…*[7] He may not be dismissed as a mystical fool. And though John writes very simply and directly and redundantly, the substance of what he has to say rises far above the shabby monotony of Gnosticism.

The Synoptic Gospel is about what Jesus taught and what he did. John's gospel is almost entirely about who Jesus is. And this is why John spends so much time in his prologue telling us who John the Baptist _is not_. Paul's way of distinguishing Jesus from John the Baptist in his first letter to the Corinthian church was to rhetorically ask: was Apollos crucified for you? Was Cephas? Was Paul? Paul's early preaching was almost entirely about the crucifixion of Christ: *But we preach Christ crucified, unto the Jews a stumblingblock, and unto the Greeks foolishness.*[8] We may even term Paul's theology a "crucifixion theology:" *For I determined not to know any thing among you, save Jesus Christ, and him crucified.*[9]

---

[5] John 6:32.

[6] This kind of thinking is found elsewhere only in Hebrews: Hebrews 9:24 For *Christ is not entered into the holy places made with hands, which are the figures of the true; but into heaven itself, now to appear in the presence of God for us.*

[7] 1st John 1:1.

[8] 1st Corinthians 1:23.

[9] 1st Corinthians 2:2.

Think for a moment about the theology of Paul as it is presented in his first block of pre-imprisonment epistles. After a preliminary emphasis on the return of Christ in Thessalonians, they become almost exclusively about reconciliation, justification and transcending the law. Where in this first block does Paul address the uniqueness of Christ in relation to these other key figures? Recall that Paul's response to the cult of John the Baptist was to offer a superior baptism – which was attended with superior charismatic manifestations. Think, too, about the Christology that is presented in James. There *is* none. What about Peter? μονογενης[10] - a term so central to the Gospel prologue of John, Peter's first preaching partner, is never found in the mouth of Peter himself. πρωτοτοκος,[11] a key theological title for Christ in Paul, Hebrews and John, is also never found in the mouth of Peter. In Matthew 16:16 Peter says to Jesus: *Thou art the Christ, the Son of the living God.* Peter never utters the phrase again. Mark begins his Gospel with this phrase yet does not put it into the mouth of Peter. Peter merely says, *Thou art Christ.*[12] Luke agrees (…*Christ of God*[13]). In a synagogue in Capernaum, John records an alternate Petrine confession: *And we believe and are sure that thou art the Holy One of God.*[14] Four times Peter calls Jesus παις ("servant" or "child") of God (in dialogue recorded by Luke in Acts), but never again does he call him "Son of God."

What got Peter into trouble in his early preaching was not blasphemy. What got him into trouble was his anti-establishment preaching. He preached that the man whom the Sanhedrin had wrongfully criminalized had been gloriously vindicated through a miraculous resurrection. And this particularly angered the Sanhedrin which was then controlled by the Sadducees, (who denied a physical resurrection), since after the death of Christ many of the seats of the Pharisee party had been vacated by conversion to "the way." Think about Peter's career as it is presented in Acts. After a burst of zealous preaching, attended with miraculous healings, Peter comes onto the stage for a lesson in missiology (the vision, the visit to Cornelius and the Jerusalem council). Then, Peter fades away as the story in Acts becomes almost entirely about Paul's career. Then, almost nothing. We hear once about Peter's shameful hypocrisy in the Antiochian affair.[15] We will not hear from Peter again until thirty years *after* the resurrection.[16]

Into this situation steps John and says: 'Jesus is the only-begotten son of God.' Yes, Christ crucified is scandalous. But what John is now saying is even more scandalous. In the Synoptics, Jesus got into trouble because he didn't wash his hands. He

---

[10] "only begotten."
[11] First born – from πρωτος (first) and τικτω (give birth).
[12] Mark 8:29.
[13] Luke 9:20.
[14] John 6:69.
[15] Galatians 2:11-14.
[16] 1st Peter. Even here we see no clear, Christological confession.

mingled with common tax collectors and sinners. He ignored the Sabbath restrictions. He did not properly respect the tradition of his elders. He blurred the lines of blasphemy by appearing to tell a man that his sins were forgiven. He appropriated the title of "Son of Man" and the prophecy of Daniel. But it is still unclear to the reader what the formal charges against him are. At the trial, the high-priest rends his robes in seeming over-reaction to what Jesus is saying. The high priest seems relieved that after parading in some embarrassing, false witnesses, he suddenly thinks that he has something upon which he can rest a conviction.

Not so in John. Early on the Jews take up stones to kill Jesus: *Therefore the Jews sought the more to kill him, because he not only had broken the sabbath, but said also that God was his Father, making himself equal with God.*[17] John has Jesus say: *before Abraham was, I am.*[18] There are no explicit statements like this in the Synoptics. The Synoptics give no sign of who Jesus is except the sign of Jonas. It is therefore difficult to see how, or even why, an enigma should be crucified.

---

[17] John 5:18.
[18] John 8:58.

Let's get back to our sentence:

ην το φως το αληθινον ο   φωτιζει παντα ανθρωπον ερχομενον εις τον
was the light   the true   which lights   all   men   coming   into   the

κοσμον
world

The sentence appears to begin without a subject. But there are three ways in which a subject is already present. 1) The reader carries over to the sentence the subject of the previous discussion. John's subject has been "the light." Now he will elaborate. 2) Verbs never come without a personal ending. That person sometimes stands in as the subject. In this example the verb is not merely "was" – but "<u>he, she or it</u> was." 3) The adjectival phrase: *who lights all men coming into the world* may also be considered as the subject of the sentence.

Note the way in which the adjective *follows* the noun that it defines. Of course αληθινον takes on the neuter ending of φως. But the main idea is "light," not "true." Sometimes in English the noun is preceded with a substantial list of adjectives. You must nevertheless wait and see what all these adjectives are defining before you can know what euphonic value you must give to the adjectives.

Note too, in our sample sentence, the presence of the article with both the noun (φως) and the adjective (αληθινον). The article is not required, but its presence tends to equalize the value of the adjective. In the lingo of grammarians, it is said that an adjective *modifies* a noun. But in the Greek the adjective does no such thing. The noun is not changed, it is more accurately *defined*. At first, the construction sounds awkward, but you will see it often. Practice saying it.

ο   We have seen the relative pronoun already in our third sentence: και χωρις αυτου εγενετο ουδε εν <u>ο</u> γεγονεν (and without him has begun not one thing **which** has become).

φωτιζει   Previously, John has said that the light shines (φαινω) in the darkness. Now he changes to a different verbal form which is more closely connected to the root word φως (sometimes called a "cognate"). This light is not shining into the uncomprehending darkness; this light is shining into the very soul of every man who makes an entrance, by ordinary biological generation, into the world. Since this word is very often use to denote "comprehension" in our literature, John is saying that this light is comprehension itself, in the most primary sense possible.

72

Luke captures this sense: *The light of the body is the eye: therefore when thine eye is single, thy whole body also is full of light; but when thine eye is evil, thy body also is full of darkness. Take heed therefore that the light which is in thee be not darkness. If thy whole body therefore be full of light, having no part dark, the whole shall be full of light, as when the bright shining of a candle doth give thee light* (φωτιζη).[19] So does the author of Hebrews, using the aorist passive participle of φωτιζω: *For it is impossible for those who were once enlightened* (φωτισθεντας[20]), *and have tasted of the heavenly gift, and were made partakers of the Holy Ghost…*[21]

Although this is the only time that John uses this verb, he will return again and again to the idea of Jesus as the light of men. And it is through this light that all knowledge exists. There is no knowledge apart from Christ. John's epistles address this idea in terms that are more familiar to modern ears. They are the terms of epistemology[22] – or, 'how we know that we know.' But in this Gospel, John has a lot of ground to cover. Jesus is the word, life and the very bread of life, true water and true wine, the light, the way, the truth, the resurrection, the door of all faithful sheep, the good shepherd, the true vine; the only begotten Son of God.

κοσμον   Here κοσμος is in the accusative case (κοσμον) since it is the object of the preposition εις. The English word "cosmos" is a direct transliteration. John uses this word 58 times in his Gospel *four times* as much as the Synoptics combined - almost always in the same sense.

<u>Exegetical Considerations</u>: Although John refers to the world in the sense of that which has been created (as he does here),[23] most of the time "the world" is seen as enemy territory into which Jesus has come to liberate the sons of God. Nevertheless, God loves the world. Just as in Pauline theology, Jesus dies for the sins of the whole

---

[19] Luke 11:34-36.

[20] In this case the θ indicates aorist passive, the ε is a connecting vowel and the ντας puts the participle in the accusative case, since it is passively receiving the action; i.e., "having been enlightened."

[21] Hebrews 6:4.

[22] In modern theories of epistemology, there is considerable emphasis on what we <u>cannot</u> know. John makes a stunning statement in his epistle about what we <u>can</u> know. And there is no other statement like this in our literature. There is no better resolution to the modern epistemological dilemma than this: και εν τουτω γινωσκομεν οτι εγνωκαμεν αυτον (*And in this we know that we know him…* 1st John 2:3). This is no more ambitious than the modern epistemological axiom: "we know for certain that we can know nothing with any certainty." Better to be thought audacious than absurd.

[23] And in 17:24 *Father, I will that they also, whom thou hast given me, be with me where I am; that they may behold my glory, which thou hast given me: for thou lovedst me before the foundation of the <u>world</u>.*

world.[24] Though Jesus declines to pray for the world, God nevertheless loves the world.[25]

This statement is sometimes construed as only loving a specialized set of men within the world. But John does not say this. Paul says that while we were yet sinners Christ died for us.[26] John says that the whole world lies in sin[27] yet here is the lamb that takes away the sins of the world.[28] John removes all doubt that Jesus' sacrifice is only for a specialized set of men: *And he is the propitiation for our sins: and not for ours only, but also for the whole world.*[29] In the Exodus from Egypt which, at length, we will see is the operating typology that is never far from the mind of John, Paul, Stephen, Timothy, etc., we understand that a man had to *do* something in order to be spared the judgment of the death of the firstborn. He had to "appropriate" the blood and spatter it upon the lintel of his house. John and Paul are saying that Jesus spattered the entire world in his blood. Now the condemnation consists solely in the *rejection* of the blood of the new covenant[30] and the active *return* to Egypt – consciously repudiating this new Moses, embracing the darkness of bondage and sin.

In the Synoptics there is very little indication that the whole world lies in wickedness. The world itself is neutral: *The field is the world; the good seed are the children of the kingdom; but the tares are the children of the wicked one.*[31] But there *is* an indication that there is something wrong with the world: *Again, the devil taketh him up into an exceeding high mountain, and sheweth him all the kingdoms of the world, and the glory of them; And saith unto him, All these things will I give thee, if thou wilt fall down and worship me.*[32] By what authority may Satan make this offer if the whole world did not lie, at least in part, under his power?

Again we must turn to a Pauline theological cognate for illumination: *Wherein in time past ye walked according to the course of this world, according to the prince of the power of the air, the spirit that now worketh in the children of disobedience.*[33] Only in John and Ephesians may we find any reference to this "prince of the world." In Luke's variant

---

[24] Romans 5:18 *Therefore as by the offence of one judgment came upon all men; even so by the righteousness of one came upon all men justification of life.*

[25] 17:9 *I pray for them: I pray not for the world, but for them which thou hast given me; for they are thine.* and 3:16 *For God so loved the world, that he gave his only begotten Son, that whosoever believeth in him should not perish, but have everlasting life.*

[26] Romans 5:8.

[27] 1st John 5:19.

[28] John 1:29.

[29] 1st John 2:2.

[30] Hebrews 10:29 *Of how much sorer punishment, suppose ye, shall he be thought worthy, who hath trodden under foot the Son of God, and hath counted the blood of the covenant, wherewith he was sanctified, an unholy thing, and hath done despite unto the Spirit of grace?*

[31] Matthew 13:38.

[32] Matthew 4:8-9.

[33] Ephesians 2:2.

of the temptation, he acknowledges this idea, albeit cryptically: *And the devil said unto him, All this authority[34] will I give thee, and the glory of them: for that is delivered unto me; and to whomsoever I will I give it.*[35] It is there also, cryptically in Matthew: *what is this possession to us and to you? Have you come to torment us before the time appointed?*[36]

This seems to be a reasonable objection in view of the fact that we read in John Jesus saying: *My kingdom is not of this world - if my kingdom were of this world, then would my servants fight, that I should not be delivered to the Jews: but now is my kingdom not from hence.*[37] The demons thus complain that Jesus is evicting them before the time that their lease on human souls expires. To what temporary lease of power and authority do these sources refer? John spends considerable space in Revelation in explanation, which could be summarized thusly: εγενοντο αι βασιλειαι του κοσμου του κυριου ημων και του χριστου αυτου και βασιλευσει εις τους αιωνας των αιωνων. (The kingdoms of this world are become our Lord's and his Christ, and he shall reign for ever.)

The important thing to see in these exegetical considerations is that John is not operating outside Synoptic and Pauline theology in a world of his own. We will see again and again that John is *shadowing* the Synoptic template - and he is, in part, *filling* it with Pauline theological cognates. Thus we see the resolution of a Synoptic theme in an apocalyptic vision of another author. Jesus is offered the power and glory of the whole world if he will merely concede some respect to Satan. Jesus says: 'no, I will not take the easy way. Because that way is wrong. You do not deserve any respect at all. I will *earn* all these things myself.' And the author of Hebrews consciously brings this theme to its perfect end: *Who in the days of his flesh, when he had offered up prayers and supplications with strong crying and tears unto him that was able to save him from death, and was heard in that he feared; Though he were a Son, yet learned he obedience by the things which he suffered; And being made perfect, he became the author of eternal salvation unto all them that obey him.*[38]

When we come to the authors of the New Testament materials, we often come influenced by the modern mindset which presupposes that these authors are individualistic existentialists who are modulating a community tradition into a personal religious system that they can live by – we thereby project our own mindset upon the authors of our literature. But this is not the mindset of the authors of our literature. They are not working in isolation. And they are not attempting to express a community consensus. They are aware that others are struggling to

---

[34] The word in the KJV is "power." But the text specifies εξουσιαν (authority) not δυναμις (power)
[35] Luke 4:6.
[36] Matthew 8:29.
[37] John 18:36.
[38] Hebrews 5:7-9.

conform themselves to something which lies wholly outside of community consensus. And they are aware of what others are, prophetically, saying. They are listening. And they are learning.[39]

This is a most important idea. The translator/exegete cannot ignore this. If we formally acknowledge that there may be theological development and perhaps even some dissonance in our literature, we cannot translate every word in a literary monotone. The New Testament documents are a tonal symphony. We must listen not only to the individual words in local context. We must listen to the local contexts as they themselves are imbedded within a larger, contextual drama. If we lift James out of this dramatic context, it becomes "an epistle of straw." But if we leave the dissonance of James *within* the larger score of the New Testament corpus, we see that at least in one sense, considerable theological pathos pivots upon this dissonance.

---

[39] John is attempting to *conform* himself to that which his spirit was once inimical. (Luke 9:54-55) But in so doing, he *transforms* the collective consciousness of a church which is drifting into apathy, doubt, fear and theological equivocation.

εν τω κοσμω ην   και ο κοσμος   δι αυτου   εγενετο   και
in   the world   was(he)   and the world   through him began   and

ο κοσμος   αυτον   ουκ εγνω
the world   him   (did) not know.

Here is the preposition εν taking the dative (τω κοσμω).

εγνω   This unusual form of the word "know" is used only 17 times in the New
            Testament materials. Of these, John accounts for 10 of them (Gospel 7x,
            1st John 2x, Revelation 1x). Just as ερχομαι is an irregular verb, so is
            γινωσκω. εγνω is its aorist form.[40] You will see this verb in all its other
            forms many times (77x) in the Johannine corpus (Gospel 49x, 1st John
            22x , 2nd John 1x, Revelation 5x). This represents nearly 40% of its
            overall appearances. Here are the forms and frequency that you will
            find this verb in John's Gospel (with various personal endings
            attached):

γινωσκεις	12	Present
γινωσκων	1	Present Participle[41]
γινωσκειν	1	Present infinitive[42]
εγινωσκεν	1	Imperfect[43]
εγνωσαν	13	Aorist
γνους	2	Aorist Participle[44]
γνω	5	Aorist Subjunctive
γνωσεσθε	6	Future
εγνωκα	6	Perfect
εγνωκειτε	1	PluPerfect[45]

[40] A key piece of information you need to complete the translation is the person. Shown here is the 3rd person singular. "The world did not know" (he she or it). This verb is basically following the 1st aorist, active indicative paradigm (see Hewett, 311), but since this is an irregular verb, it is not easy to explain the exceptions. The aorist active indicative forms you will find are this one and εγνων (I knew); εγνως (you {singular} knew); εγνωσαν (they knew).

[41] Used in an adjectival phrase defining people in 7:49 But this people who knoweth not the law (ο μη γινωσκων τον νομον) are cursed.

[42] John 2:24 But Jesus did not commit himself unto them, because he knew all. It is a reasonable conjecture that John here uses the infinitive to avoid specifying a voice for Jesus' knowledge of things, since his knowledge is timeless.

[43] Nevertheless, John changes tenses to a rare use of the imperfect in the very next sentence. And needed not that any should testify of man: for he knew what was in man.

[44] Here again is a rare usage, and in both cases (5:6; 6:15) John refers to the knowledge of Jesus.

[45] John 14:7 If ye had known me, ye should have known my Father also: and from henceforth ye know him, and have seen him. As a translator, you must rightfully ask yourself: why the change in English verbiage?

Notice that with this verb the imperfect and the aorist begin by adding a "helping" vowel at the beginning of the word. This is common with many verbs which begin with a consonant. In words which begin with a vowel, you will very often see that vowel "lengthen" to a stronger vowel. Additionally, another common feature of the aorist is that the spelling of the word *stem*[46] will also often change. Obviously, in irregular verbs like ερχομαι and γινωσκω, the spelling changes very unpredictably.

Exegetical Considerations:

Do you see the simplicity and repetitiveness of John? We are over a hundred words into his Gospel and yet in this fairly lengthy sentence there is but one new verbal idea: εγνω "know." We will not see this kind of simplicity again until we come to John's first epistle. The flow of new words into the Gospel of Mark, by contrast, is very brisk.[47] What can explain this – *style*? The simplicity and repetitiveness of John can be explained only by John's pastoral concern for all those who must undergo a radical transformation of their *own* souls. Their minds must now feed on words which are as shocking and repulsive as cannibalism. But these are the words of immortality.

John repeats the main idea of this sentence in 1st John 3:1b …*the world knoweth us not, because it knew him not.* Its closest theological cognate is Paul's first letter to the Corinthians: *For after that in the wisdom of God the world by wisdom knew not God, it pleased God by the foolishness of preaching to save them that believe.*[48] A rationalistic wisdom that attempts to ground its own humanistic sophistry ontologically,[49]

Why not translate: "If you have known me, you have known the Father…" Which is much more characteristic of John's simple style. You must have a good reason for disturbing the semantic parallelism that John is using. John will soon say: *he that <u>has seen</u> me <u>has seen</u> the father.* Ironically, John uses two different tenses here – the perfect participle and the perfect. This is part of the translator's reasoning.

[46] The verb stem of γινωσκω is γινωσκ.

[47] See *The Jonas Genre*, 69.

[48] 1st Corinthians 1:21.

[49] Here used in the sense of a self-sustaining, unquestionable, first principle. For example, Descartes said: "I think, therefore I am." There is nothing wrong with this statement except that it begins without relation to its Christological context. John would say 'I believe, therefore I am.' More specifically, he would say: 'I believe that Jesus is the Christ, the Son of God, therefore, I am.' (a modification of John 20:31). And this would be echoing Paul. Observe the similarity between these two statements: *As the living Father hath sent me, and I live by the Father: so he that eateth me, even he shall live by me.* (John 6:57) *I am crucified with Christ: nevertheless I live; yet not I, but Christ liveth in me: and the life which I now live in the flesh I live by the faith of the Son of God, who loved me, and gave himself for me.* (Gal. 2:20) Plotting these statements upon Cartesian coordinates, John is saying: 'I feed upon the "I am" through belief; therefore, I also am.' Paul is saying: 'Christ loved me and gave himself for me, therefore, I am.' Because Descartes' theory of certainty begins without relation to its Christological

eventually will come to the place where it must deny God, theologically. *But the natural man receiveth not the things of the Spirit of God: for they are foolishness unto him: neither can he know them, because they are spiritually discerned.*[50] John will soon progress to this very idea when he has Jesus ask Nicodemus: *Art thou a master of Israel, and knowest not these things?*[51] Through Nicodemus, John is explaining to an icon of Pharisaical conservatism the origin of Paul's "spiritual man." He is born again – this time, from above: *Except a man be born from above, he cannot see the kingdom of God.* On this same kind of Corinthian cue, Nicodemus scoffs at the foolishness of Jesus' preaching: *Nicodemus saith unto him, How can a man be born when he is old? can he enter the second time into his mother's womb, and be born?* Also on the same Corinthian cue, Jesus explains: *That which is born of the flesh is flesh; and that which is born of the Spirit is spirit.*[52]

Editorially, this sentence marks the beginning of a major theological theme. So far, every sentence has been positive. This is our first indication from John that something is very wrong. Here is the creative persona imminent in the very world that derives its existence through him, yet the world does not know him. Lest we begin to think that this agnosticism is due to a lack of religious development or mere ignorance, John immediately follows with: *He came unto his own, and his own received him not.* And yet John does not here conclude the troubling theological idea that he has begun. Instead he returns to one of his first editorial priorities, which is to distinguish Jesus from John the Baptist.

When we arrive at John's narrative about Nicodemus' nightly meeting with the Rabbi, we soon find that this vignette is not about Nicodemus, a secret convert from the party of the Pharisees early on. Nicodemus is, no doubt, an important figure in the early church, who has preserved important eyewitness testimony to an historical drama that not everyone has seen. Though Nicodemus is absent from the Synoptics, he reappears twice more in the Johannine Gospel in specific historical settings: as an important speaker for sympathetic Pharisees, during secret deliberations about what to do with Jesus,[53] and also paired with Joseph of Arimathaea as part of the burial party.[54] But we must note that at his first appearance in John, Nicodemus is but a symbol of the religious establishment. *Nico* means "ruler" and *demus* means "people." Nicodemus is symbol to which John attaches a teaching soliloquy. We will see John repeat this literary device often.

---

context, it must end in uncertainty. And so it has ended, not only in an epistemological crisis of the 20th century, to which we are heirs, but also in a mathematical one (see, for example: Gödel's incompleteness theorem).

[50] 1st Corinthians 2:14. Socrates could make this very same argument.

[51] John 3:10.

[52] John 3:6.

[53] 7:50-51.

[54] 19:39.

But if we follow the soliloquy, it does not resolve so much as a rabbinical conversation. It resolves as a theological theme that has begun with our sample sentence. If we see that the context for this theme stretches across narrative vignettes, we will then see a striking parallel between John's argument and Paul's argument in the prologue of Romans. Nevertheless, John is not wandering very far from the Synoptic template. In the Synoptic prologue, which Mark has dropped for other reasons, we find the same theological themes imbedded in *narrative* material, not soliloquy – the uniqueness of Christ in relation to all men, the superiority of Christ to John the Baptist, the rejection of Christ by existing institutions, the differentiation of a new people of God, etc. Note how that as the Synoptic prologue comes to a conclusion, we encounter an editorial landmark of John the Baptist's imprisonment: *Now when Jesus had heard that John was cast into prison, he departed into Galilee…* Likewise, as the Johannine prologue draws to a conclusion, we encounter the same editorial landmark - which we would have ordinarily passed by as a parenthetical narrative detail: *For John was not yet cast into prison…* John is shadowing the Synoptic template.

εις τα ιδια ηλθεν
unto his own he came

και οι ιδιοι αυτον   ου   παρελαβον
and his own him (did) not receive

ιδια   Most of the time, Matthew uses the adjective ιδιος in the sense of "private."
          But he also uses it with the connotation employed here: as an adjective which
          describes something which pertains uniquely to the subject under discussion.
          As an adjective, of course, it will take on the case of that which it defines.
          Matthew says: *And he entered into a ship, and passed over*, και ηλθεν εις την
          ιδιαν πολιν (and came to his <u>own city</u>).[55] Likewise, Mark also has both
          connotations. Here is an example of a Marcan usage in this second sense –
          describing something which pertains, or belongs to, the subject under
          discussion: *And when they had mocked him, they took off the purple from him, and
          put <u>his own clothes</u> on <u>him</u>...(*και ενεδυσαν αυτον <u>τα ιματια τα ιδια</u>).[56]

          You may be thinking: 'why this curious expression? Why not just use the
          genitive case to show possession – isn't that what the genitive is for?' In the
          case of Matthew's sentence, why didn't Matthew say: την πολιν αυτου (the
          city of him)? For one thing, you can't own a city. There is something arbitrary
          about the genitive when used to show possession. For example, one may say
          "my house," but this construction is true *only* if the current regime honors its
          social contract with the people. But if I am an architect, there will be
          something intrinsic to all my work which reflects something which pertains
          to me and to me alone. And in Mark's case, we remember that there was
          something distinctive about Jesus' clothes: *Then the soldiers, when they had
          crucified Jesus, took his garments, and made four parts, to every soldier a part; and
          also his coat: now the coat was without seam, woven from the top throughout.*[57]

          John for example, demonstrates this split between the genitive and the use of
          ιδιος. When John has Jesus first begin to talk about "his" sheep, he uses ιδιος
          three times:

          10:3 To him the porter openeth; and the sheep hear his voice: and he calleth
          his **own** sheep (<u>ιδια προβατα</u>) by name, and leadeth them out.
          10:4 And when he putteth forth his **own** sheep (<u>ιδια προβατα</u>), he goeth
          before them, and the sheep follow him: for they know his voice.

---

[55] Matthew 9:1.
[56] Mark 15:20.
[57] John 19:23.

10:12 But he that is an hireling, and not the shepherd, whose **own** the <u>sheep</u> (προβατα ιδια) are not.

From then on, he switches to the genitive or to a possessive pronoun, for example, when Jesus gently remonstrates with Peter, he twice says: *feed <u>my</u> sheep* (τα προβατα μου).

We have said that ιδιος is an adjective. And that it will agree with that which it defines. Where are the nouns that ιδιος defines in our sentence above? They must be inferred. John uses ιδια seven times, but only one of them is accompanied by a noun that fits – and it shares the same context: προφητης εν τη <u>ιδια πατριδι</u> τιμην ουκ εχει.[58] (*a prophet in his <u>own fatherland</u>, honor does not have*). The noun being defined here is πατριδι.[59] What about ιδιοι in our sample sentence (και οι ιδιοι αυτον)? We can see clearly that it is in the masculine, nominative plural, but what nominative plural noun does it define? We cannot use the same technique as before since this form is used only once. Perhaps the surrounding context will help. For now we will simply assume that John means: the men in that country. But he seems to have in mind a specific referent since he has changed cases. We will wait and see.

Exegetical Considerations: We may dismiss a discussion like the one above, regarding ιδιος and the genitive, as grammatical hairsplitting, but then how will we translate *But ye believe not, because ye are not of my sheep, as I said unto you.*[60] – in which John very heavily uses the genitive: εκ των προβατων των εμων ("of the sheep of me") For example, is John here saying that these sheep are his because they believe, or is he saying that these sheep believe because they are his? If John had not already specified these sheep as sheep which pertain to Jesus in a sense other than the mere, arbitrary act of possession, we would not be asking this question. But then we could not understand the theological consistency of John's statement here: "*he came to his own and his own received him not.*" Which would seem to be in contradiction with Jesus' statement: *But ye believe not, because ye are not of my sheep, as I said unto you.*

Consider also this exegetical issue represented by this KJV rendering: *Knowing this first, that no prophecy of the scripture is of any private* (ιδιας) *interpretation.*[61] There are many reasons why this sentence has nothing to do with forbidding the laity to read and understand the scriptures for themselves. For one thing, Peter's point is not

---

[58] John 4:44b.
[59] The case endings of πατριδι do not look familiar. This is the dative for this noun. It belongs to a special class of nouns which do not follow the ordinary patterns that we have seen so far.
[60] John 10:26.
[61] 2nd Peter 1:20.

about the *interpretation* of Scripture. His intention, both in the surrounding context and in this sentence, is to tell us that the *origin* of prophetic scripture is not *idio*matic to the prophets. He tells us in the very next sentence that the initiative of human will did not produce prophecy – whether we are talking about John the Baptist or about the apocalypse of Paul: ου γαρ <u>θεληματι ανθρωπου</u> (by the will of man[62]) ηνεχθη ποτε προφητεια (was brought prophecy). If it *were* Peter's intention to tell us that the individual should not attempt to understand the scriptures for himself, then Jesus himself becomes guilty of violating this principle: κατ ιδιαν δε τοις μαθηταις αυτου επελυεν παντα[63] (…but[64] privately to the disciples of him, he expounded all). Peter is saying that prophecy is not idiomatically filtered or distorted by the prophet who speaks it.

Consider what Satan did with the words of God in the garden. As an *interpretation* of God's word – it's not that bad. Virtually all of it was right on target: …"you will not die," "you will become as Gods," "you will know good and evil." Except that the <u>intent</u> of God's words which lay very visibly on the surface of his command – was laid aside. 'Don't eat of it.' Satan was implying that God was a linguistic docetist: 'He *said*: "don't eat." But what he *really meant* was for you to eat.'

The metamorphosis of what Peter is clearly saying - into a ban upon reading the Scriptures "idiomatically" is itself an idiomatic distortion. And though the whole world follows this distortion like a flock of birds, giving it the temporary appearance of catholicity, it doesn't make it true. Prophecy comes from God. Interpretations come from the devil. Idiomatic, interpretive distortions occur *after* prophecy becomes inscripturated, Peter says: α οι αμαθεις και αστηρικτοι στρεβλουσιν … προς την ιδιαν αυτων απωλειαν.[65] ("which the unlearned and the unstable twist to their own destruction.") Although this *may* apply to the unwashed masses that follow foolish cultic perversions of catholic sense, this is not those to whom Peter refers. By the time 2nd Peter is written, Peter has learned a very serious lesson about why "common" is not synonymous with "unclean." He has learned that foolishness is no respecter of persons. He has learned that foolishness is not confined to any social, ethnic, religious or academic class.[66]

---

[62] θεληματι is in the dative case, hence the implied preposition "by," and man is in the genitive case, hence the implied preposition "of."

[63] Mark 4:34.

[64] δε means "but." In the Greek, δε does not begin the sentence. This sounds very awkward to us, but not as awkward as our habit of beginning sentences with conjunctions would have sounded to the Greeks. The first idea in Mark's mind is "privately" not "but." Note too how the positioning of "δε" frames the prepositional phrase κατ ιδιαν together.

[65] 2nd Peter 3:16.

[66] Peter is talking about religious leaders – specifically, the Judaizers who like *Balaam the son of Bosor, who loved the wages of unrighteousness; But was rebuked for his iniquity: the dumb ass speaking with man's voice forbad the madness of the prophet. These are wells without water, clouds that are carried with a tempest; to whom the mist of darkness is reserved for ever. For when they speak great swelling words of vanity, they*

Imagine confronting the foremost scholar at some leading academic theological school to tell him: "you haven't the foggiest notion about what is going on in the New Testament materials." This is precisely what Jesus did. He came face to face with those who 'knew the scriptures'[67] and said: πλανασθε μη ειδοτες τας γραφας μηδε την δυναμιν του θεου (*you err, not knowing the scriptures neither the power of God*). The religious establishment did not know the Scriptures. But they were quite familiar with their own religious tradition, the παραδοσιν των πρεσβυτερων (tradition of the elders) which filtered everything they studied. The Synoptics set up this very παραδοσις for condemnation because it had become the official religious interpretive schemata which effectively blinded the people to the very spirit of the word of God. John takes this idea full circle - making the devil the culprit for every worldly, religious παραδοσιν: *Ye are of your father the devil, and the lusts of your father ye will do. He was a murderer from the beginning, and abode not in the truth, because there is no truth in him. When he speaketh a lie, he speaketh of his own* (εκ των ιδιων) *for he is a liar*, *and the father of it.*[68]

Paul had asked: how could the religious establishment of God have gone so completely wrong about the Lord's Christ? How could God's chosen people be rejected and the Gentiles accepted? In the Synoptics, Christ confronts the Sanhedrin to tell them that they did not know their foundational documents. And as we continue in Matthew, we find that this is not just a matter of a few errant theologians. We find that an age is coming to a close, because judgment has finally come upon the house of Israel. And 'their house is left to them desolate.' The institution of Judaism is being judged. And the verdict is one of institutional import: *The kingdom of God shall be taken from you and given to a nation bringing forth the fruits thereof.*[69] John is here explaining the consequences of: εις τα ιδια ηλθεν και οι ιδιοι αυτον ου παρελαβον.

---

allure through the lusts of the flesh, through much wantonness, those that were clean escaped from them who live in error. (2nd Peter 2:15-18) Note the imagery of instability: "wandering clouds." Jude elaborates upon this instability: *they have gone in the way of Cain, and ran greedily after the error of Balaam for reward, and perished in the gainsaying of Core. These are spots in your feasts of charity, when they feast with you, feeding themselves without fear: clouds they are without water, carried about of winds; trees whose fruit withereth, without fruit, twice dead, plucked up by the roots; Raging waves of the sea, foaming out their own shame; wandering stars, to whom is reserved the blackness of darkness for ever. While they promise them liberty, they themselves are the servants of corruption: for of whom a man is overcome, of the same is he brought in bondage.* (Jude 11-13)

[67] Primarily the Sadducees (Matthew 22:23-33) - in direct apposition to: *But this people who knoweth not the law are cursed.* (John 7:49).

[68] John 8:44.

[69] Matthew 21:43

παρελαβον   παρελαβον is the third person plural, aorist tense of παραλαμβανω,[70] a compound word formed by joining the preposition, παρα[71] (from) with the verb λαμβανω (receive). John uses παραλαμβανω only two other times. *And if I go and prepare a place for you, I will come again, and receive you unto myself.*[72] *Then delivered he him therefore unto them to be crucified. And they received Jesus and led him away.*[73] As used by John, παραλαμβανω appears to mean nothing more than "receive," yet since John uses the plainer λαμβανω in the very next sentence in the same sense, we must assume that παραλαμβανω is a strengthened form.

John has just said that the κοσμος exists in and through Christ. Yet the world, his fatherland, and men in general did not know him or receive him or receive *from* him. This word strengthens the relationship between this idea and Paul's comment in Romans: *Because that, when they knew God, they glorified him not as God, neither were thankful...*[74] Thankful for what? For all things that God has given them. In this case, it is his own Son. They are not thankful for anything which they have received <u>from</u> the father, including his own son. In present religious culture there is much talk about "receiving" Jesus. We receive him or do not receive him. In John there is no true option but to receive that which has been given to us <u>*from*</u> God. The Synoptics will capture this sense in the parable of the vineyard. The son is sent as the final representative *from* the owner to the husbandmen of the vineyard. He is not well received.

---

[70] Note the similarity with καταλαμβανω.

[71] We have said that παρα indicates "a relation which moves or stands apart from an object."

[72] John 14:3.

[73] John 19:16.

[74] Romans 1:21.

οσοι	δε	ελαβον	αυτον	εδωκεν	αυτοις	εξουσιαν
whoever,	though,	has received	him	he gave	to them	the right

τεκνα	θεου	γενεσθαι	τοις πιστευουσιν	εις το ονομα
children	of God	to become	to those believing	in the name

αυτου
of him.

οσοι   οσοι is the "reduplicated" form of the relative pronoun, ος. That is, it is the relative pronoun to which has been attached its own declension. Here we see the masculine plural ending **οι** added to the root word **ος**. So there is the combination of the idea of "he who" and "which" – hence: "whoever." This is the only time that John uses this word in this theological sense. From now on, John will use "πας ο" that is "all who" or he will use the relative pronoun or definite article with a participle form of the verb. For example: ο θελων λαμβανετω το υδωρ ζωης δωρεαν (<u>he that is willing</u>, let him take of the water of life freely[75]).

δε   Like και, δε is a primary, workhorse particle. Most of the time it is translated as either "but" or "and" (55% - 45%, respectively), depending on the context. (This shows how closely related the idea of "but" or "and" can be, therefore, do not be too restrictive in translating και, which is often used in the same sense.

Again - notice the order. "But" is the second word in, which sounds very strange to our ears. But this is the order within the Greek mind. For the Greek mind, it would be very strange to begin a sentence with a particle. The primary thought in this sentence is οσοι; why upstage it with a particle? Not so with και, which, unlike English, *often* begins a Greek sentence. There is a word for "but" - αλλα, which often begins a sentence. Therefore "δε," especially when it occurs in this subordinate position, would not be assigned the full weight of the English interruptive: "but;" therefore, it should be softened to "however" or "though" as in the above translation, or even left untranslated. But when a word is untranslated we must still deal with the intended force of the word. A Greek particle, for example, may not merit a word of its own in an English rendition, but it is not nothing. The force of the

---

[75] Revelation 22:17.

86

untranslated word will "carry over" to a word elsewhere in the sentence.

ελαβον   We have already seen καταλαμβανω ("apprehend") and "παραλαμβανω" ("receive from"). Here is the elemental word of these two compounds: λαμβανω. λαμβανω is here in the aorist tense (3rd person plural). Note the helping vowel at the beginning (ε) and the change of spelling in the middle of the word (the missing μ). These are indicators of the aorist tense. A good antonymical sentence for λαμβανω is familiar: *Blessed it is to give better than to receive.*[76] (μακαριον εστιν διδοναι μαλλον η λαμβανειν). Thus διδωμι ("give") is a good antonym for λαμβανω.

In English we sometimes think of "take" in an antonymical relationship to "receive," but in the Greek there is none; λαμβανω stands for both. There is no "give and take" in the Greek. There is only "give" (διδωμι) and "receive" (λαμβανω). This is why it is so difficult to wring any sense of "accept" from the Greek. There is nothing in God's creation merely "lying" around - in some neutral state of "not being taken." We do not "accept" or "reject" Jesus; much less do we "take" him or "choose" him, as in "choosing up sides" in a game of kickball. John says that God gave his only begotten son to the world. John says that we may either receive him or not receive him. We may either believe him or not believe him. There is no middle ground.

αυτοις   You will recognize this as the dative plural, personal pronoun ("them"). There is no accompanying preposition; just the naked, dative case. You must supply the English preposition required to complete the syntax of an indirect object. This is invariably the case with the prepositional idea of "to." Rarely, some other preposition will accompany the dative pronoun. For example, John uses παρα once and εν three times with αυτοις to specify the kind of indirect action that αυτοις receives. About 80% of the time, αυτοις is the indirect object of discourse, receiving the action of speaking (επω or λεγω or αποκρινομαι[77]) – for example: "He said to them..."

---

[76] Acts 20:35b.

[77] επω and λεγω are verbs which mean "say" and are virtually interchangeable. αποκρινομαι, however, means to give an answer or response in a dialogue format. It is a compound word combining απο (from) with κρινω (to judge) – so the speaker has first thought about a question – then gives his judgment.

εδωκεν   εδωκεν is the aorist tense of διδωμι which means "to give," the antonym of "receive" as we saw above. Most of the verbs that we will encounter will end with an omega (ω). But there are two other basic types. One is the verb which ends in ομαι. διδωμι is an example of the other basic type, ending in μι. Here are the forms of this verb found in John, again, the personal endings are random:

διδωμι	8	present[78]
διδους	1	present participle[79]
εδιδουν	1	Imperfect[80]
δωσω	6	future[81]
εδωκεν	15	aorist
εδοθη	2	aorist passive
δω	3	aorist subjunctive
δος	5	aorist imperative
δουναι	1	aorist infinitive[82]
δεδωκεν	21	perfect[83]
δεδομενον	3	perfect passive participle[84]
δεδωκεισαν	1	pluperfect[85]

Although this verb is also very irregular, you can see the same patterns as the other verbs, regardless of whether or not it is of the ω type the ομαι type or the μι type. The past tenses rely on an auxiliary "helping" vowel – ε. The future tense adds a (σ) just prior to the endings. The perfect tenses duplicate the initial consonant (in this case it is the δ)

εξουσιαν   John uses εξουσιαν - "authority" or "the right" 6 times in his gospel, yet the KJV translates this with "power" all six times. In our modern,

---

[78] In John's Gospel this verb occurs in the present tense in either this form – διδωμι – "I give" or διδωσιν – "he will give." And in each case, it is Jesus or the Father that is the one who gives.

[79] 6:33 *For the bread of God is he which is coming down from heaven, and is giving life unto the world.*

[80] 19:3b και εδιδουν αυτω ραπισματα (*and they gave to him blows*).

[81] Again, this verb occurs in the future tense in either this form – δωσω – "I will give" or δωσει – "he will give." And again, it is Jesus or the Father that is the one who gives.

[82] 6:52b *How can this man give us his flesh to eat?* All three of these verbs are in the infinitive form, which if it were translated more directly: *How to be possible this man to give his flesh to eat.* In English we designate the infinitive form by putting a "to" in front of the present tense.

[83] The first eight times John uses this verb it occurs in this form and in the 3rd person singular εδωκεν (he has given). Jesus' prayer to God in chapter 17 will show other forms, such as the 1st person δεδωκα and the 2nd person singular δεδωκας.

[84] We have already encountered the perfect passive participle in απεσταλμενος.

[85] The pluperfect of this verb occurs only one other time in our literature – Mark 14:44. Coincidently, both sentences pertain to the betrayal of Jesus.

Machiavellian thinking, "might" so often makes "right," that we do not often distinguish the two. John does. The other writers do too. Luke is very specific, using both in the same sentence: *Then he called his twelve disciples together, and gave them power and authority over all devils...*[86] Although the Synoptics use power (δυναμις) 38 times, John *never* uses it except in Revelation (12x). John is expressing a meaning other than mere power. John invokes the same connotation that Matthew invokes: *For he taught them as one having authority and not as the scribes.*[87]

τεκνα θεου   τεκνα is the common word for "children." John uses this word only three times in his Gospel and each of these three times he invokes an implicit controversy about who are the legitimate children of God. Elsewhere, only in Paul do we find this controversy. Only in Paul do we find this phrase: τεκνα θεου (children of God).[88]

<u>Exegetical Considerations</u>: Judaism insisted that the Gentiles had no intrinsic right to be called the children of God since they did not physically descend from Abraham. Paul argues in Romans that the children of God are those who believe the promise of God, irrespective of circumcision, and not those who are merely descendants of Abraham. *For he is not a Jew, which is one outwardly;... But he is a Jew, which is one inwardly.*[89] John has just made the point that Jesus came to his own people, yet they did not receive him. John will soon directly confront the Jewish establishment with an even more radical polemic – straight from the core of the Pauline argument from Galatians and Romans: *They which are the children of the flesh, these are not the children of God: but the children of the promise are counted for the seed.*[90]

In the Synoptics, we see Matthew allude to this Pauline idea: *And think not to say within yourselves, we have Abraham to our father: for I say unto you, that God is able of these stones to raise up children unto Abraham.*[91] But this allusion still appears as an argument against nominalism or hypocrisy. John goes much further than this. Not

---

[86] Luke 9:1.

[87] Matthew 7:29.

[88] For example: *The Spirit itself beareth witness with our spirit, that we are the children of God* (Romans 8:16) Characteristically, it also appears twice in 1st John. Even if we add the article (τεκνα του θεου), the distribution remains unchanged (John 1x; Romans 1x, 1st John 2x).

[89] Romans 2:28a; 29a

[90] Romans 9:8 This is the genesis of the Johannine argument that we will next consider. But it is just a beginning. It appears to maintain that to be born of the seed of Abraham is not *enough*. The Judaizers had no difficulty with this part of Paul's argument. They said: 'You're exactly right Paul, it <u>isn't</u> enough. You must also keep the law of Moses in order to inherit the promises. The Gentiles may become proselytes (προσηλυτος), but they may not bypass this requirement.'

[91] Matthew 3:9.

only has God raised up children from rocks; he has announced that Abraham is not the spiritual father of the children of the current religious establishment of Judaism:

I know that ye are Abraham's seed; but ye seek to kill me, because my word hath no place in you. I speak that which I have seen with my Father: and ye do that which ye have seen with your father. They answered and said unto him, Abraham is our father. Jesus saith unto them, If ye were Abraham's children, ye would do the works of Abraham. But now ye seek to kill me, a man that hath told you the truth, which I have heard of God: this did not Abraham. Ye do the deeds of your father.... Ye are of your father the devil, and the lusts of your father ye will do.[92]

In the very next sentence, John will introduce that which goes well beyond even the Pauline argument. Compared with Paul's passing metaphor of grafting a wild Gentile branch upon the natural, Jewish olive tree,[93] through some forensic process of adoption[94] or theological (though subjunctive) argumentation,[95] John's idea threatens to destroy the very core of the Judaizing argument against which Paul has struggled so long. John maintains that ultimately, it matters not to be of the physical seed of Abraham at all, since the children of God must be born from above: *Except a man be born from above, he cannot see the kingdom of God.[96]* John will soon elaborate in his soliloquy between Jesus and Nicodemus. And John will repeat this idea five times in his first epistle.

This idea was implicit in the central parable of the Synoptic template - the parable of the sower, in which the seed (σπερμα) of God is sown in the very heart of man:[97] *The field is the world; the good seed are the children of the kingdom; but the tares are the children of the wicked one; The enemy that sowed them is the devil...* The idea was also implicit in yet another passing metaphor in Paul: *My little children, of whom I travail in birth again until Christ be formed in you.[98]* It is almost an indelicate suggestion – that we should

---

[92] John 8:37- 41a; 44a.

[93] Romans 11:24 *For if thou wert cut out of the olive tree which is wild by nature, and wert graffed contrary to nature into a good olive tree: how much more shall these, which be the natural branches, be graffed into their own olive tree?*

[94] The word is υιοθεσια a compound of υιος (son) and τιθημι (to put or place) (probably). But contrary to popular theological opinion, especially among Protestants, the idea is not well developed in Paul. And it is not really clear that Paul is invoking the Roman idea of adoption. For example, consider: Romans 9:4 *Who are Israelites; to whom pertaineth the adoption, and the glory, and the covenants, and the giving of the law, and the service of God, and the promises.*

[95] For example consider the argumentation of Romans 8:17: *And if children, then heirs; heirs of God, and joint-heirs with Christ; if so be that we suffer with him, that we may be also glorified together.* There are a lot of "ifs" (some which are implicit in the subjunctive mood) in this sentence.

[96] John 3:3b.

[97] Matthew 13:38-39. But be careful here in your exegesis. Both Luke (8:11) and Mark (4:26) gravitate to σπορος - a seed with no sexual connotation.

[98] Galatians 4:19. In the Synoptic template we become as children (ως τα παιδια). In Paul, we become theologically fathered in this process 1st Corinthians 4:15b *...for in Christ Jesus I have begotten you*

be pregnant with God through Paul. Paul takes this no further. John is fearlessly explicit. We must be born of God.

In Paul we become children of God because we died in a watery baptism and rose to <u>follow</u> the spirit.[99] In Paul we are *reckoned as* the σπερμα of God (αλλα τα τεκνα της επαγγελιας <u>λογιζεται</u>εις σπερμα[100]). In John we find that the waters of baptism are the amniotic fluid from which we burst forth as a genetic child of the very spirit of God. John is so insistent about this[101] that he imperils the theological substance of his own Christology. John says that Jesus is the only-begotten (μονογενης[102]) of God. How then can *we* also be born of the spirit? But John uses this term only four times in his Gospel and only once more in his first epistle, again, as a <u>title</u>. By the time we come to Revelation, John has dropped "only–begotten" and adopted a word that has been forged in one of Paul's prison epistles: πρωτοτοκος ("firstborn") – specifically: πρωτοτοκος εκ των νεκρων – the "first born from the dead." Hebrews, which displays a very close linguistic relationship to Colossians, in which this word originates, inserts πρωτοτοκος precisely where μονογενης would have (or could have) been.

By the time we arrive at the table-talk with Christ in John's Gospel (chapters 13-16), all sense of having been grafted unnaturally into the root of Jesse is gone: John 15:5 *I am the vine, ye are the branches: He that abideth in me, and I in him, the same bringeth forth much fruit: for without me ye can do nothing.* And this is because we are no longer *reckoned* as the seed of Abraham. We <u>are</u> the seed of God himself: *That which is born of the flesh is flesh; and that which is born of the Spirit is spirit.*[103]

γενεσθαι   We have already encountered this verb before in John's 3rd sentence: παντα δι αυτου εγενετο (aorist) και χωρις αυτου <u>εγενετο</u> ουδε εν ο <u>γεγονεν</u> (*all things through him <u>began</u> and without him <u>began</u> not one thing which <u>has become</u>*), and again in the 6th: εγενετο ανθρωπος απεσταλμενος παρα θεου ονομα αυτω ιωαννης (*There was a man having been sent from God – named John*).

---

through the gospel). In John these metaphors are synthesized and become flesh. When John addresses his audience in his first epistle he uses τεκνιον (little children) 7 times. Outside of John this word is used only here in Galatians. Only Paul and John refer to their charges as τεκνια μου ("my children") We will see this theological and linguistic synthesis over and over again in John.

[99] Romans 8:14: *For as many as are led by the Spirit of God, they are the sons of God.*

[100] Romans 9:8b. (*but the children of the promise are **counted** for the seed.*) This word "counted" (λογιζομαι) is *very* Pauline. But here again, it is a weaker term. In Paul's first block of epistles, we are *counted* (reconded) as children of God. But John goes further: 'there is no legal fiction here. We <u>are</u> the children of God.'

[101] He repeats that we have been born of God 8 times in his first epistle.

[102] from μονος which means "only" and γενναω which means "to be born."

[103] John 3:6.

91

The form that we see here in our sample sentence is the infinitive (_to_ become). Specifically it is the 2nd aorist middle infinitive. It is the "middle" voice since the action of becoming, in the sense that John is using it, is part active, part passive. We know that it is the aorist because 1) there are the spelling changes characteristic of the aorist, and 2) there is no reduplication of the first consonant, a sign of the perfect (as in γεγονεν). John will later use this form in a highly theological sentence: Jesus said unto them, Verily, verily, I say unto you, Before Abraham γεγονεν (had begun to be), I am.[104] This is very much stronger than the AV: ..._before Abraham was, I am_.

For continuity, let us repeat the sentence:

οσοι δε ελαβον αυτον εδωκεν **αυτοις** εξουσιαν τεκνα θεου γενεσθαι **τοις πιστευουσιν** εις το ονομα αυτου

Next in the sentence there is τοις πιστευουσιν. This phrase fragment goes hand in hand with the previous pronoun in this sentence, αυτοις, in two ways. Firstly, John is elaborating who "them" is, beyond the descriptor: "those who received him." Secondly, all three words are both in the dative. Thereby we know that this is an additional, defining phrase which is tacked on to the end of the sentence. Here is a case in which the present participle in the dative is spelled exactly like the present tense 3rd person plural. Only the dative article can here clarify this word as a participle.

Exegetical Considerations: This is the second time that John has employed the verb πιστευω – "believe." In its first occurrence, John is editorializing as to why John the Baptist has come. _He came for a witness, to bear witness of the Light, that all men through him might believe._[105] "Witness," "light," "believe" – these are the key words. But what is it that men must believe? In view of the fact that John never uses the noun, πιστις, (belief), perhaps John is saying that we need not have any indirect object to the act of believing. Perhaps for John, the act of believing is merely an act of obedience. Perhaps John means that the important thing is not what you believe but that you _do_ believe. Perhaps he is again alluding to Paul, where he says that Love...believes all (παντα πιστευει) things.[106] Perhaps John is saying that believing is the good thing and that "doubt" or "skepticism" is the bad thing. We must ask these hypothetical questions in order to illuminate the context for such a critical word in our literature.

---

[104] John 8:58.

[105] 1:7.

[106] 1st Corinthians 13:7.

Thus this sentence is important because this is our first sentence in which John specifies an object of our believing. John could have easily ended the sentence after γενεσθαι, yet he added an amplificatory phrase: *to those believing in the name of him.* Just as in the case of Luke's use of "power" and "authority" in the same sentence, John's use of "receive" and "believe" in the same sentence means that these are two different acts. Following backward through John's account, we find that the object of "receive" is logos. In this sentence the object of believe is *his name* (το ονομα αυτου). εις pre-positions this object. ονομα is in the accusative case; therefore, the direct object. And we must think not only about the object, but about how it is pre-positioned. Again, it is very easy to say that we believe *in* something. But this is because it has become a colloquialism, since we would be hard pressed to explain why the preposition "in" is necessary at all. And the more you think about it, the more "in" seems like such an odd word to pre-position the object of an act of belief. And εις is a much stronger form of "in" (εν), meaning "into" or "unto." So we are believing *into* the name of him. There is no mere tipping of the hat of "intellectual assent" to Christ. It is like "buying into" an idea. John will soon go much further than this. He will say that we must *eat* his ideas.

The important thing that we have been saying is that here we see that there is an object of belief that may be *prepositioned* as if it were receiving some sort of action. Though "believe" has taken on some of the functions of an adjective in this phrase, since John is using it as a participle, and is therefore declined like an adjective, it still, necessarily, retains its verbal idea. Furthermore, this means that belief is an action which, like love and obedience, requires an object. Therefore, though we often think of the "act" of believing as entirely intransitive,[107] it does retain a transitive component. This transitive element in this verb becomes absolutely crucial in understanding the argument between Paul and the Judaizers.

Paul argues that we are justified by belief apart from works of the law:[108] (πιστει δικαιουσθαι ανθρωπον χωρις εργων νομου). The more sophisticated arguments of the Judaizers remonstrated: 'yes, but there is a sense in which belief is *itself* a work. In James' argument, for example, we are not necessarily seeing an argument for faith *plus* something else.' We are seeing (among other things) an argument that the act of belief without works is a theological abstraction which cannot have a life of its own in the world in which we must live. James concludes such an argument succinctly: ωσπερ γαρ το σωμα χωρις πνευματος νεκρον εστιν ουτως και η πιστις χωρις των εργων νεκρα εστιν (*just as, therefore, the body without the spirit is dead, so also belief without works is dead*).[109] What remains is a heated argument: Was Abraham justified

---

[107] That is, diction that does not take a direct object.
[108] Romans 3:28
[109] James 2:26.

by works (εξ εργων εδικαιωθη[110]) or by faith apart from works? We shall, at length, see what John has to say about this.

If we read Paul's argument closely – that we are justified apart from the works of the law – we see that he is not attempting to "intransitize" belief. Paul is attempting to decouple belief not (necessarily) from works per se, but *works of the law* (εργων νομου). Only once does Paul fail to couple works with the law that was given through Moses: *Even as David also describeth the blessedness of the man, unto whom God imputeth righteousness without works.*[111] But this statement is buried deep into the context of Paul's argument about works of the law, and should not be construed as a generalized abstraction. Paul goes beyond this. Paul argues that believing is a law unto itself: *Where is boasting then? It is excluded. By what law? of works? Nay: but by the law of belief.*[112] John is elaborating this law. The law of believing is that it <u>actively</u> rests in the name of Christ, from whence we passively, and umeritoriously, derive our righteousness before God.

Belief, hope, and love – these are not abstractions that may be picked off a theological tree, isolated and put into an academic basket. Paul unequivocally declares that faith without love is nothing. God is not merely an idea, he is a *living* God. God *is* life. Likewise love. God defines love because God *is* love. We are baptized not just in the name of Christ,[113] but <u>into</u> the name of Christ. Consider this sentence. Paul says: κατα το ευαγγελιον της δοξης του μακαριου θεου ο επιστευθην εγω (*According to the glorious gospel of the blessed God, which <u>was committed</u> to my trust.*)[114]

---

[110] In your Greek New Testament, look carefully at Romans 4:2 and James 2:21, 25. Paul and James use exactly the same construction. This demands clear, exegetical resolution, or we have a very serious problem.

[111] Romans 4:6.

[112] Roman 3:27.

[113] See for example Romans 6:3 and 1st Corinthians 1:13. Paul later says that we are baptized in Christ just as the Hebrews were baptized by crossing the Red sea. Note the transitive nature of such a crossing over. Though there is the theoretical possibility of believing Moses apart from crossing the sea, the act of crossing the sea is itself the act of belief. The two cannot be severed, although they are two and not one. The author of Hebrews will resolve the controversy between belief and works by arguing that belief is an act – but it is an act of affirming the trustworthiness of God. And, as such, cannot (easily) be construed as a *meritorious* act. The Pharisees indeed believed that there was something intrinsically meritorious in their worship. But such a belief was easily ridiculed and destroyed: *The Pharisee stood and prayed thus with himself, God, I thank thee, that I am not as other men are, extortioners, unjust, adulterers, or even as this publican. I fast twice in the week, I give tithes of all that I possess….*(Luke 18:11-12).

[114] 1st Timothy 1:11 See also Titus 1:3. Also Romans 3:2. There are only six occasions where πιστευω assumes the aorist passive form. Yet the aorist passive is not an usual form. You will encounter it over 600 times in our literature.

What are we to make of ο επιστευθην εγω? Should we translate: "which I have believed"(?) We cannot do this because πιστευω is in the aorist *passive*.[115] That is, the εγω of this phrase, which means "I," is the passive *receiver* of action. But what sort of transitive action could be attached to the phrase: "I *was* believed?" This doesn't sound right, does it?

Yet if the coach calls me off the bench and sends me into the game with a clutch play in which I am the principle participant, this indicates to me that the coach *believes* that I am capable of executing the play. If he did not believe this, he would have sent someone else. We may also deduce from his call that he has confidence that I am capable of executing the play. He has committed to me his confidence that I will execute the play. In the sense that Paul has used it, the coach has "believed" me into the play. We say that "he has sent (πεμπω) me into the into the game. But just because we would not say that "he believed me into the play" does not change the fact that Paul does say this very thing. The student of Greek must accept this, because it is there.

Even if we are believing a mathematical axiom, the axiom is still the receptor of action. For example, the Pythagorean theorem. My mind relates itself to this theorem as it does to any other truth, whether that truth be a black hole or the Grand Canyon. The mind actively bends the knee of worship and praise of the beauty of truth. The mind decks itself with expectancy that such a theorem will guide the soul upon the path to the very author of this truth - to Truth itself. It does not merely "hope" that the theorem is true. It *knows* that the theorem is true. It rests its confidence upon this hope just as it is willing to rest its cars and trucks upon the bridges that are built upon the Pythagorean theorem.

This is not the tepid "I hope so" of modern parlance. This is confidence. It is to this confidence that John refers: *And every man that hath this hope in him purifieth himself, even as he is pure.*[116] The very act of believing necessarily involves a component of worship and confident hope. John will qualify the act of believing in yet another way in his epistles. Believing is an act of *love*. εν τη αγαπη ("in love") is a phrase which occurs only in John.[117] With John it is not so much "keeping the faith" as it is abiding (μενω) *in love*. Here again resounds a common Corinthian theological motif: *And now abideth belief (πιστις), hope (ελπις), love (αγαπη), these three; but the greatest of these is love.*[118] Only John says that we "abide in Christ." *I am the vine, ye are the*

---

[115] You may derive this from the Strong's number amplifier included with every verb in the OnlineBible program, or you may refer to Hewett.

[116] 1st John 3:3. This is the only occurrence of hope (ελπις) in John. It is Paul that develops the theological implications of hope. It does not occur in the Gospels.

[117] John 15:9-10; 1st John 4:16,18.

[118] 1st Corinthians 13:13.

branches: He that abideth in me, and I in him, the same bringeth forth much fruit: for without me ye can do nothing.[119] We abide in his love.[120] We abide in his light.[121] Yet what is it about believing that produces the righteousness of the law which the law itself could not produce in us? The New Testament authors say that mere legalism can only produce a sterile orthodoxy and spiritual hypocrisy. And there was simply no fruit to show for this. John synthesizes the Synoptic and Pauline argument. *Ye shall know them by their fruits*, Matthew says.[122] *That the righteousness of the law might be fulfilled in us, who walk not after the flesh, but after the Spirit*, Paul says.[123] John is more intimate: *Abide in me, and I in you. As the branch cannot bear fruit of itself, except it abide in the vine; no more can ye, except ye abide in me.*[124]

Modern linguistic theories believe that words can be "field stripped" – like a piece of artillery – into its component parts – into individualistic monads.[125] But language is not like a machine. Words share in the meanings of other words just as in the Trinity itself. When you have seen the act of believing, you have also seen the transitive act of hope, love and worship. Therefore, as we strip "believe" down to its essential meaning, we may not throw away its transitive component. If we do, we will be unprepared when we come to the exegetical argument between James and Paul.

Both in John and in Paul we see that "believe" requires an object. And that object receives the action inherent in the recessive but transitive nature of "believe." This is why we cannot speak of "believe" as mere intellectual assent. When we "believe" something in the sense of these writers, we are not merely making a statement about our relative warmth or enthusiasm about a proposition. All sorts of transitive actions occur. Paul says that when we believe Christ, we are immersed, or rather "baptized" in him. He says: There is therefore now no condemnation to them which are in Christ (εν χριστω) Jesus.[126] We live in him. We "fall asleep" in him. *Therefore if any man be in Christ, he is a new creature: old things are passed away; behold, all things are become new.*[127]

We not only enter into (εις) Christ through (δια) belief. We now believe *from within* him. This is not just the jargon of theological existentialism. These men are saying something absolutely essential about the nature of belief. Belief admits of no "media via." We either believe or we do not believe. Paul says: any act which does not flow

---

[119] John 15:5.
[120] 15:10.
[121] 1st John 2:10.
[122] Matthew 7:16a.
[123] Romans 8:4.
[124] John 15:4.
[125] Here used in the sense given to it by Gottfried Leibniz.
[126] Romans 8:1. Paul accounts for 72 of 75 occurrences of εν χριστω. Peter concedes to this theological usage in the closing benediction of his first epistle: *Peace be with you all that are in Christ Jesus.*
[127] 2nd Corinthians 5:17.

out of belief from within Christ - is sin.[128] John says: *He that believeth on him is not condemned: but he that believeth not is condemned already, because he hath not believed in the name of the only begotten Son of God.*[129]

---

[128] Romans 14:23.
[129] John 3:18.

Chapter 3 Vocabulary Review

Let us review the words (Strong's numbers in parenthesis) which we have encountered so far in John and in this text. Fill in the meanings from the discussion or from any other source:

Word	Meaning
πιστις (4102)	
ελεος (1656)	
γενναω (1080)	
τυπος (5179)	
αρχη (746)	
λογος (3056)	
αρχη και τελος (746 & 5056)	
ο πρωτος και ο εσχατος (4413 & 2078)	
προς (4314)	
δια (1223)	
ουτος (3778)	
αυτου (846)	
γινομαι (1096)	
ποιεω (4160)	
χωρις (5565)	
ουδε (3761)	
ζωη (2222)	
αιωνιον (166)	
εχω (2192)	
φως (5457)	
ανθρωπων (444)	
σκοτια (4653)	
σκοτος (4655)	
φαινει (5316)	
καταλαμβανω (2638)	
λαμβανω (2983)	
αποστελλω (649)	
παρα (3844)	
ονομα (3586)	
ερχομαι (2064)	
μαρτυριαν (3142)	
εις (1519)	
αληθης (227)	

ινα (2443)
περι (4012)
πιστευω (4100)
ουκ (3756)
αλλ (235)
εκεινος (1565)
μεσσιας (3323)
αληθινος (228)
αρτον (740)
παις (3816)
φωτιζω (5461)
κοσμος (2889)
γινωσκω (1097)
ιδιος (2397)
παραδοσις (3862)
παραλαμβανω (3880)
οσοι (3745)
διδωμι (1325)
εξουσιαν (1849)
τεκνα (5043)
σπερμα (4690)
λογιζεται (3049)
μονογενης (3439)
πρωτοτοκος εκ των νεκρων (4416 ... 3498)
εργων νομου (2041 &3551)
εξ εργων εδικαιωθη (2041 & 1344)
ο επιστευθην εγω (Titus 1:3)
ελπις (1680)
αγαπη (25)

Chapter 4: John 1:13 – 1:14

οι ουκ εξ αιματων ουδε εκ θεληματος σαρκος ουδε εκ θεληματος
who not out of blood   neither out of the will   of flesh neither out of the will

ανδρος αλλ εκ θεου   εγεννηθησαν
of man   but   out of God they have been born

Let's first consider our new words: blood, will, flesh, man.

αιματων   This is the only time that "blood" (αιμα) occurs in the genitive in our literature. We therefore immediately suspect that we are dealing with an expression of "poetic diction" which is slightly deforming the word from its ordinary use. If we scan the sentence, we see that it begins as a negative series of things. We see ουκ, ουδε…ουδε…αλλ – that is, "not this, neither that, neither that, but…" The sentence begins with οι, which can be construed as the masculine plural relative pronoun or the masculine plural article, but in either case can be translated as "the ones who" or "who," respectively. Since John has just used the construction τοις πιστευουσιν (τοις being the dative plural form of the article), it is probably the article.

Exegetical Considerations: John is further elaborating upon those to whom God has given the authority to become the sons of God – in this case, the *nature* of such a becoming. They are begotten of God. This is not a progeny derived from blood – i.e., Abraham's seed. But it is also not a progeny conceived or achieved from the resources of man's will. John is saying that there is something much more here than being sorry for sin, or "turning over a new leaf." The will of man submits to Christ, but it is incapable of achieving this new birth. To submit to Christ is an active (i.e., transitive), believing submission. It is the same kind of submission of which Mary is the τυπος (type): γενοιτο μοι κατα το ρημα σου. (Let it be done unto me according to your word.)

When the will of man bows itself in believing submission, it is implanted with God's seed. John again is alluding to the metaphor of the parable of the sower. It is the σπερμα of God which is received – the very logos of God. As before, the image which lurks just below the surface here is pregnancy. It is offensive to speak of a man being pregnant with the sperma of God, but it is not nearly so offensive as drinking his blood and eating his flesh. As we mentioned before, Paul has used the metaphor of pregnancy with the Corinthian church: *for in Christ Jesus I have begotten you through the gospel.*[1] Now John is saying: 'this kind of pastoral begetting is just a metaphor, but the kind of begetting from above is no metaphor. It is not a self-

---

[1] 1st Corinthians 4:15.

induced pregnancy. Nor is it achieved by any other human agency. The father of these children is God.'

"Flesh and blood" occur together as an expression ten times in our literature – five of which are Johannine. Yet the other five are theologically significant and well known. Jesus tells Peter that his preliminary understanding of his identity as Christ has come from God, not from within his own experience: *Blessed art thou, Simon Barjona: for flesh and blood hath not revealed it unto thee, but my Father which is in heaven.*[2] In Paul's pivotal section of his first letter to Corinth, speaking about the resurrection, in which the corruptible "puts on" incorruption, he announces ominously: *Now this I say, brethren, that flesh and blood cannot inherit the kingdom of God; neither doth corruption inherit incorruption.*[3] That is, unless our perishable flesh and blood is clothed in an imperishable, spiritual body[4] - we will never see God.

But it is to some seemingly mundane dialogue in Galatians to which this Johannine sentence is most closely connected: *But when it pleased God, who separated me from my mother's womb, and called me by his grace, To reveal his Son in me, that I might preach him among the heathen; immediately I conferred not with flesh and blood: Neither went I up to Jerusalem to them which were apostles before me...* The setting for this dialogue is Paul's bitter letter to the Galatians, in which he opened maintaining that his apostleship was not derived ουκ απ ανθρωπων ουδε δι ανθρωπου αλλα δια ιησου χριστου (not from man neither through man but by Jesus Christ). Notice the structure: not…neither…but.

In his Ephesian Letter, Paul says that even as we were mere men, driven by the desires (επιθυμια) and intentions (θελημα) of the flesh and were thus children of wrath, God quickened (ζωοποιεω) us into a new kind of resurrected life in Christ. Indeed the basic phraseological structure of this sentence; i.e., *not…flesh and blood…but,* can only be found in Matthew and Ephesians. And the expression: the "intention(s) of the flesh" can only be found in our sample sentence and in Ephesians. And the structure and substance of the phraseological *series* (*not … neither … but*) can only be found in Galatians. Paul's apostleship was not derived from flesh and blood (Galatians 1:16), nor from (απ) or through (δι) the other Apostles (1:1). These are not just interesting phraseological details. These are the only places in which both the phraseological structure and theological substance of John converge. There is simply too much coincidence here.

---

[2] Matthew 16:17b.

[3] 1st Corinthians 15:50 Here is the Corinthian connection again. We will soon encounter a very close linguistic and theological cognate in the Nicodemus soliloquy: *Except a man be born of water and of the Spirit, he cannot enter into the kingdom of God. That which is born of the flesh is flesh; and that which is born of the Spirit is spirit.* (John 3:5b-6).

[4] 15:44 *It is sown a natural body; it is raised a spiritual body. There is a natural body, and there is a spiritual body.* The discussion here is very close to what will be attempted in the Nicodemus soliloquy.

θελημ ατος   θελματος is the genitive form of θελμα which means "will," "intention." The genitive form of this neuter noun is used 13 times – only once in John and 12 times throughout the epistles of Paul. Most of the time θελματος is imbedded in the phrase: δια θελημ ατος θεου (through the will of God; 7x) or its close equivalent: του θελημ ατος αυτου (of his will; 4x) – the "his" referring to God in all cases.

Note the similarity between John's phrase - εκ θελημ ατος ανδρος and a phrase which we have already come across in Peter: ου γαρ θελημ ατι ανθρωπου. Except that in John it is "will" that it is in the genitive; in Peter it is "man." In Peter's phrase, "will" is in the dative which beckons forth the English preposition "by." Therefore we have: "not by the will of man." What's the difference? Semantically, none. But there are two probable reasons why John chooses the genitive. First, it makes "will" part of the genitive series in this sentence, agreeing with "blood," also in the genitive. So the parts of John's series are "blood," "will" and "will" – not "blood," "flesh" and "man." Secondly, if we strip away the qualifiers to get at John's basic construction we get: "who have been born of God." If John had used the dative, we would translate: "who have been born by God." See the difference? The Red Sea was also parted by God, but through the *intermediate* agency of an east wind.[5] Since John uses the genitive, he brings the birth of his subjects as close to the agency of God as they could possibly be.

<u>Exegetical Considerations</u>: In the Nicodemus soliloquy, we will learn that the agency of our birth is the very spirit of God, that same spirit which overshadowed Mary. When Mary asks Gabriel (in Luke) how she will become pregnant, he says that the Holy Spirit will come upon (επελευσεται) her. But this is also the same word that Luke uses to describe the Pentecostal phenomena: *But ye shall receive power, after that the Holy Ghost is <u>come upon</u> you...*[6] Mary is "overshadowed" by the spirit, but so are the apostles by the cloud in which God himself spoke to them.[7]

John has clearly distinguished Jesus as the "only begotten" son of God. But then he immediately places everyone who submits to and believes Christ into the same category. In Paul there is always a discernable difference of kind between the true son and the adopted son; the natural branch and the wild branch. In John, the sonship of the children of God is organically kindred to Christ. Except that in John, Jesus' "biological" father is also somehow God. This is, possibly, one of the reasons

---

[5] Exodus 14:21.
[6] Acts 1:8.
[7] Luke 9:34.

for John's short-lived use of μονογενης (only-begotten). Jesus' fleshly form begins with Mary. But contra the Arians, Christ had no beginning. By the spirit, Jesus descends into the womb of Mary; by that same spirit we ascend through the amniotic waters of this world and are born into a world which is completely above and beyond this one – as very sons of God.

σαρκος   σαρκος is the genitive form of σαρξ which means "flesh." So far we have seen three types of nouns. The reason that we have not discussed them until now is because they have been pretty easy to categorize. Until now. The grammarians have invented a good word that is very helpful here: "declension." Greek grammarians place Greek nouns into one of three declensions.

"Declension One" is composed mostly of feminine nouns (but there are a few exceptions that look like masculine nouns). "Declension Two" is composed mostly of masculine nouns, but also contains many feminine and neuter nouns. We have already seen the basic forms for these two declensions. But we have also already come across the *Third* Declension, which contains nouns in all three genders (masculine, feminine and neuter). The endings for third declension nouns show considerable variation.

Our first Third Declension noun which we encountered in John was "φως"(light) a neuter noun we called "this somewhat unusual noun." There was even a third declension adjective which mixed first declension and third declension endings: πας, so we gave all the forms that John uses. It is simply too complicated to approach the variations of the declensions by means of charts alone. We therefore unreservedly recommend Hewett's summary chart of *nine* frequently occurring Third Declension forms in Hewett, 140. Take a moment to look them over and review Hewett's discussion of the third declension (15.2-5), focusing particularly on the underscored uniformities which he notes.

Again, it is better to become familiar with the individualized forms of the words as they occur in the texts than it is to first memorize the forms divorced from their contexts. Words are like people. We learn each one individually. It is only *after* we have met so many of them that we begin to see personality *types*. Then we say things like: 'you remind me so much of my neighbor in Pittsburgh.' We do not say that the process of knowing individual people is to "memorize" them. Nor should we speak of first learning words individually as memorization. Likewise with children it is only well after they can read the first book of Beaupre's Nursery rhymes[8] that we should teach the rules about "vowels walking together." When we begin to teach children about irregular verbs and the inversion of subjunctive subject/verb agreement, it is already too late. They have already intuited their own memory schemes from their reading and our speaking. Let yourself learn Greek this way. It will cease to be foreign.

σαρξ is here in the genitive(σαρκος) because it belongs to the phrase: ουδε εκ θεληματος σαρκος ("neither out of the will of the flesh"). As we noted above, only in Ephesians is there a similar phrase: τα θεληματα της σαρκος.[9] But there are two things different about Paul's phrase. Firstly, if you have looked at Hewett's chart, you will correctly divine that θεληματα is either the nominative or the accusative plural form. If we look backward in Paul's phrase: εν ταις επιθυμιαις της σαρκος ημων ποιουντες τα θεληματα της σαρκος (in the desires the flesh of us, doing the wills of the flesh), we will see that θεληματα is, like επιθυμιαις (desires), the object of the preposition εν. Here again Paul, like John, is objectifying "will" - not flesh.

ανδρος   Although ανηρ, yet another third declension noun, is often interchangeable with ανθρωπος (man), ανηρ carries with it an emphasis upon gender, whereas ανθρωπος is a more universal term which corresponds to our non-gender specific "mankind." About a quarter of the time, ανηρ is properly translated "husband" to reflect this. Beware, however, Luke uses the two terms without much distinction, *preferring* ανηρ to ανθρωπος two to one, even though all other authors reverse this by a factor of about 4 to 1 in favor of ανθρωπος.

Predictably, the formal designation of Christ - "Son of Man" <u>always</u> uses ανθρωπος. John *does* follow this gender convention, preferring ανθρωπος to ανηρ by a factor of 6 to 1. He uses ανηρ only 8 times – 5 of these times it is properly translated "husband" since it refers to the "significant other" of the woman at the well. And here we can say that Jesus is not saying: "Go, call thy man." Otherwise the woman would not have said "I have no man."[10]

---

[8] Book 1, *The Bookhouse For Children*, © 1920.

[9] Ephesians 2:3.

[10] Yes, she *could* have been lying. But it doesn't fit the context. Jesus is not making a point about legitimacy as much as he is making a point about her lack of permanency of will. Would there be any

John appears to carry a neutral use in 1:30 *This is he of whom I said, After me cometh a man (ανηρ) which is preferred before me: for he was before me.* But remember - he is making a direct quote of the verbiage of John the Baptist. And in 6:10b John is probably following a Matthean convention. *And Jesus said, Make the men (ανθρωπους[11]) sit down. Now there was much grass in the place. So the men (ανδρες[12]) sat down, in number about five thousand.* In the Synoptic template version, Matthew continues: … ησαν ανδρες ωσει πεντακισχιλιοι χωρις γυναικων και παιδιων (…were men about 5000 apart from women and children). This is probably why John abruptly switches from ανθρωπους to ανδρες in the same sentence – because Matthew has already distinguished the "men" from the women and children with ανδρες. This leaves only our sample sentence to consider. Why does John use ανδρος here instead of ανθρωπου? Because it carries the distinction of gender and this is consistent with the underlying figure of *conception*.[13]

εγεννηθησαν   This is the aorist passive (3rd person plural) of γενναω "beget." In the Nicodemus soliloquy John will repetitiously elaborate what it means to be begotten of God in relation to our earthly generation. We are born from above (γεννηθη ανωθεν). He repeats this twice. We are born of the spirit (εκ του πνευματος). He repeats this three times.

Note the spelling similarities between γινομαι, (to become) γενναω (to beget) and γινωσκω (to know).

Exegetical Considerations: No other author says what John is here saying. At least not explicitly. In James, God is the "father of lights." In Paul, God is "our father," but this expression is almost always imbedded in an opening blessing[14] and is not theologically developed. Indeed, for Paul, God is *the* Father of all things.[15] But in the Synoptic template, we encounter God as *our* father 17 times in the Sermon on the

---

point in giving the water of everlasting life to a woman who cannot be true to an institution for even a few short years?

[11] This is the accusative plural form.

[12] This is the nominative plural form.

[13] John's preference for the generic term ανθρωπος, therefore, is not chauvinistic. If he had said that Jesus 'lights up every ανηρ that comes into the world', we would have evidence of chauvinism.

[14] Which is some variant of: χαρις υμιν και ειρηνη απο θεου πατρος ημων και κυριου ιησου χριστου (*Grace to you and peace from God the Father of us and of the Lord Jesus Christ*).

[15] Specifically: ο πατηρ εξ ου τα παντα (the ου is a relative pronoun in the genitive. See Chapter 1 Review). Therefore we have: "*out of whom…τα παντα.*" When we studied πας, πασα, παν it may have seemed odd to have a plural form for the idea of "all." How can there be more than one all(s)? Nevertheless, this explains why τα παντα is invariably translated "all things."

Mount, which is a significant theological development. The model prayer, for example, beckons us to say "our father." But even the nominal Jew would have said: 'isn't that a bit informal to be addressing God in this manner?' Nevertheless, Matthew continues in familiar, if not disconcerting terms: *For it is not ye that speak, but the Spirit of your Father which speaketh in you.*[16] Yet nowhere in Matthew is it clearly explained how it is that God is our father in this sense. And there, also, Jesus constantly addresses God as *"my"* father. If God is also *our* father, why is a possessive pronoun necessary between full-blooded brothers? Perhaps it is just a metaphor, as in: *For whosoever shall do the will of my Father which is in heaven, the same is my brother, and sister, and mother.*[17] Perhaps it is just an allegory, as it is in Paul: *Which things are an allegory: for these are the two covenants; the one from the mount Sinai, which gendereth to bondage, which is Agar....But as then he that was born after the flesh persecuted him that was born after the Spirit, even so it is now.*[18] John is explicit. God has begotten us. This is no metaphor. This is no allegory. And just as μονογενης has become a formal title by the time we reach 1st John, so being "born of God" has become a formal, pastoral *principle* in 1st John. He there repeats it seven times.

---

[16] Matthew 10:20.
[17] Matthew 12:50.
[18] Galatians 4: 24-29.

και ο λογος σαρξ εγενετο και εσκηνωσεν εν ημιν   και εθεασαμεθα
and the word flesh became and dwelt   in us   and we beheld

την δοξαν αυτου δοξαν ως μονογενους παρα   πατρος πληρης χαριτος
the glory of him, glory as only-begotten from   the father full   of grace

και αληθειας
and truth

και ο λογος σαρξ εγενετο

<u>Exegetical Considerations</u>: There are no new words in this construction, but we have here one of the most scandalous assertions that has ever been put into human language. It utterly transcends any pantheism or any materialism the mind of man has ever made. Paul had said that the crucifixion of the Lord's Christ was foolishness to the Greeks, but he did not entirely explain why. In his first letter to Corinth, Paul's subtle reversal of the ordinary categories of wisdom and foolishness, contrasting the wisdom of the world with the wisdom of God, continues for so long, that the argument itself becomes unstable.[19] In his bell-weather epistle, Romans, Paul opts for a much less subtly ironic presentation, which entirely re-stabilizes the argument:

For the invisible things of him from the creation of the world are clearly seen, being understood by the things that are made, even his eternal power and Godhead; so that they are without excuse: Because that, when they knew God, they glorified him not as God, neither were thankful; but became vain in their imaginations, and their foolish heart was darkened. Professing themselves to be wise, they became fools…

In Romans we clearly see that the Corinthian reversal of wisdom and foolishness labels, was itself a rhetorical device. Paul does not take up this device again. In Ephesians he returns to the ordinary use of these categories, condemning "foolish talk" (μωρολογια). And in his letter to Titus and in his second letter to Timothy, Paul specifically warns about the dangers of entertaining foolish (μωρας) questions.

But the question remains: what is it about the "Christ event" that the Greeks find so offensively foolish? Now that we understand how sobriety can appear to be foolishness to a drunk, there is still something offensive about sobriety even to the sober. In Romans, Paul adopts another word to describe it: σκανδαλον. For Paul

---

[19] 1st Corinthians 1:17 – 2:16. The proof of this is that this instability has come down to us in the form of an almost intractable argument about faith versus reason. The argument maintains that faith is irrational *per se*. Even Chesterton is defensive, saying, in *Orthodoxy*: "Reason is itself an act of faith."

there is but one offense, and that is the offense of the cross (σκανδαλον του σταυρου[20]). For Matthew there is the one typological offense of Peter's betrayal of the Lord's Christ. If the Gospel is such good news, and the salvation of God is such a blaze of gory, why was it that none of the apostles stood with him when for envy he was so ignominiously silenced by the religious establishment? Carnality has always been scandalous. Cowardice has always been scandalous. But was there no true grit in all of Israel? None at the docks? None in the custom's house? None in the religious orders of the day? Soldiers have always been found to die for righteous causes. If Roman rule and religious hypocrisy inspired such hatred among the common folk from which Jesus chose his students, couldn't one be found to die for a righteous prophet that so gloriously stood up to these things?

John is helping us to understand why none of the disciples stood with Christ. It is for the same reason that the Jerusalem Christian church stood negligently by while Paul was betrayed into the hands of the Romans - and why the Pauline bishopric unraveled at the end. Because Paul was an offensive man. Paul's righteousness was a hard saying – who could hear it? For John there had been so many offenses to *his* Jewish sensibilities. There was not only his own carnal sense of retribution, so inimical to spirituality sobriety.[21] There is the offense of our spiritual generation, in which we are sired by God. There is the descent of God into human flesh. There is the drinking of the blood and the eating of the flesh of God. And there is the "I am"-ness of Jesus. At first, Paul was no less offensive to John than he was to the Judaizing establishment. John is explaining the inertia of unbelief. But now the tabernacling of God among men has ceased to be a sentimental piece of religious existentialism. It has happened. The Lord's Christ has come – in the flesh – and dwelt in us. The enfleshment of God was the rock of offense upon which even the Apostles had dashed their foot. This was the Lord's doing - and it was scandalous in their eyes.

εσκηνωσεν This is the aorist of the verb σκηνοω, which means "dwell." Only John uses this verb to specify the mode of what we have come to call the "incarnation" or "enfleshment." But its precise meaning is not hard to discern from its cognates found throughout our literature. Even then we must first consider this antonymical construction of "earthly" from John: ει <u>τα επιγεια</u> ειπον υμιν και ου πιστευετε πως εαν ειπω υμιν <u>τα επουρανια</u> πιστευσετε (*if I have told you <u>earthly things</u> and you do not believe, how if I tell you <u>heavenly things</u> will you believe*[22]) This provides the linguistic context for another statement in Paul which twice

---

[20] Galatians 5:11.
[21] Luke 9:51-56.
[22] John 3:12.

employs the noun form (σκηνος) of σκηνοω - but deformed from its ordinary use:

οιδαμεν γαρ οτι εαν <u>η επιγειος ημων οικια του σκηνους</u> καταλυθη οικοδομην εκ θεου εχομεν οικιαν αχειροποιητον αιωνιον εν τοις ουρανοις και γαρ οι οντες <u>εν τω σκηνει</u> στεναζομεν βαρουμενοι επειδη ου θελομεν εκδυσασθαι αλλ επενδυσασθαι ινα καταποθη το θνητον υπο της ζωης

"For we know that if <u>our earthly house of this tabernacle</u> were dissolved, we have a building of God, an house not made with hands, eternal in the heavens. For we that are <u>in this tabernacle</u> do groan, being burdened: not for that we would be unclothed, but clothed upon, that mortality might be swallowed up of life."

The ordinary use of σκηνος is "tabernacle." But Paul's "poetic diction" is making it stand for our physical body. And this is a key elaboration about our "earthly tabernacle." Contrary to the expectations of the Gnostic form of Platonism - the body is not merely a prison from which we seek to be free. If there were something intrinsically dirty about our fleshly tabernacle, it would be philosophical foolishness to insist that God enfleshed himself within it. And, indeed, this encompasses much of the foolishness and scandal of the Gospel as Paul depicts it in his first letter to Corinth.[23]

Our earthly tabernacle is not, in fact, dissolved, but swallowed up by an *eternal* tabernacle.[24] Thus when Paul says: "flesh and blood cannot inherit the kingdom of God" we should understand – '*in its present form.*' It is no wonder that some early churchmen drifted towards docetism – that is, that Christ only *appeared* to enflesh himself in an earthly tabernacle. And it is not just John who takes pains about insisting that Christ became true man. Luke narrates that after the resurrection Jesus says: *Behold my hands and my feet, that it is I myself: handle me, and see; for a spirit hath not flesh and bones, as ye see me have… and they gave him a piece of a broiled fish, and of an honeycomb. And he took it, and did eat before them.*[25]

σκηνος is cognate to σκηνη - a more specific form of tabernacle. Hebrews employs this form to refer not to Paul's earthly body and

---

[23] 1st Corinthians 1:23 *But we preach Christ crucified, unto the Jews a stumblingblock, and unto the Greeks foolishness.*
[24] 2nd Corinthians 5:4.
[25] Luke 24:39, 42-43.

heavenly body, but to the earthly tabernacle built by Moses according to the pattern shown to him upon the mount, its form derived from the heavenly tabernacle, which the Lord built and not man.[26] And this is what makes Peter's suggestion at the Transfiguration to build Christ a tabernacle so silly. Luke says that Peter simply did not know what he was talking about (μη ειδως ο λεγει). But John gives every evidence of knowing exactly what he is talking about here. Jesus did not just appear as a ghost or a vision among us. He *tabernacled* with us. *Hebrews*, possibly well versed in the Gospel of John, therefore confidently asserts: *Forasmuch then as the children are partakers of flesh and blood, he also himself likewise took part of the same...*[27] Even Paul, who has never said anything like this in his first two blocks of letters[28] says: θεος εφανερωθη εν σαρκι (God was manifested in the flesh).[29]

ημιν

This is the dative form of the first person plural pronoun – "us." Since it is in the dative, it receives indirect action – in this case, via the preposition εν. The most common meaning for εν is "in." We should, with few exceptions, adhere to this even though it may sound strange to our ears. Otherwise, translational bias will come in. The AV has "among." But "among" does not touch the intimacy of the incarnation. Likewise Luke has Peter say that David's sepulcher is "in us" to this day. The AV has "with us."

The AV translates the preposition εν many times as "by" or "with" when it should clearly be "in." Observe this example. Note the connecting string of **εν**'s: αλλ **εν** παντι συνιστωντες εαυτους ως θεου διακονοι **εν** υπομονη πολλη **εν** θλιψεσιν **εν** αναγκαις **εν** στενοχωριαις **εν** πληγαις **εν** φυλακαις **εν** ακαταστασιαις **εν** κοποις **εν** αγρυπνιαις **εν** νηστειαις **εν** αγνοτητι **εν** γνωσει **εν** μακροθυμια **εν** χρηστοτητι **εν** πνευματι αγιω **εν** αγαπη ανυποκριτω. Yet suddenly, in the middle of the string, the AV switches to another English preposition: "But in all things approving ourselves as the ministers of God, **in** much patience, **in** afflictions, **in** necessities, **in** distresses, **in** stripes, **in** imprisonments, **in** tumults, **in** labors, **in** watchings, **in** fastings; **by** pureness, **by** knowledge, **by** longsuffering, **by** kindness, **by** the Holy Ghost, **by** love unfeigned."

---

[26] Hebrews 8:1-5.

[27] Hebrews 2:14.

[28] The closest that he has come to this is something like Romans 1:3 *Concerning his Son Jesus Christ our Lord, which was made of the seed of David according to the flesh.* Or like Romans 8:3b *God sending his own Son in the likeness of sinful flesh...* The statement in 1st Timothy is categorically novel. *God* has appeared in the flesh.

[29] 1st Timothy 3:16.

There is no justification for switching to "by." It is translational inconsistency such as this which sometimes makes it so difficult to see connections between John and Paul. It is probably translational inconsistency such as this which hinders us from seeing that we are not baptized "with" the Spirit. We are baptized *in* the Spirit. As Paul says: [they] were baptized into Moses in the cloud and in the sea (και παντες εις τον μωσην εβαπτισαντο **εν** τη νεφελη και **εν** τη θαλασση)[30] If prepositions are translated consistently, John's constant injunction to "abide *in* Christ" will not sound so foreign.

We have already encountered the 3rd person forms of the personal pronoun (he, she or it). Now we must fill out our chart with the 1st and 2nd forms.

	Singular			*Plural*	
N	εγω	*I*		ημεις	*we*
G	μου	*my*		ημων	*our*
D[31]	μοι	*me*		ημιν	*us*
A	με	*me*		ημας	*us*

	Singular			*Plural*	
N	συ	*you*		υμεις	*you*
G	σου	*your*		υμων	*your*
D	σοι	*you*		υμιν	*you*
A	σε	*you*		υμας	*you/we*

εθεασαμεθα   This is the aorist form of θεαομαι, which means "see" or "behold." The aorist tense is formed by the addition of the helping vowel **ε** at the very beginning of the word and by the addition of a **σ** before the personal endings. That's the easy part. The confusing part is the endings. We have discussed "transitive" and "intransitive" in terms of action flowing from a verb to an object. We must now discuss the idea of "active" and "passive" more fully in terms of action which necessarily flows from the verb to the *subject*. Because this is a verb, which, although is translated in the active voice ("to see", versus "to be seen"), has passive endings. We must sort this out.

---

[30] 1st Corinthians 10:2.

[31] You will find the dative used with verbs that require in its capacity to express itself as the object of indirect action such as the verb give or follow or show. Or *believe*.

We spoke of three "types" of verbs in the koine – the ω verbs, the oμαι verbs, and the μι verbs. This is an oversimplification. And the problem with oversimplifications is that they sometimes complicate matters further. So it is better to deal with the complications as soon as we must. The most common category of verbs in Koine are those which end in ω. More properly, we must speak of the ordinary verb in which the stem takes an ordinary set of endings. These endings distinguish _who_ is initiating the action. The "ω" ending, itself, means that _I_ am doing the action. If _you_ are doing the action, the stem of the verb will end in "εις." Here are all the ordinary endings:[32]

	Singular		_Plural_	
ω	_I_		oμεν	_we_
εις	_you_		ετε	_you_
ει	_he, she it_		oυσι	_they_

Eventually, the arbitrary distinction of verbs into three "types" i.e., those ending in ω, those ending in oμαι and those ending in μι will get us into trouble. It is better to speak of _all_ verbal ideas as being distinguished by various sets of endings than it is to speak of inviolable categories of verbs.

If we take a verbal idea like crucify (σταυροω[33]), and we are told that it is an ω verb, we should like to know _why_ it is classified as an ω verb. Why isn't it a μι verb. i.e., σταυρωμι – or even an oμαι verb – σταυρομαι? The problem with this question is that it already presupposes the answer. A language is not assembled like an automobile – where every part has a specific, discrete function. Nor may a language be disassembled like an automobile in which this discrete function may be observed in isolation from the rest of the car. The interrelation of language with human culture is organic; therefore, to disassemble a language into discrete units invariably results in the dissolution of those discrete units. And to speak of a language as if it were a mechanistic assembly of discrete mechanical parts, creates the illusion that etymology is irrelevant.

The etymology of a word (i.e., its historical evolution) is organically connected to the function and meaning of that word. Yet our understanding of the evolution of _any_ historical language is, at best, vague. And this is especially true in that we do not perfectly understand the etymology of our own language. Finally, we may not speak as if the rules of a language follow this particular λογικος (logic) or that particular λογικος, when we know that the culture to which a language belongs follows its own λογικος, which is, in many respects, sociologically and historically inscrutable.

---

[32] There is another school of thought about how "endings" came to be (see Hewett, xv) but for didactic purposes we use the conventional approach.

[33] Grammarians further specify this verb as a "contract" verb, because its final vowel contracts with the endings that are added to it to form endings that are slightly different than normal. You may find a grammatical discussion of contract verbs in Hewett 147-153. Observe, but do not memorize.

And this is especially true in that we do not fully understand the sociology of our own culture. We do not even understand our own *psychology*.

Therefore, when we try to understand the etymology of a word, and in this case, the etymology of a language rule, we ought not to think that language has been mechanistically assembled. And we surely ought not to think that it has been mechanistically assembled by grammarians. You will often hear grammarians speak of a language as if this were so; nevertheless, we must approach our own rule-making and paradigm-formation with both humility *and* confidence: the humility which admits that language comes before language rules; confidence that we may create our own, provisional paradigms in which an organic language might enflesh itself in our minds.

We may confidently say, for example, that the μι verbs were in the process of dying out in the Koine period, but we must humbly admit that we do not know whence they came and wither they goeth. We may also confidently speak of the verbs that invariably take the ομαι endings as verbs which have "put off" ("deposed" as some grammarians have suggested) their active endings, but we must humbly admit that we do not know why verbs can become so unruly as to depose their own endings. Thus, we may speak of σταυροω as a verb that may very well have been in the process of becoming a "deponent" verb, since in our own literature it is used almost exclusively in the passive voice (since it is much, much more common to be crucified as it is to crucify).

But the head of that which we have been speaking (κεφαλαιον δε επι τοις λεγομενοις[34]) is this: when we want to distinguish who is the subject of an ordinary verb in the active voice (who is doing the action), we use the active endings above. When the subject becomes primarily a *receiver* of the verbal action (passive voice), we use the passive endings below.

Singular			*Plural*	
μαι	*I*		μεθα	*we*
σαι	*you*		σθε	*you*
ται	*he, she it*		νται	*they*

Thus, I am crucified with Christ is not χριστω συνεσταυρω; it is χριστω συνεσταυρ*ωμαι*. There will be some variations to these endings throughout the various tenses of a verb, but this is the basic paradigm with which we must become familiar.

---

[34] Hebrews 8:1.

114

Now when these passive endings have become *permanently* affixed to a verb (for whatever etymological reason) we may then speak provisionally of our second class of verbs – the ομαι type – of which εθεασαμεθα is an example. But what happens when we want to put one of <u>these</u> verbs, which have permanently adopted the passive endings - into the passive voice? That is, if these verbs, which have passive endings, are ordinarily translated in the active voice, how will we distinguish *them* when we want to make them truly passive? Matthew has a clear example of our verb θεαομαι. Jesus says that we should beware not to do our good works before men <u>*to be seen*</u> of them.

Matthew distinguishes the passive voice of this verb, which already carries the passive endings, by using a special construction in the aorist passive *infinitive* tense: το <u>θεαθηναι</u> αυτοις (*to be seen by them*). But this doesn't explain everything. It is not just that Matthew has switched to a special infinitive construction to push θεαομαι into complete passivity. For example, what if you were wanting not *to be seen* – but *to see*. What about those who "went out" (aorist tense) "to see" (infinitive mood) John the Baptist? (And Matthew must also use the same verb which already begins with passive endings) People went out into the desert not "to be seen" θεαθηναι but "<u>to</u> see." Matthew then switches to a set of aorist endings that are slightly different than the aorist passive. Grammarians call these endings the aorist <u>*middle*</u>. Matthew says θεασασθαι.[35] Hewett, 311-12 gives all the tenses. Observe, but do not memorize. Look at the aorist middle infinitive and the aorist passive infinitive forms. This chart gives us an accurate paradigm of how to understand what Matthew is doing when he switches from the passive to the active voice when using a verb which has already deposed its ordinary endings in favor of fixed passive endings.

When grammarians use the term "middle" they mean that the "voice" of the verb is somewhere midway between active and passive. Normally you don't see the grammar for the middle tense because the form for the middle and passive is the same for the present, the imperfect, the perfect and the pluperfect. The fact that a verb has already deposed its ordinary endings in favor of passive endings already tells us that it is a verbal idea that is somewhere midway between passive and active – that there is already a significant load of action which comes back upon the subject. We must then allow context to be our guide in expressing how much of the action goes to the subject; how much to the object. But in the future and the aorist tenses, there are recognizable grammatical differences to help us to express some of this differential.

---

[35] What Matthew avoids here is the more complicated construction that really gets to the essence of what is happening. The Pharisees went out to the wilderness "to be seen to be seeing" John the Baptist. How would Matthew express this? Happily, this is precisely what this course is not about (how would we express this - *hypothetically*). Because Matthew has already given us an answer. He has <u>separated</u> the idea of the hypocrisy of the Pharisees (to be seen of men) - from the act of going out to the wilderness to be a spectator of John the Baptist.

The confusing thing about how passivity is expressed in Koine is that English has more rigidly defined the categories of active and passive. Using our sample verb, we say. "I beheld." To switch to the passive voice, we insert the state of being verb – I was beheld. But in the Koine, it is much easier to see that <u>all</u> verbal ideas carry with them an intrinsically reflexive, or passive idea. Some more. Some less. It is the verbs that carry "somewhat more" of this reflexive component which have, etymologically, evolved into the deponent class of verbs – the so-called ομαι verbs.

Think for a moment about the verbal ideas of "crucify" and "behold." If we crucify someone, our attention is focused upon the object of the action. But when we *behold* something... Do you see the shift? The subject of the sentence has become much more important. Ironically, much of modern rhetoric is plagued with the overuse of the passive voice. For example, "It has been determined." English teachers will tell you that what is wrong with this phrase is that one of the most important things about the word "determined" is not only *what* has been determined, but *who* determined it. Think about "determine" for a moment. Here is a word that intrinsically carries a high level of reflexive force. To leave out the subject of this verb is not only irritating – it is disingenuous. The determiner is as important as what has been determined. But if Jesus "was crucified" (passive voice), we really don't need to know the soldier's name. "John Doe" is sufficient. For that matter, we don't care which nation is more at fault – the Jews or the Romans. The important thing is that Jesus was crucified by violent hands.

To summarize: let us say that deponent verbs; i.e., those which have permanently taken on the passive endings, are verbal ideas which *intrinsically* carry somewhat more of a passive component than other verbs. In order to push these verbs further into the passive voice, which is particularly relevant in the past (aorist) tense, John and others will then use special infinitive constructions, or in the case of the aorist and the future, special "middle" endings and special "passive" endings to distinguish them.

There is no need to be intimidated by deponent verbs, especially since John uses so few of them. Many of the deponent verbs convey a subtle balance between the passivity of the subject and the transitivity of action received by the object. One of the reasons that John is a good place to start is that he is not particularly subtle. And he is not particularly sophisticated. And perhaps John is not particularly Greek. Having continued so long with the Judaizing contingent in Jerusalem, he had, perhaps, very little reason to exercise his academic Greek. Yet later in his life we find him influential in Ephesus, affirming Pauline theology, writing from the isle of Patmos, and here writing a Gospel in Koine which looks very much like it is intended for an intelligent, Greek audience.

John uses just 34 deponent verbs in his gospel - a third of them (13) only once (marked in gray). Six more he uses only twice. Seven more are merely variants of ερχομαι (marked in italics) which we have already seen. Only three are used more than a half a dozen times (bold and enlarged): αποκρινομαι, δυναμαι, and θεαομαι - our sample verb. Take a moment to review them.

αγωνιζομαι	fight[36]
αλλομαι	spring up[37]
ανερχομαι	ascend[38]
απαρνεομαι	deny[39]
απερχομαι	depart[40]
αποκρινομαι	answer[41]
απτομαι	touch[42]
αρνεομαι	deny[43]
αρχομαι	begin[44]
βουλομαι	will, would, intend[45]
γευομαι	taste[46]
δαιμονιζομαι	possessed[47]
δεχομαι	make welcome, receive[48]
διαλογιζομαι	consider[49]

---

[36] Used once in 18:36 *My kingdom is not of this world: if my kingdom were of this world, then would my servants fight* (ηγωνιζοντο; imperfect, middle/passive).

[37] Used once in 4:14 *...but the water that I shall give him shall be in him a well of water springing up* (αλλομενου; present, middle/passive participle) *into everlasting life.*

[38] Used once in 6:3 *And Jesus went up* (ανηλθεν; aorist active indicative) *into a mountain, and there he sat with his disciples.* We have already seen ερχομαι of which this is but a minor variant.

[39] Used once in 13:38 *Verily, verily, I say unto thee, The cock shall not crow, till thou hast denied* (απαρνηση; future middle) *me thrice.*

[40] Another variant of ερχομαι. (26x)

[41] This is a very common word. It is often used (246x) in the narrative format of the Gospel/Acts sequence. It is only used twice outside of that sequence. It is almost formulaic. A typical construction in all the Gospels, for example: ο δε αποκριθεις ειπεν – *but he, answering, said...*

[42] Used once in 20:17 *Touch* (απτου; present middle imperative) *me not; for I am not yet ascended...*

[43] John uses this thrice – once of John the Baptist and twice concerning Peter's denial.

[44] John uses this only twice; once concerning the woman taken in adultery and once at the foot washing.

[45] Used once in 18:39b *...will* (βουλεσθε; present middle/passive) *ye therefore that I release unto you the King of the Jews?*

[46] John uses this twice – once at the marriage feast and once in 8:52: *If a man keep my saying, he shall never taste of death.*

[47] Used once in 10:21 *These are not the words of him that hath a devil* (δαιμονιζομενου; present middle/passive participle)

[48] Used once in 4:45 *Then when he was come into Galilee, the Galilaeans received* (εδεξαντο; aorist middle) *him.*

[49] Used once in 11:49b-50a *Ye know nothing at all, nor consider* (διαλογιζεσθε; present middle/passive) *that it is expedient for us, that one man should die for the people, and that the whole nation perish not.*

διερχομαι	pass through[50]
δυναμαι	can, be able[51]
εισερχομαι	enter[52]
εκδεχομαι	wait[53]
εκλεγομαι	choose[54]
εκπορευομαι	go forth[55]
εμβριμαομαι	be angry[56]
εντελλομαι	command[57]
εξερχομαι	go out[58]
εξηγεομαι	relate, explain, elaborate[59]
επιλεγομαι	call, choose[60]
εργαζομαι	work[61]
ερχομαι	come[62]
εσομαι	shall be[63]
θεαομαι	behold, see[64]
ιαομαι	heal[65]
καθεζομαι	sit[66]
συγχραομαι	consort[67]
συνεισηλθεν	go with[68]
συνερχομαι	come together[69]

---

[50] John uses this twice – once saying that Jesus need to <u>go through</u> Samaria and that when the people attempted to stone Jesus he <u>passed through</u> the midst of them. Another variant of ερχομαι.

[51] 36x.

[52] 14x Another variant of ερχομαι.

[53] Used once in 5:3 *In these lay a great multitude of impotent folk, of blind, halt, withered, <u>waiting</u>* (εκδεχομενων; present middle/passive participle) *for the moving of the water.*

[54] 4x.

[55] 2x - 5:29 *And shall <u>come forth</u>; they that have done good, unto the resurrection of life…* 15:26 *But when the Comforter is come, whom I will send unto you from the Father, even the Spirit of truth, which <u>proceedeth from</u> the Father.*

[56] John uses this twice to describe what Jesus was feeling at the raising of Lazarus.

[57] 4x.

[58] 30x. Another variant of ερχομαι.

[59] Used once in 1:18 *No man hath seen God at any time; the only begotten Son, which is in the bosom of the Father, he hath <u>declared</u> him.* Only Luke uses this term (5x).

[60] Used once in 5:2 *Now there is at Jerusalem by the sheep market a pool, which is <u>called</u> in the Hebrew tongue Bethesda.*

[61] 6x.

[62] 142x.

[63] 6x.

[64] 7x.

[65] 3x.

[66] 3x.

[67] Used once in 4:9 *…for the Jews <u>have</u> no <u>dealings with</u> the Samaritans.* The prefix συγ means "with" so this verb is an extension of χραομαι, which is the general word "use" as in: Acts 27:17 *…they <u>used</u> helps, undergirding the ship.*

[68] Used twice – another variant of ερχομαι.

[69] Used twice – another variant of ερχομαι.

και εθεασαμεθα[70] την δοξαν αυτου δοξαν ως μονογενους παρα[71]
and we beheld the glory of him glory as (the) only begotten from

πατρος πληρης χαριτος και αληθειας
the father full of grace and truth

δοξαν   δοξα (glory) is in the accusative case here because it receives some of the action of "beheld." While glory can be something which is passively beheld, it is also something which can be actively given, as in 5:41 *Glory from man I do not receive* (δοξαν παρα ανθρωπων ου λαμβανω). The AV has *I receive not honour from men.* But this is not the word that John is using here. There *is* a word for "honor" which John does use once in 4:44: *For Jesus himself testified, that a prophet hath no honour* (τιμη) *in his own country.* "Honor" is a weaker word than "glory," sometimes meaning just "value" (as in: Matthew 27:9 *Then was fulfilled that which was spoken by Jeremy the prophet, saying, And they took the thirty pieces of silver, the price* (τιμην) *of him that was valued, whom they of the children of Israel did value*). Or "importance" (as in: 1st Corinthians 12:23 *And those members of the body, which we think to be less honourable, upon these we bestow more abundant honour* (τιμην) *and our uncomely parts have more abundant comeliness*). Or it may mean "price" (as in: 1st Corinthians 7:23 *Ye are bought with a price* τιμης).

"Glory" is a word that the AV translators have also pressed into the service of translating καυχαομαι, but John never uses this word. It would have been better that καυχαομαι had never meddled with "glory," but left as "boasting" (as it is in translating many of Paul's usages) or some derivative of pride (good or bad).

Matthew succinctly captures the character of "glory" in 6:28b-29: *Consider the lilies of the field, how they grow; they toil not, neither do they spin: And yet I say unto you, That even Solomon in all his glory was not arrayed like one of these.* Consider how John uses the word in its Old Testament context: *And the temple was filled with smoke from the glory of God, and from his power; and no man was able to enter into the temple, till the seven plagues of the seven angels were fulfilled.*[72] Now compare this with Exodus 40:35: *And Moses was not*

---

[70] See discussion, John 1:14.
[71] See discussion, John 1:6. John says παρα του πατρος nine times (once in 2nd John; once in Revelation), yet here he says simply παρα πατρος (with no article), which diminishes the genitive idea of possession and strengthens the prepositional idea, or relational idea of "from" (παρα).
[72] Revelation 15:8.

119

able to enter into the tent of the congregation, because the cloud abode thereon, and the <u>glory</u> of the LORD filled the tabernacle.[73] This is glory.

When John says: "we beheld his glory" he is using this in the same sense as Peter's:

For we have not followed cunningly devised fables, when we made known unto you the power and coming of our Lord Jesus Christ, but were eyewitnesses of his majesty. For he received from God the Father honour and <u>glory</u>, when there came such a voice to him from the excellent <u>glory</u>, This is my beloved Son, in whom I am well pleased.[74]

Remember that John was one of the three who witnessed the transfiguration of Jesus, saw the figures of Moses and Elijah and heard the voice coming from the cloud.[75]

Paul contrasts the sufferings of this life with the glory which is to come.[76] He also contrasts the dishonor of biological life with a resurrection into glory.[77] He also juxtapositions glory with shame.[78] From these, it is clear that by "glory," John means an illuminating splendor deserving of awe and joyful worship as in: Revelation 18:1 *And after these things I saw another angel come down from heaven, having great power; and the earth was lightened with his glory.* And also in Revelation 21:23 *And the city had no need of the sun, neither of the moon, to shine in it: for the glory of God did lighten it, and the Lamb is the light thereof.*

ως   ως is an adverb which means "as" or "like." It is therefore used to set up a simple simile: *If a man abide not in me, he is cast forth <u>as</u> a branch.*[79] It also is used to express the idea of similarity inherent in an approximation: *So*

---

[73] The LXX translators properly use δοξης here.

[74] 2nd Peter 1:16-17. The word he uses for "honor" is τιμη.

[75] See Luke 9:28-31.

[76] Romans 8:18 *For I reckon that the sufferings (παθεμα) of this present time are not worthy to be compared with the <u>glory</u> which shall be revealed in us.* Similarly, he contrasts the suffering inherent in persecution with glory as in: 2nd Corinthians 4:17 *For our light affliction (θλιψις), which is but for a moment, worketh for us a far more exceeding and eternal weight of <u>glory</u>.*

[77] 1st Corinthians 15:43 *It is sown in dishonour (ατιμια); it is raised in <u>glory</u> it is sown in weakness; it is raised in power.* In his second letter to Corinth he also contrasts ατιμια with δοξα: 2nd Corinthians 6:8 *By <u>glory</u> and <u>dishonour</u>, by evil report and good report: as deceivers, and yet true.*

[78] Philippians 3:19 *Whose end is destruction, whose God is their belly, and whose <u>glory</u> is in their shame (αισχυνη), who mind earthly things.*

[79] John 15:6.

120

when they had rowed <u>about</u> five and twenty or thirty furlongs.[80] Often this approximation is an estimate of time, or as often, an estimate of the relationship of two events in time: *But <u>when</u> they came to Jesus, <u>and</u> saw that he was dead already, they brake not his legs.*[81] John's idiomatic expression, which more assertively expresses two events in time, is ως ουν[82] (therefore when).

<u>Exegetical Considerations</u>: *...the glory as of the only begotten of the Father.* Translated thusly, it potentially leaves the mistaken impression that since this was an inferior glory, then Jesus was only *like* an only-begotten Son of the Father. This expression could be corrected by substituting *...a glory befitting the only begotten of the Father.* This also clears up why John twice repeats "glory." John is specifying the *level* of glory that they saw. Particularly, he is alluding to the glory that they saw at the transfiguration, which he will elaborate – not in his Gospel, but in his Apocalypse:

And in the midst of the seven candlesticks one like unto the Son of man, clothed with a garment down to the foot, and girt about the paps with a golden girdle. His head and his hairs were white like wool, as white as snow; and his eyes were as a flame of fire; And his feet like unto fine brass, as if they burned in a furnace; and his voice as the sound of many waters.[83]

Although the miracles revealed the glory of Christ (*This beginning of miracles did Jesus in Cana of Galilee, and manifested forth his <u>glory</u> and his disciples believed on him.*[84]), John makes it very clear that this was only the beginning: *Father, I will that they also, whom thou hast given me, be with me where I am; that they may behold my <u>glory</u> which thou hast given me: for thou lovedst me before the foundation of the world.*[85]

μονογενης   Some lexical discussions have this word as a compound of μονος (only) and γινομαι (be), and its meaning as "unique." But most probably it is a compound of μονος and γενναω, and its meaning is "only-begotten" as the AV translators assert. Even if we had an etymological commentary from the period, we still would not know

---

[80] John 6:19.
[81] John 19:33.
[82] Of seven occurrences of this phrase, John uses six of them. A much weaker form is ως δε (but when). John uses this expression six times. But the phrase is more characteristic of Luke's style – he uses it 30 times of its 37 occurrences.
[83] Revelation 1:13-15.
[84] John 2:11.
[85] John 17:24.

for sure. But one thing we do know for sure is that Luke uses this word thrice in its ordinary sense – "only child."[86] John is surely aware of Matthew's parable of the wicked tenants, which is a thinly veiled reference to Christ and his rejection by the Jews. None of the Synoptic accounts use μονογενης to distinguish Christ in this parable. All three are exactly synchronous at this point, saying: ουτος εστιν ο κληρονομος δευτε αποκτεινωμεν αυτον (this is the heir – come let us kill him). Whether the vineyard owner's son is his only son or his first born son is irrelevant to the parable. He is the _heir_. That is the important thing. Though there is considerable equivocation on the part of Peter regarding Christ – calling him merely παις[87] in his early preaching, the Synoptic tradition clearly distinguishes the uniqueness of Christ. It is therefore unnecessary that John specify this uniqueness by means of the _nature_ of his generation. And this is especially true because John very much distinguishes both the uniqueness and the nature of Christ by other means. For example, John will shortly say in just four more sentences: _No man hath seen God at any time; the only begotten Son, which is in the bosom of the Father, he hath declared him._[88] While there remains ambiguity about the precise meaning of μονογενης, and thus what has become known as the "eternal generation" of Christ, there is no ambiguity in John about the _relation_ that Christ stands to the Father and to the world of created men.

πατρος   This is the genitive form of πατηρ, another third declension noun, which means "father." John uses this word almost as much as the Synoptics combined. And like Matthew, who accounts for almost half the occurrences in the Synoptic material, John uses this word much more often to refer to _God_ the father. Anterior to the Gospels, Paul has already well-defined God as father. The idea has even become part of a formal Pauline benediction which is repeated in nine of his thirteen

---

[86] 7:12; 8:42; 9:38 Also the author of Hebrews uses it in the same way – to refer to Isaac, the only begotten son of Abraham (11:17).

[87] "child" or "servant."

[88] John 1:18. Also consider John's editorial statement: _Therefore the Jews sought the more to kill him, because he not only had broken the sabbath, but said also that God was his Father making himself equal with God._ (John 5:18) This despite the fact that Matthew's Sermon on the Mount encourages us to call God "our Father." Ultimately, John does not rely on μονογενης to distinguish the Son. John _contextually_ parses the "unique" nature of Christ's sonship. For example: _...all men should honour the Son, even as they honour the Father_ (5:23) Also: _I and my Father are one._ (10:30) Also: _Jesus saith unto him, Have I been so long time with you, and yet hast thou not known me, Philip? he that hath seen me hath seen the Father_ (14:9) Also: _He that hateth me hateth my Father also._ (15:23) Though many men in our literature address God as father – even _abba_ (father) as Christ did at Gethsemane, no one but Christ makes statements like these concerning his unique sonship, which are recorded in John.

letters: χαρις υμιν και ειρηνη απο θεου πατρος ημων και κυριου ιησου χριστου (*grace to you and peace from God our Father and from the Lord Jesus Christ*).

πληρης   Of the 17 times this word occurs in the literature, 10 of them are theological and thus may be categorized as poetic diction, which deforms ordinary usage. But what is the ordinary usage for this word? Matthew gives a good, clear example: *And they did all eat, and were filled: and they took up of the fragments that remained twelve baskets full.*[89]

χαριτος   This is the genitive of χαρις, a third declension noun,[90] which means "grace," or "favor." But what does grace mean? Though very common in the Pauline corpus, Matthew and Mark don't use it at all. In John, this word occurs only three times – all three in this chapter. None of these uses elaborate very much about the nature of grace, except to say (3 sentences later) that there is a contrast between grace and the law of Moses.[91] But there is no further elaboration here either. Yet there is a very strong linguistic connection precisely at this point with the core of Paul's argument in Romans and in Galatians, which contrasts the law of Moses with grace. Only John and Paul contrast these two terms. Here is a representative example from a Pauline argument: … *for sin shall not have dominion over you: for ye are not under the law, but under grace.* There is no need for John to define a theological term which has already been very rigorously defined by Paul.

"Grace" appears once more in 2nd John in a formal introductory benediction,[92] and once in Revelation in an opening and a closing benediction. If we examine these benedictions closely we will see that they are quotations of well established Pauline formularies. For example the combination of grace (χαρις), mercy (ελεος) and peace (ειρηνη) occur only in Paul, once in the opening benediction of each of the pastorals (1st Timothy, 2nd Timothy and Titus). Yet this is the only place that "mercy" appears in the Johannine corpus. Let us call this

---

[89] 14:20.
[90] Which is one of Hewett's examples – see Hewett, 16.4.
[91] 1:17 *For the law was given by Moses, but grace and truth came by Jesus Christ.*
[92] 1:3 ***Grace** be with you, **mercy, and peace**, from **God the Father**, and from the **Lord Jesus Christ**.* The words synchronous with Paul (which appear in the pastoral benediction) are bolded. Note that the KJV translators split grace from mercy and peace. There is no reason for this. Particularly in view of the fact that John is phraseologically synchronous with Paul. In both authors it appears in the Greek thusly: χαρις ελεος ειρηνη.

phenomenon a "source alignment pin."[93] <u>A source alignment pin is a preferential word of one author which makes a very rare appearance *in a synchronous passage* of another author</u>. The author showing preferential treatment for that word might be the source of the synchronous passage and therefore might be the source for the theological idea contained in that passage. If this phenomenon occurs sufficiently distinctly and sufficiently often, then that "*might be* the source" may be upgraded to "*probably is* the source." This phenomenon is of particular concern in a study of the "Synoptic problem" in which three separate authors share many synchronous passages.

There is further alignment between John and Paul. In John's opening benediction in Revelation, he is almost certainly quoting Paul: ... χαρις υμιν και ειρηνη απο ... (grace to you and peace from ...).[94] This phrase occurs only in Paul - but in fully ten of his thirteen epistles.[95] But there is more. The *closing* benediction in Revelation appears only in Paul as the closing formulation in seven of his epistles: η χαρις του κυριου ημων ιησου χριστου (*The grace of our Lord Jesus Christ...*).

If we have strong circumstantial evidence like this that John is theologically aligned with Paul, then we must look into the Pauline corpus for definition of words like χαρις which remain undefined in John.[96]

αληθειας   With this word, "truth," we come to a theological word which receives considerable emphasis from John. It is a feminine noun that occurs

---

[93] We are calling such fragments of apparent vocabulary tracking in synchronous passages "source alignment pins" since they tend to positively "pin" a phenomena of <u>possible</u> vocabulary dependence to the phenomena of <u>actual</u> vocabulary *preference*; i.e., the importation of someone else's vocabulary. If we know, or strongly suspect that John is, at this point, either looking at Paul's pastorals or is subconsciously thinking about them as he composes 2nd John, we must ask - why? Are there any higher order linkages of content or style between them? And is this linkage of sufficient force and kind to suggest that 2nd John is chronologically linked to the Pauline Pastorals? If our circumstantial evidence begins to accumulate to support such a suggestion, then this also drives the dating of John's Gospel in the direction of the early 60s.

[94] Revelation 1:4.

[95] All in the opening benediction.

[96] Since Matthew and Mark do not use this word, we have very little choice. Luke uses it untheologically, which will help us to fill in some of its color, but even here we cannot escape the presumption that since Luke was Paul's constant companion as his secretary, it is logical that there will be a very strong vocabulary relationship between Luke and Paul. And there certainly is. We will explore this relationship in our New Testament textbooks. For now, let us simply note that John does not develop the word "grace" and move on in our translation of John.

almost 100 times in the Biblical materials, 37 times in John's Gospel and in his epistles. Of the 25 occurrences of αληθης, a close adjectival cognate, 16 are Johannine. Of the 25 occurrences of αληθινος, an even closer adjectival cognate, which we encountered previously in John's sentence: *That was the <u>true</u> light, which lighteth every man that cometh into the world,*[97] 20 are Johannine. αληθως is the adverbial cognate, which almost always[98] occurs with a state of being verb derived from ει (is). Almost half its occurrences are Johannine.

<u>Exegetical Considerations</u>: It is in this word that we come as close as we may to the modern equivalent of "really." In a world which has been hopelessly bifurcated into that which is real and that which is unreal[99] by the philosophy of Hegel, Descartes, and Eastern philosophical categories migrating into the Western mind, it is difficult to understand how far short the idea of "really" falls to express the philosophical category of αληθως. It is John only who attempts an explanation of truth itself. It is only in John that we find such an engaging philosophical question: τι εστιν αληθεια; that is, "what is truth."[100] It is only in John that we can know of a surety (αληθως) that Pilate is not asking: "what is real?"

John says that Jesus was "*full* (πληρης) of grace and truth," which explains why both grace and truth are in the genitive. But the modern idea of "reality" is indeclinable. A man cannot be "full of reality." But he can be full of himself - as Satan was: *Ye are of your father the devil, and the lusts of your father ye will do. He was a murderer from the beginning, and abode not in the truth, because there is no truth in him. When he speaketh a lie, he speaketh of his own: for he is a liar, and the father of it.*[101] For John, the antithesis of truth is not that which is "unreal." The antithesis of truth is <u>lie</u>. And this is not confined to John. In our literature there are false brothers (ψευδαδελφος), false apostles (ψευδαποστολος), false teachers (ψευδοδιδασκαλος), false witnesses (ψευδομαρτυρ), which bear false witness (ψευδομαρτυρεω; ψυεδομαρτυρια), false prophets (ψευδοπροφητης), and false Christs (ψευδοχριστος).

It is not so much the *result* of the lie which concerns John in his Gospel.[102] It is the lie itself. It is the liar (ψευδης[103]), who changes the truth of God into a lie (ψευδος[104]). In the modern, dialectical idea of truth, a thesis is in an eternal codependent relationship with its antithesis. In John, the antithesis of truth is eternally repudiated

---

[97] See discussion, John 1:9.
[98] 14 of 19 occurrences.
[99] See for example discussions of Schrödinger's Cat.
[100] 18:38.
[101] 8:44.
[102] This changes in his Revelation.
[103] NT 3x = Acts 1x/Rev 2x.
[104] NT 9x = Paul 4x/ John 5x.

in hell.[105] No lie is of the truth,[106] nor ever can be, world without end. According to John, the rejection of Christ is not an understandable existential orientation – it is the work of a liar[107] (ψευστης[108]).

Whatever Hegel might have meant by his dialectical theory of truth, these words of John are no longer acceptable in polite society. Yet John insists that they should be a crucial part of our consciousness and of our dialogue. We say that "to err is human." John says, no. To err is demonic. And there are many deceivers at large which deny Christ.[109] There are no Koine equivalents for the bland and neutral words of "mistake" and "incorrect," there are simply πλαναω (deceive) and πλανη (deception) which are themselves possessed of a malignant spirit.[110]

Even πλανητης, from which we derive "planet" – to describe a somewhat picturesque, but wandering, celestial body, has very strong connotations of wickedness in Koine: *Woe to them…these are…raging waves of the sea, foaming out their own shame; <u>wandering</u> stars, to whom is reserved the blackness of darkness for ever.*[111] God is not angry with us because we make a mistake doing our sums. He is angry with us because we refuse his correction - to go back to the place where we made our mistake and begin again.[112] He is angry with us because we purposely deceive ourselves, transforming the truth of God into a lie,[113] and therefore, the truth does not dwell in us.[114] They called Christ a deceiver.[115] John says that the light enlightens every man that comes into the world, and that in order to escape that light of truth, which we have all done to some extent, we must at least insinuate that Christ is a liar.[116] If we did not subconsciously believe that Christ was lying or wrong (or

---

[105] Since Hell itself is a repudiation of truth. C. S. Lewis' *The Great Divorce* is a very clever suggestion about how this could be so.

[106] 1st John 2:21.

[107] 1st John 2:22 *Who is a <u>liar</u> but he that denieth that Jesus is the Christ? He is antichrist, that denieth the Father and the Son.*

[108] NT 10x = Paul 3x/ John 7x.

[109] 2nd John 1:7 *For many <u>deceivers</u> are entered into the world, who confess not that Jesus Christ is come in the flesh. This is a <u>deceiver</u> and an antichrist.*

[110] 1st John 4:6 *We are of God: he that knoweth God heareth us; he that is not of God heareth not us. Hereby know we the spirit of truth, and the spirit of <u>error</u>.*

[111] Jude 11-13.

[112] This illustration comes from Lewis' Preface to *The Great Divorce*.

[113] Romans 1:25.

[114] 1st John 1:8; John 8:37.

[115] Matthew 27:63; John 7:12.

[116] 1st John 1:10 *If we say that we have not sinned, we make him a liar, and his word is not in us.* We try to make this more palatable by saying that Christ is not lying, he is simply wrong. But how is he wrong without actively deceiving himself? We *wish* he were wrong. Our self-image suffers considerable abuse at his hands: he says he wants to marry us but then he says that we must first acknowledge that we are wretched, and miserable, and poor, and blind, and naked (Revelation 3:17). What kind of marriage proposal is that (we ask)? He says that we are spiritual prostitutes. In anger, we say 'to hell with you!' He says: this was precisely what I have done. Otherwise, *you* must go.'

possibly irrelevant and ignorant), what would be our rationale for embracing the destructive darkness of sin and bondage as an alternative to him?

Christ is full of truth, but Adam and Eve were, at first, mere earthen vessels. God had much to tell them, but they could not then bear to hear it all.[117] It would take time for their legs of clay to bear an eternal weight of glory.[118] Satan suggested to Eve that God was doing more than simply keeping them in the dark about their destiny. He suggested that he was unrighteously keeping them in a state of sullen servitude - by deception.[119] If error is intrinsic to the manishness of man (i.e., 'to err is human'), then the Son of Man is the Son of sin itself and Satan then assumes a messianic role in leading humanity on an exodus from superstition and utterly dependent slavery, to a land of autonomous freedom. Satan promised them freedom, but gave them death. Truth died in the mouth of Satan. But in the sacrificial death of truth, the power of deception was itself destroyed, and Adam's children revived (αναξαω). And if the truth make us free, we will be free indeed.[120]

---

[117] John 16:12 *I have yet many things to say unto you, but ye cannot bear them now.*
[118] 2nd Corinthians 4:17.
[119] Genesis 3:4-5.
[120] John 8:36.

Chapter 4 Review

Read aloud, *with comprehension*, the passage below. Go as slow as needed in order to maintain comprehension. If you have forgotten a word, stop, take the time to look it up, and resume the exercise.

εν αρχη ην ο λογος και ο λογος ην προς τον θεον και θεος ην ο λογος ουτος ην εν αρχη προς τον θεον παντα δι αυτου εγενετο και χωρις αυτου εγενετο ουδε εν ο γεγονεν εν αυτω ζωη ην και η ζωη ην το φως των ανθρωπων και το φως εν τη σκοτια φαινει και η σκοτια αυτο ου κατελαβεν εγενετο ανθρωπος απεσταλμενος παρα θεου ονομα αυτω ιωαννης ουτος ηλθεν εις μαρτυριαν ινα μαρτυρηση περι του φωτος ινα παντες πιστευσωσι δι αυτου ουκ ην εκεινος το φως αλλ ινα μαρτυρηση περι του φωτος ην το φως το αληθινον ο φωτιζει παντα ανθρωπον ερχομενον εις τον κοσμον εν τω κοσμω ην και ο κοσμος δι αυτου εγενετο και ο κοσμος αυτον ουκ εγνω εις τα ιδια ηλθεν και οι ιδιοι αυτον ου παρελαβον οσοι δε ελαβον αυτον εδωκεν αυτοις εξουσιαν τεκνα θεου γενεσθαι τοις πιστευουσιν εις το ονομα αυτου οι ουκ εξ αιματων ουδε εκ θεληματος σαρκος ουδε εκ θεληματος ανδρος αλλ εκ θεου εγεννηθησαν και ο λογος σαρξ εγενετο και εσκηνωσεν εν ημιν και εθεασαμεθα την δοξαν αυτου δοξαν ως μονογενους παρα πατρος πληρης χαριτος και αληθειας

Chapter 5: John 1:15 – 1:18

ιωαννης μαρτυρει περι¹ αυτου
John   witnesses concerning him

και κεκραγεν λεγων
and had cried saying

ουτος ην² ον εἰπον
this   was the one of which I said³

ο   οπισω μου ερχομενος εμπροσθεν μου γεγονεν
the one after me coming   before   me was

οτι   πρωτος μου   ην
because first   of me he was

μαρτυρει   We have already seen this word in John's seventh sentence: *The same came for a witness, to* bear witness *of the Light*, and in his eighth sentence: *He was not that Light, but was sent to* bear witness *of that Light*. But in both these cases μαρτυρεω is in the aorist subjunctive. Here it is the simple present tense, 3ʳᵈ person singular. John (he) bares witness… But this is not a case of the "historical present," in which the editor employs the present tense in describing past events in order to move his audience closer to them. This is a case of using the present tense to state a timeless, tenseless fact.

For example, John does not say: I *was* the alpha and I *will be* the omega. In both cases, Jesus *is* the alpha and the omega. The events which concern John's audience are half a generation removed from the events themselves. John the Baptist was beheaded approximately 30 years ago. John *could* speak in the past tense concerning John's role. But the Baptist's role *per se* is a timeless fact.⁴ But for John the Apostle, John the Baptist's role is re-iterated in the present tense, not only because the events have only recently transpired, and not only because the

---

¹ See John 1:7.

² John has already used ουτος ην (*this one was*) in 1:2.

³ John the Baptist will make this point three times. Here he mentions that he has already said this outside of the Johannine record, which makes four times.

⁴ This may be yet another reason for John's unusual construction ονομα αυτω ιωαννης – "name to him, John" – instead of employing the past tense: his name *was* John. His name still *is* John. It will *always* be John. And this is because John the Baptist's role will always be relevant.

Baptist's role is a timeless fact, but because the Baptist's role is a *timely* fact. The cult of John the Baptist is, in John's ministry, still having its present effect.

κεκραγεν   Is the perfect tense of κραζω, which means to "cry out." The perfect tense is generally formed by repeating the primary consonant. Generally a κ is added just before the final endings, but in many cases, such as with κραζω, the spelling changes slightly at the end of the stem.[5]

A very close synonym to κραζω is βοαω. Matthew describes the crying out of Jesus on the cross with the verbal idea of κραζω: *Jesus, when he had cried* (κραξας) *again with a loud voice, yielded up the ghost.*[6] Yet Mark uses βοαω to describe a very similar crying out: *And at the ninth hour Jesus cried* (εβοησεν) *with a loud voice, saying, Eloi, Eloi, lama sabachthani?*[7] John will use both terms to describe the confession of John the Baptist – here, and also repeating the Synoptic prophecy concerning John the Baptist in his 23rd sentence.[8] Another close synonym for κραζω is κραυγαζω, which John uses thrice. You can gauge its closeness by comparing John's *But they cried out* (εκραυγασαν), *Away with him, away with him, crucify him*[9] with Mark's: *...and they cried out* (εκραξαν) *again, crucify him.*[10]

λεγων   λεγω is another workhorse narrative[11] word meaning "say" or "tell." Here it is in present participle, nominative singular[12] form. Although λεγω is a very common word, it is highly irregular.[13] (You can see its various forms in Hewett, 310). You will not see much of this irregularity in John since he uses the present tense or the aorist tense almost exclusively. And in the aorist, you will almost always see it

---

[5] See Hewett, 12.2.2.
[6] Matthew 27:50.
[7] Mark 15:34.
[8] Isaiah 40:3 *The voice of him that <u>crieth</u> in the wilderness, Prepare ye the way of the LORD, make straight in the desert a highway for our God.*
[9] 19:15.
[10] 15:13.
[11] For example, of its 153 occurrences, only 5 are outside the narrative genre of the Gospel/Acts sequence.
[12] Since it describes the subject of this sentence – John the Baptist.
[13] It is so irregular that the OnlineBible program makes it two different words (contrary to the GNT and Hewett)

either as "he said" (ειπεν) or "I, they[14] said" (ειπον). The present tense and the aorist tense often appear together in the same sentence, as it does in our sample sentence. For example, Matthew says: *What* λεγω *you in darkness, that* ειπατε *in light*.[15] A very common formation in the Gospel genre is: ειπεν… αμην λεγω υμιν (*he said...verily I say to you*). Distinctively, (only) John augments this phrase seven times with an additional amen: ειπεν… αμην αμην λεγω υμιν. He repeats αμην αμην λεγω υμιν 20 times. John once repeats λεγω in this *same* phraseological construction: και <u>λεγει</u> αυτω αμην αμην <u>λεγω</u> υμιν.[16]

ον	Here is the relative pronoun again, this time in the accusative singular. Note how just the relative pronoun is used. English must put in a few words to express its accusative function, hence the extra words: "the one of" - to go along with "which" in order to make sense.
ο	And here is the relative pronoun yet again in the nominative. It is distinguished from the nominative article by context alone. We saw this form in the third sentence (και χωρις αυτου εγενετο ουδε εν <u>ο</u> γεγονεν; (1:3). Notice how John is setting up the upcoming phrase with this relative pronoun.
οπισω	This word is part of the Synoptic template concerning John the Baptist. Matthew says: ο δε <u>οπισω</u> μου ερχομενος (but the one <u>after</u> me coming …) Also well known - in Matthew - Jesus says to Peter: δευτε <u>οπισω</u> μου (come <u>after</u> me), but he later completely alters the connotation of this very word through context alone: υπαγε <u>οπισω</u> μου σατανα (get behind me, Satan). οπισω is an adverb; therefore, concerning the relationship between Jesus and John, the verbal idea of coming (ερχομενος), as well as the surrounding context, makes it clear that John is saying that Jesus is coming after John in time and not *as a disciple*. John repeats the substance of this relationship twice more in this paragraph.
μου	The genitive form of the personal pronoun is used because the coming behind of Christ is something which stands in relation, or pertains, to John's own coming – or the coming of John – or the ερχομενου ιωαννου. John couples a phrase about chronology: "*The coming behind of me*" to a phrase about theology "*before me he was*" εμπροσθεν μου

---

[14] Yes, in this paradigm the first person singular and the third person plural are identical – ειπον. It will be an easy matter to decide from context which is which.
[15] Matthew 10:27 *What I tell you in darkness, that speak ye in light.*
[16] 1:51.

γεγονεν), about which he has just been teaching. 'Yes, Jesus came after John the Baptist, but Jesus nevertheless stands as the logos before all things.' This is a much stronger statement than the Synoptic template. We will shortly compare the Johannine and Synoptic contrast between Jesus and the Baptist.

ερχομενος   Here is ερχομαι in present middle, or passive participle form. We cannot tell from the word alone whether it is middle or passive since it is already a deponent verb. When it occurs, grammarians simply designate it as being in the M/P form, as Hewett does.[17] We have said that a participle is a verbal adjective, and therefore the participle will take on the case of the noun or pronoun that it defines – in this case it is defining the relative pronoun **o** which is in the nominative case. We now have completed our phrase: ο οπισω μου ερχομενος (the one after me coming). Yet a participle still retains much of its verbal idea. Otherwise οπισω (after), an adverb, would have nothing to define.

εμπροσθεν   We also know then that εμπροσθεν, another adverb meaning "before" must go with γεγονεν, a verb we have already seen. John's second, contrasting phrase εμπροσθεν μου γεγονεν (before me was) is also now complete. There is obviously some word play, or poetic diction going on here, at which we must take a closer look. How can a man be coming after, yet at the same time have come before? John then pushes an expression formed by word play into a theological enigma by answering his own implicit, rhetorical question: because he [Jesus] was first (of me). (οτι πρωτος μου ην) notice how John puts "me" into the genitive to achieve the same effect as before. That is, John the Baptist is saying: 'in relation to things pertaining to me' he comes after, yet he is before. John links all three phrases (underlined) with this genitive (bolded):

ο οπισω **μου** ερχομενος // εμπροσθεν **μου** γεγονεν // οτι πρωτος **μου** ην. John has linked οπισω ("after") with εμπροσθεν ("before") three times (1:15, 27, 30).[18]

---

[17] Hewett 19.3.3.

[18] This linkage occurs only once in Paul - Philippians 3:13 *Brethren, I count not myself to have apprehended: but this one thing I do, forgetting those things which are <u>behind</u> and reaching forth unto those things which are <u>before</u>…*

οτι   οτι is word that is used over 1000 times in our literature. It is a conjunction which means "that," or often, as is the case here, means "because."

πρωτος   Most of the time, πρωτος means numerically first. Although μια is once contrasted with "second" by Paul: *A man that is an heretick after the first* (μιαν) *and* <u>*second*</u> (δευτεραν) *admonition reject,*[19] normally, it is this word, πρωτος. For example: *This is the* <u>*first*</u> (πρωτη) *and great commandment. And the* <u>*second*</u> (δευτερα) *is like unto it…,*[20] or as Luke uses it: *When they were past the first* (πρωτην) *and the second* (δευτεραν) *ward…*[21]

A very common, but enigmatic Synoptic formula which does not appear in John's Gospel, but makes prominent appearance in the Apocalypse, is the contrast between πρωτος (first) with last (εσχατως).[22] It would be very tempting to assume that John has in mind the Apocalyptic formula: *I am Alpha and Omega, the beginning and the end, the first* (πρωτος) *and the last* (εσχατος).[23] But then, he hasn't been given this formula yet. Neither does he appear to be harboring any anticipatory thought forms. Yes, he has already said in his Gospel that Jesus is the "beginning" (αρχη), but nowhere in his Gospel does he say that Jesus is the "end" (τελος).

There is another clear but infrequent connotation of πρωτος, seen most often in Acts, which means "most important" or "top ranking official" or simply "chief" (as the AV translators invariably use). For example: και <u>τους πρωτους</u> της πολεως is translated "and <u>the chief men</u> of the city" (or <u>the firsts</u> of the city).[24] Also τω πρωτω της νησου is translated "the chief man of the island."[25] There is also the well known: *This is a faithful saying, and worthy of all acceptation, that Christ Jesus came into the world to save sinners; of whom I am chief.*[26] (ων πρωτος ειμι εγω) "of whom first I am."

Notice that in all three cases that the AV has chosen "chief" to stand for πρωτος, it is occurring in a *genitive* construction. πολεως (city)

---

[19] Titus 3:10.
[20] Matthew 22:38-39.
[21] Acts 12:10.
[22] For example: Matthew 20:16 *So the last shall be first and the first last.*
[23] Revelation 22:13.
[24] Acts 13:50.
[25] Acts 28:7.
[26] 1st Timothy 1:15.

νησου (island) and the relative pronoun, ων, are all in the genitive. Thereby we know that πρωτος is not being used to describe mere numerical order (i.e., "first"). In these constructions, πρωτος is being used to express *rank*. Paul is not saying that he is the *first* sinner. He is saying that he is the *greatest* sinner. Likewise, when John uses the same construction, he is explaining how that one coming after John the Baptist can be before him: οτι πρωτος μου ην – 'because in relation to me, he takes *precedence*.' Inconsistently, the AV has translated: *He that cometh after me is preferred before me: for he was before me.* This is the only place in our AV translation where πρωτος is translated as "before." Since the AV has used "before" to stand for both εμπροσθεν and πρωτος, it apparently attempts to avoid inexplicable redundancy by inserting a "preferred" to go along with εμπροσθεν. There are two problems with this strategy. Firstly, it has broken off the connotation of *precedence* which belongs to πρωτος and attached it to εμπροσθεν, where it does not belong. Secondly, the importation of the word "preferred" brings in a connotation which suggests that Jesus' precedence is the *preference* (or popularity) which is derived from an unstated subject – whether that be his father or the people.

Within the cult of John the Baptist which lingered in Ephesus, John the Baptist was more popular than Jesus. For some, even Apollos was more important.[27] This is *five years after* the Jerusalem council.[28] For now, we have no theory about how this could be so. We see only that the Apostle John is belaboring the categorical difference between John the Baptist and Jesus – even in relation to the Synoptic differentiation of these two characters.

Since this will come up again and again in John's extended prologue, let's examine John's effort to distinguish Jesus from John the Baptist in relation to the differentiation we see in the Synoptic template:

Synoptic Template	John
	John's prologue: Christ is the word; he is God; all things made through him; the light and life of men. 1:1-4
	John was not that light, but came to bear witness to the light, which is Christ. 1:6-9
	John declares that he that comes after him takes precedence over him. 1:15

---

[27] 1st Corinthians 1:12.

[28] If we accept the general dating of 1st Corinthians at around 55 or 56 AD.

The direct encounter: *I have need to be baptized of thee, and comest thou to me?*[29]	
The transfiguration distinguishes Jesus from Moses and Elijah.[30]	Jesus counterpoised with Moses. 1:17
	Only Jesus has seen the father. 1:18

1) Applies the prophecy of Isaiah 40:3 to John[31]
2) Has John the Baptist say that the one coming after him
   a. 1) is stronger[32]
   b. 2) is more worthy[33]
   c. 3) and has a baptism of the Holy Ghost which is far superior to his water baptism[34]
	John the Baptist Soliloquy to the Priests and Levites 1:19-28:
	
	1) I am not the Christ
	2) Appropriates Isaiah 40:3
	3) Repeats the substance of 1:15 – Jesus takes precedence.
	4) I am not worthy to unloose his sandals

---

[29] Matthew 3:14b.

[30] Luke adds what Jesus talked to them about. He told them of his exodus (εξοδος) from Jerusalem.

[31] But it is not clear what John the Baptist is heralding from this passage except general statements: "the glory of the Lord will be revealed" Matthew says that John the Baptist's message is this: *Repent ye: for the kingdom of heaven is at hand.* But when Jesus hears that John is thrown into prison, he goes to Capernaum and begins to preach the exact same message: *Repent: for the kingdom of heaven is at hand.* (The Greek is identical.) Mark sees the problem. He adds three things to the account: *Now after that John was put in prison, Jesus came into Galilee, preaching* [1] *the gospel of the kingdom of God, and saying,* [2] *the time is fulfilled, and the kingdom of God is at hand: repent ye,* [3] *and believe the gospel.* (Mark 1:14b-15)

[32] ισχυροτερος.

[33] A connotation of ικανος is being used here.

[34] There is also in the Synoptic template the implication that Jesus will somehow judge Israel. Matthew says: *Whose fan is in his hand, and he will thoroughly purge his floor, and gather his wheat into the garner; but he will burn up the chaff with unquenchable fire.* Mark omits this, but Luke quotes almost verbatim. Being more intimately familiar with the erroneous cult of John the Baptist, Luke prefaces John the Baptists words with an editorial explanation: *And as the people were in expectation, and all men mused in their hearts of John, whether he were the Christ, or not…*which strongly differentiates the two. John's Gospel has John the Baptist answer this question directly. Indeed, the subject of Luke's first two chapters has been to differentiate these two characters.

The decent of the spirit in the form of a dove. The voice from heaven; *this is my beloved Son in whom I am well pleased*[35]	John the Baptist's Soliloquy the next day 1:29-34: 1) "Behold the Lamb of God, which taketh away the sin of the world" 2) Again repeats the substance of 1:15 (Jesus takes precedence) 3) John the Baptist did not know him but only his role to make him manifest to Israel 4) "I saw the Spirit descend from heaven like a dove" 5) "I baptize with water, but God has told me that he upon whom the spirit descends and remains is he that baptizes with the Holy Spirit" 6) "This is the Son of God"
	John the Baptist's Soliloquy the next day again 1:35-42 1) "Behold the Lamb of God" 2) Two who had been listening to John, follow Jesus – Andrew and another 3) Andrew finds his brother Peter and says that they have found the μεσσιας
Jesus distinguishes himself as the bridegroom; John the Baptist is not; thus his disciples fast[36] John sends envoys from prison asking if Jesus in Christ[37] Jesus applies Malachi 3:1/4:5 to John and says that he was the "Son of Man" and that John was not, and implied that John was the last of the Old Testament order[38]	John the Baptist's soliloquy 3:23-36 1) "I am not the Christ but am sent before him" 2) "Christ is the bridegroom; I am merely the friend of the bridegroom" 3) "He must increase and I must decrease" 4) "He is from heaven and is above all"
	John the Baptist did bear witness to Christ, yet Christ has a greater witness to himself than John. 5:33-41
	*John did no miracle: but all things that John spake of this man were true.*10:41b

---

[35] Matthew 3:16-17 John hears the voice from heaven, but not here. When Jesus begins to speak of his "glorification" he prays: *Father, glorify thy name. Then came there a voice from heaven, saying, I have both glorified it, and will glorify it again.* (John 12:28).
[36] Matthew 9:15. Mark more aggressively answers the rhetorical question posed in Matthew and adds: *as long as they have the bridegroom with them, they cannot fast.* (Mark 2:19)
[37] Matthew 11:2.
[38] Matthew 11:7-15; 18-19;17:12.

<u>Exegetical Considerations</u>: In this sentence John makes reference to a narrative detail that he has not yet given: *John bare witness of him, and cried, saying, this was he of whom I spake…* But the reader asks – 'where in the narrative flow have you spoken of him?' This is a witness to the fact that this narrative detail lies *outside* this account; in this case, John's referent is the Synoptic template, which editorially invokes Isaiah 40:3 to explain the relationship between Jesus and John.

In the past we have tended to smear the details of one account with another account; one letter with another letter. But now that we are translating, exegeting and doing literary analysis, we must be very mindful of the unit of literature with which we deal. It is that unit of literature which gives a word its primary context beyond mere syntax and general lexical meanings. We must also be very mindful of the sociological and historical situation which, in turn, gives context to each unit of literature. If we reach into another account or another letter in order to achieve sharper definition, we must be able to positively link the two accounts together; that is, we must be able to prove dependence or influence by another author. In our sample sentence, for example, it very strongly appears as if John is elaborating the categorical difference between John the Baptist and Jesus found in the Synoptics in order to resolve the persistent error of the cult of John the Baptist represented by that which Paul found in Ephesus, years later. Based on what we see here, we may, for example, (tentatively) lay down a principle that if two accounts are very closely (i.e., based on synchronous phraseology) elaborating a story, one dependent and mindful of the other, the details of the source account will sometimes be assumed but omitted in the following account.

We have made some tentative literary deductions about John's relation to the Synoptics. This is important in order to help clarify word definitions. For example, does John mean the same thing that Matthew would mean when he uses a word? Sometimes a computer analysis will show us relationships that would otherwise be very difficult to see. If we can bolster our deductive conclusion with inductive data, we can have more confidence in the refinement of word meanings. Figure 3: "John's Vocab Print" is an example of a computer assisted analysis of all the significant words that John uses[39] in relation to all other literary units of our literature:[40]

---

[39] i.e., 35 times or less.
[40] This chart does not adjust for book length.

John Vocab Print

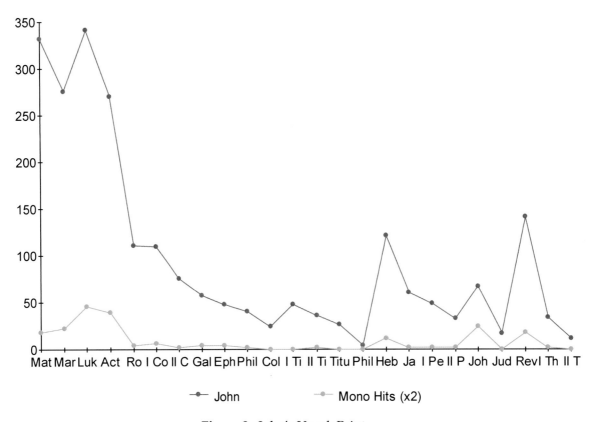

Figure 3. John's Vocab Print

As seen in **Figure 3**, though there is very little synchronous phraseological activity outside the "Passion Week" block, John's vocabulary correlates *very strongly* with the Synoptics. The overlap in technical terms required to tell an indicative mood story will certainly account for much of John's Synoptic correlation, but there is considerable correlation with "non-technical" terms – words that could easily be employed in any genre. There is also a considerable number of words which seem technical but could - and were - easily deformed by poetic diction (figures of speech) and pressed into the service of theological metaphor. So even though the structure and style of John is quite different from the Synoptic Gospel, John's overwhelming Synoptic vocabulary correlation is truly strong. Note the "monohits" with John's epistles and Revelation)[41]

---

[41] For a fuller discussion of these relationships see *A Vesture Dipped in Blood* (41ff).

καὶ ἐκ   τοῦ πληρωματος αὐτου ἡμεις[42] παντες ἐλαβομεν
and from   the fullness   of him we   all   have received

καὶ χαριν ἀντι χαριτος
and grace   for   grace

ἐκ   Although we have already seen this word four times in 1:13, we did
             not formally define it. From context we inferred that it was a
             preposition which means "of" or "out of" or "from." John says ἐκ του
             ουρανου ("out of heaven," or "from heaven") 13 times in his Gospel.
             He says ἐκ του κοσμου 11 times[43] and ἐκ των μαθητων[44] (of the
             disciples) 9 times. ἐκ is always used with its object in the genitive.
             Sometimes you will see this word presented as ἐξ, but this is for
             euphony only. ἐξ is almost always followed by a word that begins with
             a vowel. There are four cases in which this does not hold, but this is
             because ἐξ is also a homonym for "six."

             This preposition, combined with God, becomes an important
             theological expression for John, especially in his first epistle, where he
             uses this expression (ἐκ του θεου) *sixteen* times. Adding the state of
             being verb "is" yields an expression that only John uses and again
             links his work together (1x John; 3x 1st John; 1x 3rd John).

πληρωματος   πληρωματος is the genitive form of πληρωμα which means "fullness."
             But what is it that Jesus is full of, which we have received? Jesus is full
             of grace and truth (1:14). And by this we know that 1:15 is a
             parenthetical insertion of the editor. Otherwise we could not easily tell
             if John the Baptist was simply continuing his dialogue about Jesus.
             There is also an uncommon connotation of και which would fit much
             more nicely into the expression that John is executing. Listen to this
             dialogue: *Then said Martha unto Jesus, Lord, if thou hadst been here, my
             brother had not died. But I know, that even (και) now, whatsoever thou wilt
             ask of God, God will give it thee.* Do you see how that in this case "and"
             or "also" simply does not rise to the occasion of this pathos? Therefore
             we do find και translated about 2% of the time as "even." This would
             be a good place for it. *...and of his fullness we have all received, even grace*

---

[42] See Hewett 7.2.1.

[43] This is a monohit with 1st Corinthians 5:9-10: *I wrote unto you in an epistle not to company with
fornicators: Yet not altogether with the fornicators of this world, or with the covetous, or extortioners, or with
idolaters; for then must ye needs go out of the world.* Note the dovetailing with John 17:15 *I pray not that
thou shouldest take them out of the world, but that thou shouldest keep them from the evil.*

[44] Only John uses this expression.

141

upon grace. The AV translators thought it well to put it in place of καɩ in the following sentence: *That as sin hath reigned unto death, even* (καɩ) *so might grace reign through righteousness unto eternal life by Jesus Christ our Lord.*[45]

---

[45] Romans 5:21.

There are only two places in which grace is received: Romans 1:5 *By whom we have <u>received grace</u>* (ελαβομεν χαριν) *and apostleship...* and Romans 5:17 *For if by one man's offence death reigned by one; much more they which <u>receive</u> abundance of <u>grace</u> and of the gift of righteousness shall reign in life by one, Jesus Christ.* We have already seen very strong linkages between John and Paul, especially in this word "grace." We noted the monohit[46] of "grace" and "law" between John and Paul. The example we gave then is from Romans 6:14, but there is yet another Romans' example just three sentences away from 5:17 where "law" and "grace" are combined – Romans 5:20: *Moreover the law entered, that the offence might abound. But where sin abounded, grace did much more abound.*

In 5:17 we have the "abundance of grace;" in 5:20 we have "grace much more abounding." Since there are these phraseological linkages, we may permit ourselves to feel the linguistic kinship between John and Paul. We don't have to explain it just now, but we can use this kinship to sense what χαριν αντι χαριτος (grace for grace) could possibly mean. This is especially true in that John, only, pairs αντι with grace.

He will also use words that have taken up αντι into a compound formation – for example the well-known αντιχριστος (antichrist). In compound form we see that αντι carries with it a connotation of "in place of." For example Matthew says that Archelaus reigned in Judea αντι (in the place of) his father Herod.[47] If we combine the phrase kinship with Paul with the connotation of αντι in Matthew with John's stated idea that we are receiving a fullness of something from Christ, we can then understand that John is constructing a figure of speech. We would say that Job received sorrow upon sorrow. John is saying here that from Christ we have received "grace *upon* grace."[48]

---

[46] We said that a "monohit" was a word that two – and only two - authors share. But this can also be expanded to include a combination of words, a specific phrase or even an idea that only two authors share.

[47] Matthew 2:22.

[48] The figure of speech may even be an ironic play on words. There are four other places in which αντι is flanked by the same word first in the accusative case, then in the genitive – all of them bad: 1) κακον αντι κακου (evil for evil); 2) λοιδοριαν αντι λοιδοριας (reviling for reviling); 3) οφθαλμον αντι οφθαλμου (eye for eye) and 4) οδοντα αντι οδοντος (tooth for tooth).

οτι ο νομος δια μωσεως εδοθη
because the law through Moses was given

η χαρις και η αληθεια[49]
-[50] grace and - truth

δια ιησου χριστου εγενετο
through Jesus Christ was

οτι	We have said that οτι (meaning "because", "for" etc.) is a conjunction, therefore, John is linking this sentence to the previous sentence. We have received grace upon grace from the fullness of Christ, because Christ is the source of grace, not Moses. The law can be brokered to men through men and angels, but who can broker the favor of God himself? This also helps explain the purpose of John's next sentence – Moses has declared the law; Christ declares God himself.
νομος	νομος almost always refers to the law of Moses. Luke also calls it the "law of the Lord."[51] But in John the law also embraces the non-Pentateuchal writings. For example when Jesus says: "Is it not written in your law, I said, Ye are gods?"[52] He appears to be quoting the Psalms.[53] Note too in this quotation, that Jesus refers to the law as "*your* law." Only in John do we find Christ speaking of the law in this way.

Exegetical Considerations: In the Sermon on the Mount, Jesus says that: *Whosoever therefore shall break one of these least commandments* [of the law], *and shall teach men so, he shall be called the least in the kingdom of heaven.* Yet in the Synoptic *Plucking Ears of Grain on the Sabbath* pericope, Jesus appears to be doing this very thing. The Pharisees object to Jesus that he is allowing his disciples to do that which is unlawful to do on the Sabbath. The Synoptic response is not that the Pharisees have

---

[49] Here is "truth" in the nominative form.

[50] Sometimes we add words to clarify our translation; sometimes we omit them, for example here. Saying the article with the word - "the grace," would be awkward, so we leave it out.

[51] Luke 2:23 *As it is written in the law of the Lord, Every male that openeth the womb shall be called holy to the Lord.*

[52] John 10:34.

[53] Psalms 82:6 *I have said, Ye are gods; and all of you are children of the most High.*

misinterpreted the law – it is that the Son of Man is Lord of the Sabbath. Jesus' response could not have been more confrontational if he had said: 'I am above the law.' In Matthew, Jesus does say more: *here is one greater than the temple*.[54] But in Matthew, it is not clear how this can be so. In Pauline theology, we are not above the law, nor are we under it.[55] But through an cathartic process of spiritual death, we become buried with Christ[56] and die to the law.[57] The Jerusalem church officially supported Paul's contention that Gentile converts to the Gospel of Christ need not keep the law of Moses,[58] but they balked at applying Paul's crucifixion theology to Jewish converts.[59] They may die to sin, but not to the law of Moses.

It is not until *Hebrews* that we may resolve the Matthean dilemma of how Jesus can be above the law (and the temple). In *Hebrews* the office of both priest and king are reunited - after the ancient order of Melchizedec. Here too we find an answer to that which is most difficult to understand in Paul: how may we make an exodus from the law of Moses without becoming lawless? Because there is a new Joshua that will finally give us rest from works righteousness, yet perfect in us the righteous work of God. Moses, like the law itself, was a faithful guide[60] until his successor appeared, the Apostle and High Priest of our profession. The law of Moses and the Temple were but shadows[61] of the things which have now appeared in flesh and dwelt among us.

John will later explain that the body of Jesus is a new temple.[62] This is why we can become dead to the law of Moses through the body of *Christ*.[63] This is why Jesus is a law unto himself. This is why Jesus is the Lord of even the Sabbath. And this is why John has Jesus speaking of the "law of the Jews" as if it were no longer of direct concern to him. And this is why there is so much distance between the Koine gospels and the world of Judaism from which they have made an exodus. It is because those to whom the conversation in Koine is addressed have been given a new covenant and a new altar – from which those who continue to embrace the old

---

[54] Matthew 12:6.

[55] Romans 6:15 *What then? shall we sin, because we are not under the law, but under grace?*

[56] Romans 6:4 *Therefore we are buried with him by baptism into death...*

[57] Romans 7:6 *But now we are delivered from the law, that being dead wherein we were held; that we should serve in newness of spirit, and not in the oldness of the letter.*

[58] Acts 15: 23-24 *And they wrote letters by them after this manner; The apostles and elders and brethren send greeting unto the brethren which are of the Gentiles in Antioch and Syria and Cilicia: Forasmuch as we have heard, that certain which went out from us have troubled you with words, subverting your souls, saying, Ye must be circumcised, and keep the law: to whom we gave no such commandment...*

[59] Acts 21:20-26.

[60] Galatians 3:24.

[61] Hebrews 10:1.

[62] John 2:19-21 *Jesus answered and said unto them, Destroy this temple, and in three days I will raise it up. Then said the Jews, Forty and six years was this temple in building, and wilt thou rear it up in three days? But he spake of the temple of his body.*

[63] Romans 7:4.

law have no right to eat.[64] This new people are making an *eisodus* (entrance) into the Sabbath rest of God. And now that the priesthood has been changed, there is by necessity a *change* also of the law.[65]

As the daystar rises in the hearts of the apostles,[66] the long shadows of the temple of Judaism begin to recede. The shadows of a carnal (fleshly) commandment[67] written in stone, give way to Jeremiah's prophecy[68] - of words written in the fleshly tablets of the heart.[69] "Every mountain will be made low." Particularly, Mt. Sinai. "Every valley shall be filled," particularly, the valley of the shadow of death. The law came by Moses, but grace and truth came by Jesus Christ. The condemnation of the law has been destroyed by its complete fulfillment:[70] The condemnation of our conscience has been destroyed by the blood of the Levitical Lamb of God himself,[71] that taketh away the sin of the world.

μωσεως	The Johannine contrast between "Moses," here shown in the genitive, and Christ more openly harmonizes with the Pauline contrast between the law of Moses and the law of faith: *Received ye the Spirit by the works of the law, or by the hearing of faith? Are ye so foolish? having begun in the Spirit, are ye now made perfect by the flesh?*[72] Indeed, the curse of the law is obviated only by Christ himself becoming a curse for us: *Christ hath redeemed us from the curse of the law, being made a curse for us: for it is written, Cursed is every one that hangeth on a tree.*[73] John will soon allude to this very idea: *And as* μωσης *(Moses) lifted up the serpent in the wilderness, even so must the Son of man be lifted up: That whosoever believeth in him should not perish, but have eternal life.*[74]

ιησου χριστου	Only twice do we find Jesus in close proximity to Joseph, his supposed biological father (ιησους ο υιος ιωσηφ {Jesus, the Son of Joseph}) and this is in John. We do find the same, somewhat formalized title

---

[64] Hebrews 13:10.

[65] Hebrews 7:12.

[66] 2nd Peter 1:19.

[67] Hebrews 7:16.

[68] Hebrews 8:10-12 which is a quotation of Jeremiah 31:31-34, the longest quotation in the New Testament and the *only* mention of this pivotal prophecy.

[69] 2nd Corinthians 3:3.

[70] Matthew 5:17 *Think not that I am come to destroy the law, or the prophets: I am not come to destroy, but to fulfil.*

[71] Hebrews 9:14 *How much more shall the blood of Christ, who through the eternal Spirit offered himself without spot to God, purge your conscience from dead works to serve the living God?*

[72] Galatians 2:2b-3.

[73] Galatians 2:13.

[74] John 3:14-15.

elsewhere of others, for example, Peter: σιμων ο υιος ιωνα (Simon son of Jona).[75] We can see that by the time the Gospels are written, the more formal "Jesus the Christ"[76] has simply been contracted to "Jesus Christ." This, of course, is not to be confounded with the English surnaming process; i.e., "John Smith."

Just as "Caesar" became attached to many Roman heads of state, "Christ" remains a title. This can be seen in the Pauline corpus, which precedes the Gospels, when Paul distinctively *reverses* the terms and refers to Jesus as "Christ Jesus."[77] In the naming of Simon by Christ, "rock" begins and ends as a *characteristic* which Jesus saw in Peter, not a title. Lebbaeus was called Thaddaeus, Judas was called Iscariot, and Joses was called "the son of consolation"[78] just as Simon, son of Jonah was called Simon "the stone." If this argument is true, then Petros alone would be the equivalent of a nickname: "Rocky."

John is clear that this character name was assigned to Peter from the very beginning, and not as a result of a later confession.[79] Peter is never referred to as Rock Simon - as if it were a title. And though he is called κηφας[80] (a Greek transliteration of the Aramaic original; the English transliteration being "Cephas") or πετρος, he is often referred to as "Simon Peter." Just as "Christ" as a formal title has become attached to "Jesus" in ιησου χριστου, dropping the interior article, so "Petros," as a formal *characteristic*, has become attached to "Simon."

John, perhaps, wants to be very clear that the intricate verbiage in Matthew's confession[81] is not understood as a formal name change, as

---

[75] John 1:42.

[76] Found in 1st John 5:6, 1st Corinthians 3:11, Acts 9:34, and Matthew 16:20.

[77] Likewise we have Augustus Caesar or Caesar Augustus.

[78] Acts 4:36.

[79] John 1:42 *And he brought him to Jesus. And when Jesus beheld him, he said, You are Simon the son of Jonah: you shall be called Cephas, which is by interpretation, a stone.*

[80] Outside of John's record of the assignment of his character name, this name is confined to four occurrences in 1st Corinthians and one in Galatians – all of them closely connected to Judaizing controversy.

[81] συ ει πετρος και επι ταυτη τη πετρα οικοδομησω μου την εκκλησιαν (*thou art Peter, but upon this rock I will build my church*). We have spoken of the importance of keeping track of article and pronoun gender for good reason. Matthew's word play could not be understood without such discipline. πετρος is masculine. Yet Matthew has Christ change to a _feminine_ demonstrative pronoun (ταυτη), which draws και towards its sometimes contrast function of "but." But what is this feminine alternative "rock" to which ταυτη refers? It is the belief (πιστις) that Jesus is Christ, the Son of the living God. It is the confession (ομολογια) of the doctrine (διδαχη) which Christ has been teaching them. These three words: "belief," "confession," and "doctrine" - are all feminine. This is the πετρας upon which Christ builds his church.

it had become with the changing of Saul to Paul. Thus John carries the name "Simon Peter" 17 of its 20 usages. Very late in his career, a fully converted man humbly refers to himself as "Simon Peter." In contrast, shortly after the commissioning of Saul to depart on his first missionary journey, Luke suddenly drops the name of "Saul" and switches to "Paul" for the remainder of his narrative and never refers to Saul again except as a quotation in an address by Paul telling of his conversion from his life *as* Saul. Paul is never called "Saul Paul."[82] Simon the stumbling stone, who once seemed to be first, fades completely from the narrative, and Saul, the 'least desired,'[83] obtains the pre-eminent name in the establishment of the word of Christ in the world. The last became first; the first last.

---

[82] Although he could have. For example, consider the dative construction σεργιω παυλω (Sergius Paulus) Acts 13:7.

[83] From combining the transliterated Aramaic "σαουλ", meaning "desired", and "παυλος" meaning "little" or "least."

θεον ουδεις   εωρακεν πωποτε
God   no man has seen   at any time

ο   μονογενης   υιος
the   only-begotten son

ο ων   εις τον κολπον   του πατρος
the one in   the bosom   of the father

εκεινος εξηγησατο
this one   has declared

ουδεις	ουδεις contracts ου (not) δε (but) and εις (one) together to form the pronoun "no man." Of course there is a feminine form, ουδεμια. But this is used only four times in the New Testament and in each case the feminine referent is given. ψυχης ουδεμια (not one life), ουδεμια … εκκλησια (not one church), ουδεμια πηγη (not one fountain), and finally John says in his first epistle that there is not any darkness in God, he uses the feminine form of darkness, hence: σκοτια … ουδεμια.
	The neuter form, ουδεν, is seen much more often as "nothing." It seems odd to call "nothing" a pronoun, but no more odd than to say that "it" is the third person, singular, neuter pronoun in English. If one wanted to emphasize the "thingness" of nothing, such that it could stand alone as a noun, one would simply separate the contraction into "no thing," just as John has done in the Greek in his third sentence: χωρις αυτου εγενετο <u>ουδε εν</u> ο γεγονεν (without him has begun <u>not one *thing*</u> which has become).
εωρακεν	When the κ appears just before the personal endings, suspect the "perfect" tense. When verbs start with a vowel we will not see the "reduplication" feature of the perfect tense, but we do see here the presence of ε. It could be part of the word, or it could be the helping vowel added to throw the verb into one of the past tenses. If we strip off the κ along with the ε we will come very close to the root word, οραω. We now see too that the o in οραω has changed to an ω – a spelling change, which is another sign of the aorist or perfect. οραω means "see." The difference between οραω and its close synonym βλεπω is the difference between our "look" and "see." For example, if someone were translating our language 1000 years after it had become a dead language, he would be hard pressed to distinguish

the difference if he came across a sentence: "Go look and see what time it is." Mark uses them both in a sentence saying: *And he charged them, saying, Take heed* ορατε *beware* βλεπετε *of the leaven of the Pharisees, and of the leaven of Herod.*[84] And again Marks says: *And he looked up, and said, I see* (βλεπω) *men as trees, I see* (οραω) *them walking.*[85] Generally, βλεπω is the commoner verb, and though the meanings of the words are very close, *generally* speaking οραω lends itself to more of a figurative use. Both of these rules do not hold for John. And his reverse preference for οραω holds into 1st John as well.[86]

πωποτε

Occurs only 6 times, once in Luke, four times in John and once in first John. It may be translated "at any time" in all six places. The infrequency of this word binds the phraseological connection between John and 1st John ever more closely. They share the phrase: θεον ουδεις … πωποτε.[87] But in his epistle, John switches to the word θεαομαι, which John, in his Gospel, has just used four sentences ago: *and we beheld his glory*, which, in turn invokes the contracted opening of John's first epistle which also resonates with John's Gospel prologue. Look at them together:

John 1:14 *And the Word was made flesh, and dwelt among us, and we beheld his glory, the glory as of the only begotten of the Father, full of grace and truth.*

1st John 1:1 *That which was from the beginning, which we have heard, which we have seen with our eyes, which we have beheld, and our hands have handled, of the Word of life*

And note too the apparently intrusive positioning of this idea in both cases. *No man has seen God at any time…* But what has this to do with the flow of John's gospel paragraph? It resolves in the underlying point that John is trying to make. Only Christ has seen and has declared God to us. In 1st John, the underlying idea is that it does not matter what any man might say of visions or communion with God. It is only those that love one another in truth in whom God dwells.

---

[84] Mark 8:15.

[85] 8:24.

[86] And here we have a linguistic feature that tracks from John to 1st John which would have been almost impossible for an imposter to track. Therefore we have tentatively proved that the author of 1st John and John is the same.

[87] 1st John 4:12 *No man hath seen God at any time.*

John will repeat the idea of Christ as the "sole declarer" of God in many ways in subsequent dialogue. For example: *Not that any man hath seen the Father, save he which is of God, he hath seen the Father.*[88] and: *Jesus saith unto him, I am the way, the truth, and the life: no man cometh unto the Father, but by me.*[89]

But it is important to understand that this is not a distinctively Johannine idea. John is *shadowing* the Synoptic template. The idea is first there: *All things are delivered unto me of my Father: and no man knoweth the Son, but the Father; neither knoweth any man the Father, save the Son, and he to whomsoever the Son will reveal him.*[90] But though this is not a distinctively Johannine idea, it receives a distinctively Johannine emphasis and elaboration.

It is difficult not to infer a physical, literary connection between John's tremendous emphasis upon the idea of the sole-declarer-ship of Christ and the sudden appearance of a very close theological cognate late in the Pauline corpus – the sole *mediatorship* of Christ: *For there is one God, and one mediator (μεσιτης) between God and men, the man Christ Jesus.*[91]

ο ων   Here John combines the singular masculine article with the present participle of ειμι, thus we translate "he being." The subject is missing, of course, but this often occurs. Since the subject is obvious

---

[88] John 6:46 John says that no man has seen God except the son. Paul will soon confess the logical corollary: no man except Jesus is <u>able</u> see the Father: *Who only hath immortality, dwelling in the light which no man can approach unto; whom no man hath seen, nor can see: to whom be honour and power everlasting. Amen.* (1st Timothy 6:16) The Old Testament established that no man can fully see God and live. (Ex 33:20) But we *may* see the express image (χαρακτηρ) of his person (υποστασεως), the very ειχον of God. When Philip therefore asks Jesus – 'show us the Father,' Jesus replies: *If ye had known me, ye should have known my Father also: and from henceforth ye know him, and have seen him… he that hath seen me hath seen the Father.* (John 14:7,9b).

[89] John 14:6.

[90] Matthew 11:27. The parallel is deeper. Consider Jesus' prayer in Matthew, in which these words are embedded (25-30). Now read Jesus' "high priestly" prayer in John (17:1-26). Structurally, there are many parallels. And in the larger structural flow of each Gospel they are positioned similarly. In Matthew, after the prayer, Jesus initiates open conflict with the religious establishment. The cornfield incident immediately follows. In John, the prayer concludes the extended period of table-talk and Jesus finally rises to present himself for the scene of his betrayal.

[91] 1st Timothy 2:5 This is the first and only time that the role of mediatorship of Christ clearly appears in Paul. Hebrews picks up both the "new covenant" which is in a passing metaphoric, embryonic state in 2nd Corinthians 3:6 and this word, "mediator," and the universalistic but problematic justification of Romans 5:18 and synthesizes them into theological fruition: *And for this cause he is the <u>mediator of the new testament</u>, that by means of death, <u>for the redemption of the transgressions that were under the first testament</u>, they which are called might receive the promise of eternal inheritance.* (Hebrews 9:15)

from context, the definite article alone "stands for" the subject.[92] The participle defines the subject – here the state of being verb is itself the adjectival idea. Although the present participle ων is a common word, ο ων[93] is almost exclusively Johannine, occurring 7 times in his Gospel and 6 times in his Revelation. Four of those constructions in Revelation repeat the formal formula: "who is and who was and who comes" (ο ων και ο ην και ο ερχομενος).

κολπον "Bosom" is a hard word to get the sense of. It does not occur in our language except as an anachronism, which preserves the difficulty. Certainly, when we read that the author of this Gospel "reclined in the bosom of Jesus" at the last supper, the difficulty appears. For us, to eat a meal in the reclining position is already foreign. And most bodily contact between males (except in sports) is taboo in our culture. But not for Greek men. We find it difficult to imagine why there would be two men in one bed together, but this is unremarkable for Luke: *I tell you, in that night there shall be two men in one bed…*[94] For the Greek mind, to take rest from a peripatetic ministry under the shade of a tree in the heat of the day and rest one's head on the chest of the teacher is no more remarkable than for a boy to fall asleep in his father's lap.

Four times John refers to himself as that disciple whom he (Jesus) loved (ον ηγαπα), and he also specifies that Martha, her sister and Lazarus as those whom Jesus loved in some special sense.[95] It is hard for us to imagine how the Son of God could be a respecter of emotional relationships, yet with John, this is also unremarkable. The disciples know that John is more intimate with Jesus, and use this intimacy to try to pry out of Jesus which one of them is the traitor, so Peter motions to John in order to exploit this intimacy. Once again John specifies who Peter is motioning to by saying: *the one lying on Jesus' breast* (στηθος)[96] Here he changes from "bosom" to "chest" – the part upon which one might beat in anguish: *And the publican, standing afar off, would not lift up so much as his eyes unto heaven, but smote upon his breast …*[97]

---

[92] Grammarians call this the "substantive" use of the article.

[93] It occurs once in 2nd Corinthians and once in Romans.

[94] Luke 17:34.

[95] John 11:5 *Now Jesus loved Martha, and her sister, and Lazarus.*

[96] John 13:25.

[97] Luke 18:13.

As the chest is like a shield, so the bosom is like a hallow into which the children were gathered by the encircling (εναγκαλιζομαι[98]) arms of Christ. It would be easy to call this a place of honor, intimacy and rest - as it was for Lazarus, who was gathered into Abraham's bosom when he died.[99] But there is also the connotation of protection, as a woman feels protected in the harbor of her husband's arms, even as a ship rests her anchor in the hollow of land, protected by the sea.[100]

John is personalizing the relationship of Jesus as the sole-declarer of God. As we shall see, John places a tremendous emphasis on Christ as mediator in every sense. Jesus has not only declared God. He has not only reconciled us to God. It is *through* Christ, and through Christ alone, that we live and move and have our being in God. This is far beyond anything that has been said so far about the mediatorship of Christ.

εκεινος	is a demonstrative pronoun meaning "that" or "those" and takes the same endings as ουτος (see Chapter 1, John 1:2). This word (εκεινος)[101] first occurred in 1:8. Why doesn't John use αυτος, the ordinary pronoun for "he"? John uses εκεινος for emphasis, preferring it to αυτος much more than Matthew, for example – especially in reference to Christ. The same preference appears also in 1st John. The distinction is everywhere lost in the KJV translation. These special emphatic contractions beckon forth a translation of "this one" or "this man." *This* is the sole declarer of God.
εξηγησατο	is the aorist of εξηγεομαι. This verb is used but once by John and five times by Luke. From context, and from its component parts, εξ and ηγεομαι, we infer that this word means "speak" or "declare authoritatively." The KJV translates this word as "declare" 5 of 6 times, which does seem to encompass what John is saying. It would be difficult to describe how "declare" is different from "tell." Only the colonists could declare their intentions for independence; likewise, only he who possesses the luggage can make a declaration to the customs official. But only the son can *authoritatively* declare what the father is like to those who have never seen him in person. In the Synoptic template, we see that the people immediately pick

[98] Only Mark uses this word (2x).
[99] Luke 16:22.
[100] Acts 27:39.
[101] Hewett 8.2.2.

up the sense of this: *the people were astonished at his doctrine: for he taught them as one having authority, and not as the scribes.*[102]

Thus ends an intense section of editor/reader dialogue. These first eighteen sentences may be called John's prologue. But they also present a summary survey of what his Gospel will be about.

---

[102] Matthew 7:28b-29.

Chapter 6: John 1:19 – 1:28

και αυτη εστιν η   μαρτυρια του ιωαννου
and this is the witness   of John

οτε   απεστειλαν οι ιουδαιοι
when sent   the Jews

εξ   ιεροσολυμων ιερεις και λευιτας
from Jerusalem   priests and Levites

ινα   ερωτησωσιν αυτον
that   they might ask him

συ τις ει
you,who are (you)

αυτη	the feminine, demonstrative pronoun,[1] "this," is a pronoun which refers to "witness." This phrase: αυτη εστιν η μαρτυρια occurs only here and twice in 1st John.
εστιν	We have seen the imperfect tense of this verb (ην) and the present participle (ων), but till now we have not seen John use the present tense of ειμι.[2]
μαρτυρια	This is the feminine form of "testimony" or "witness." John uses this almost exclusively as a formal theological term; i.e., the witness concerning Christ – in his Gospel, in his epistles and in his revelation.[3] Likewise John uses the verb, μαρτυρεω almost exclusively in the same theological sense.
του ιωαννου	It may seem awkward to see the article included with the noun, but this is the convention. If it were "my witness" or "your witness," then the definite article is dropped (since a pronoun is, by nature,

---

[1] See John 1:2 discussion; Hewett 8.2.

[2] Hewett, 5.8.

[3] Mark uses it three times, Luke twice, and it occurs twice in the pastorals, but only in one of these is it used theologically. John uses it 14x in his Gospel, 3x in his first epistle and 1x in his third epistle, and 9x in his Revelation - all of which are theological. In contrast, John uses the neuter version of "witness" (μαρτυριον) only once (Revelation 15:15) in its twenty New Testament occurrences.

155

indefinite). We rarely speak or write the definite article along with a proper noun, but many other languages, including Koine, do. Therefore you will see: αυτη εστιν η μαρτυρια του θεου...[4] (*this is the witness of* [the] *God...*) and το μαρτυριον του χριστου...[5] (*the witness of* [the] *Christ*).

οτε   οτε is an adverb which is almost always translated "when." A very close variant is οταν, which runs together οτε and the particle αν. The purpose of the article αν, which has no English equivalent, is to add the mood of conditionality to a verb, pushing it in the direction of the subjunctive. As αν combines with οτε to form οταν, you will always find οταν used whenever a sense of conditionality is being expressed. But in a narrative, οτε will be used. Only once are they combined and you can see this conformation: *When* (**οτε**) *thou wast young, thou girdedst thyself, and walkedst whither thou wouldest: but when* (**οταν**) *thou shalt be old, thou shalt stretch forth thy hands, and another shall gird thee.*[6]

απεστειλαν We have already encountered αποστελλω (send) in the perfect passive participle form in John's 6th sentence. Here it is in the aorist. We see that here also there are spelling changes that indicate that this verb has been shifted into a past tense. There is no helping vowel (ε) at the beginning of the word, but it *has* appeared in place of the o; that is, instead of απο we see απε. The internal spelling has also changed from στελ to στειλ, and a λ has dropped out. Affixed is the personal ending for "they," (αν).[7] Below is a paradigm of αποστελλω in the 1st aorist, with all the personal endings (although the first and second person plural is not used in our literature). Confirm these endings again with Hewett.[8]

Singular			Plural	
απεστειλα	*I sent*[9]		απεστειλαμεν	we sent
απεστειλας	*you have sent*[10]		απεστειλατε	you sent
απεστειλεν	*he sent*[11]		απεστειλαν	*they sent*

---

[4] 1st John 5:9.
[5] 1st Corinthians 1:6.
[6] John 21:18.
[7] 1st aorist endings. See Hewett, Appendix 6, 311.
[8] Ibid.
[9] John 4:38.
[10] Only John attaches the singular 2nd person ending to this verb – 7 times; all in prayer to God, 6 in Jesus' prayer in chapter 17.
[11] John 3:17.

Just as we mentally carry a number in a multi-column addition, so our minds must carry the awareness of the personal endings for the verbs we see, even though the subject of the verb will very often be given. We carry the awareness in anticipation that the subject will be given. As soon as we see this verb, for example, we will begin looking for a 3rd person plural subject. In this sentence, the subject is οι ιουδαιοι – "the Jews."

It is important to maintain translational discipline because, until now, the word order has aligned with English syntax; that is, we have simply translated in the order that John has written and this has resulted in perfectly understandable English syntax. As soon as we see the introductory particle οτε, we must prepare our minds for a philosophy of syntax that is different from our own.

If *we* had been writing this sentence, we would have probably chosen this word order: …'when the Jews sent priests and Levites out of Jerusalem.' Subject/Verb/Indirect Object/defining phrase. But for John the priority is the verb first, then the subject. Likewise, the place of origin (from Jerusalem), then the indirect object (priests and Levites). But does John mean: the "Jews from Jerusalem" or the "priests and Levites from Jerusalem?" Again, we must maintain the discipline of consistency within the phrase. It is verb/subject; place of origin/indirect object. The priests and Levites are being sent from Jerusalem.

οι ιουδαιοι   There is another reason why John is not specifying "the Jews from Jerusalem" as opposed, say, to "the Jews from Jericho." As soon as John's readership encountered οι ιουδαιοι, they would have known that this is not the subject of a defining phrase. They would have known that John was putting considerable distance between himself and "them." Of the 35 times that this phrase is used in the literature, John uses it 25 times. Of the nine times Luke uses it in Acts, it is in highly confrontational episodes between the Jews on one side and Paul on the other. There is only one other place where οι ιουδαιοι occurs – in Mark. Listen closely to the context: *And when they saw some of his disciples eat bread with defiled, that is to say, with unwashen, hands, they found fault. For the Pharisees, and all <u>the Jews</u>, except they wash their hands oft, eat not, holding the tradition of the elders.* It will become increasingly evident that Mark is writing to a non-Jewish audience. And so is John.

Of all the authors, John's editorial distance from the Jews is greatest. Only John uses "in the Hebrew tongue" (εβραιστι) to translate "Bethesda," "Gabbatha" and "Golgotha." Three times he translates (ερμηνευω) fairly obvious Jewish terms ("Rabbi,"[12] "Cephas" and "Siloam"). He explains basic Jewish liturgy: *And the Passover, a feast of the Jews, was nigh.* He explains the Jewish custom (εθος) of burying. He even translates (μεθερμηνευω) "Messias" to "Christos." In John, Christ refers to *your* law, not *the* law. For example: *Jesus answered them, Is it not written in your law, I said, Ye are gods?*[13] Christ refers to *your* father, Abraham.[14] He refers to "the Jews" (in all variants) a total of *sixty-four* times. Matthew,[15] Mark,[16] and Luke[17] do this but once.

"The Jews" is a phrase that has become John's substitute phrase for Matthew's variants of: 'Scribes, Pharisees and Elders.' John uses "scribes and elders" only once and never mentions the Sadducees. Matthew says: *Then cometh he to his disciples, and saith unto them, Sleep on now, and take your rest: behold, the hour is at hand, and the Son of man is betrayed into the hands of sinners.* John clearly specifies who this sinful "enemy" is, to whom Jesus is handed over. It is not the Romans. The answer comes when Pilate specifically asks Jesus whether he is the King of the Jews: *Jesus answered, My kingdom is not of this world: if my kingdom were of this world, then would my servants fight, that I should not be delivered to the Jews: but now is my kingdom not from hence.*[18] The enemy is of his own household. The enemy is "the Jews." In John, the divorce between the editor and his one-time homeland is total. This explains why he can refer to Judaism as the "synagogue of Satan" in the Revelation[19] and to Jerusalem as "Sodom" and "Egypt."[20]

---

[12] This occurs *twice* for two variants of this word.

[13] Only Pilate and Gallio display this detachment.

[14] John 8:56.

[15] Matthew 28:15 *So they took the money, and did as they were taught: and this saying is commonly reported among the Jews until this day.*

[16] Mark 7:3 *For the Pharisees, and all the Jews, except they wash their hands oft, eat not, holding the tradition of the elders.*

[17] Luke 23:51 (*The same had not consented to the counsel and deed of them;) he was of Arimathaea, a city of the Jews: who also himself waited for the kingdom of God.*

[18] John 18:36.

[19] Revelation 2:9; 3:9.

[20] Revelation 11:8.

Concerning John's Gospel, the editor is clear about who the author is. We have seen hints already that the place of writing is Ephesus. We now have a clear indication of John's perspective and his audience.[21]

εξ ιεροσολυμων

Here Jerusalem is in the genitive. Normally, (in 8 of 10 cases) this takes the preposition απο (from), but here and once in Acts[22] it is coupled with εξ, though John, too follows the convention that to designate where someone is *from*, he uses απο. Lazarus was *from* Bethany (λαζαρος απο βηθανιας), Philip was *from* Bethsaida (απο βηθσαιδα), and Joseph was *from* Arimethea (απο αριμαθαιας).

ιερεις και λευιτας

Although "priest" (ιερευς), here shown in the accusative plural), is used 30 times in our literature,[23] Levite (λευιτης) is used only 3 times, once here, once in Luke's Good Samaritan parable, and once regarding Barnabas, a Levite from Cyprus, one-time colleague of Paul.

ερωτησωσιν Although the aorist subjunctive is used many times, this is the only time in our literature that the aorist subjunctive for "ask" is used.[24] A stronger word for ask, αιτεω, is more often used by authors other than John. But John prefers ερωταω for "ask" and reserves αιτεω for petitions addressed to God, rejecting altogether (in his Gospel, his three epistles and in the Revelation) the more commonly accepted

---

[21] That the science of Biblical criticism is in crisis is clearly evident by the fact that despite all the technological improvements in materials and instruction, the world is no closer to finding the historical Jesus as it was when Albert Schweitzer first wrote his book – *The Quest for the Historical Jesus*. Modern biblical criticism is no closer to solving the Synoptic Problem than were the Church Fathers. It is no closer to solving the authorship of Hebrews than the guess work of Erasmus and Luther. It is no closer to dating John, than the earliest controversies doubting his Apocalypse. And instead of doing the hard work of internal linguistic analysis, it casually brings the authorship of almost every New Testament document into serious question upon the most tenuous conjecture, obviating the need. Internally, every Pauline epistle bears his unmistakable stamp, yet instead of doing the hard work of accounting for disparities in style and content, modern Biblical criticism invokes the *deux ex machina* of "The Forgerer." Likewise with John – instead of accounting for how the one-time intimate of Jesus can be found in Ephesus completely detached from his fatherland – modern Biblical criticism invents multiple Johns – or ignores the problem altogether. Unless we confront these literary realities - genre, authorship, sitz im leben, etc., we cannot be truly serious about translating John.
[22] Acts 28:17b *I was delivered prisoner from* (εξ) *Jerusalem into the hands of the Romans.*
[23] Only *Hebrews* directly refers to Christ as a priest. All other uses refer to the Aaronic order of priests except three references in Revelation which assert that all believers have been made priest.
[24] See Hewett, chapter 17.

word for "pray" (προσευχομαι). (Although he does use the primary cognate ευχομαι once in 3rd John: *Beloved, I wish above all things that thou mayest prosper and be in health…*

As we examine the grammatical landmarks of this word, we first observe the verb in the present tense: ερωταω. We then note the internal spelling change – the **α** just before the personal ending changes to an **η**, a sure sign that the verb is in a past tense. We then note the presence of the coupler, σ, which signifies either the future or the aorist. But even more noteworthy is the spelling change within the personal ending. We remember the third person plural ending of ουσι for both the present and the future tense – but what is this ωσι(v)? Whenever we see an ω appear in the personal ending, we should suspect that the verb has moved out of the normal indicative mood.[25] And since, as we discussed, there is the conditional ινα lurking in close proximity, we can be sure that this is the <u>subjunctive</u> mood.[26]

τις   τις is the nominative form of what is called the *indefinite*, or *interrogative* pronoun; that is, we do not know, exactly, to whom, to what, to which or to what purpose the pronoun refers. Here it is simply "who." Logically, in context, the indefinite pronoun helps to form an interrogative sentence. As in English, you must hear from context whether the indefiniteness of this pronoun pushes the sentence into the form of a question.[27] And you must "hear" the Greek as the English – without the euphonic variations.

---

[25] This also works (almost) for η. Whenever you see it without a θ – expect subjunctive.

[26] Take a moment to review personal endings in Hewett, Appendix 6, 311.

[27] Most grammars make two categories for this word – the indefinite pronoun and the interrogative pronoun, but they distinguish the two by accent marks which *translators* have added. Therefore you must decide based on context.

Here is the indefinite/interrogative pronoun in most of its forms (bold denotes those forms used by John):

	Singular			*Plural*	
N[28]	τις[29]/τι[30]	*who*		**τινες**[31]	(some of) *who*
G	**τινος**[32]	*of whom*		**τινων**[33]	(of) *whom*
D	**τινι**[34]	*to whom*		τισι(ν)	(of) *whom*
A	**τινα**[35]	*whom*		τινας	(of) *whom*

συ[36] τις ει[37]   We have translated this "who are you?" There is no question mark. There are no quotation marks. Twice John asks συ τις ει (who are you); but once he (and he alone) uses a weaker form: τις ει – the "you" being

---

[28] τις asks about people. τι asks about things.

[29] John uses τις 50 times. We will develop familiarity and confidence in translating this from context as we go on.

[30] τι, used 51 times, is the neuter form, translated "why," "what," "whatsoever."

[31] John uses this 9 times. A representative construction: τινες δε εξ αυτων ειπον (*some of them said*)

[32] John uses this twice: 13:22 *Then the disciples looked one on another, doubting of whom he spake.* (απορουμενοι περι τινος λεγει.) In this sentence, there is not enough to push this sentence into a direct quotation of a question. It would have been different if John had written: 'Then the disciples looked on one another, saying to themselves…περι τινος λεγει?' Then we would translate: "*of whom does he speak?*" John also uses τινος in 19:24: *They said therefore among themselves, Let us not rend it, but cast lots for it, whose it shall be:* (τινος εσται) *that the scripture might be fulfilled.* Here again, there is not enough to push this sentence into a quotation of a direct question.

[33] Used only once in John 20:23a *Of whom you may forgive sins, they are remitted …*

[34] John uses τινι once in 12:38 - a quotation from Isaiah: …*to whom revealed?* (τινι απεκαλυφθη)

[35] John uses this only 8 times. A representative use occurs when Jesus goes out of the garden to meet the arresting party: ειπεν αυτοις τινα ζητειτε he said to them: whom do you seek? Here there are sufficient evidences that this is a direct question – for example, ειπεν (he said) and ζητειτε are in different tenses.

---

[36] Hewett, 7.2.1.

	Singular			*Plural*	
N	συ	*you*		υμεις	*you*
G	σου	*your*		υμων	*your*
D	σοι	*you*		υμιν	*you*
A	σε	*you*		υμας	*you*

[37] Hewett, 5.8.

	Singular			*Plural*	
ειμι	*I am*		εσμεν	*we are*	
ει	*you are*		εστε	*you are*	
εστι(ν)	*he, she, it is*		εισι(ν)	*they are*	

161

understood in the "to be" verb, ει.[38] And once συ τις ει occurs in John as an *indirect* quotation: *And none of the disciples durst ask him, Who art thou?* (συ τις ει) *knowing that it was the Lord.*

Paul twice asks a rhetorical question: *Nay but, O man, who art thou* (συ τις ει) *that repliest against God?* and *Who art thou* (συ τις ει) *that judgest another man's servant?* Likewise James rhetorically asks: *who art thou* (συ τις ει) *that judgest another?* Note the word order: "you who are." This seems odd to us only because there is no clear distinction in the English between the relative pronoun "who" and the interrogative pronoun "who" except word order. But in Koine, there is.[39]

But even when word order denotes an English question, there is still ambiguity. Consider the English question "who are you?" Where is the emphasis? Is the question "who *are* you?" or is it "who are *you*?" In the Koine, the word order clearly indicates the latter; that is, the question is slightly pejorative; that is, who are *you* to be preaching about God? Who are *you* to be baptizing? In Matthew, Jesus turns the tables: 'you tell *me*, the baptism of John - from whence was it?' (το βαπτισμα ιωαννου ποθεν ην). It is the same word order. It is the same euphonic emphasis. "*the baptism of John* – where was it from?"

Exegetical Considerations: *...and this is the witness...* (και αυτη εστιν η μαρτυρια) is a phrase that elsewhere appears only in 1st John 5:11.[40] The witness of the apostle John is that *God hath given to us eternal life, and this life is in his Son.* The witness of John the Baptist begins with a negative: I am <u>not</u> the Christ. Yet John was asked "who are you?" – not: "who aren't you?" So great was John the Baptist's influence, that Herod once originally thought that Jesus *was* John, risen from the dead.[41] Luke makes it clear that there were many that once thought that John *was* the Christ: *And as the people were in expectation, and all men reasoned in their hearts concerning John, whether he were the Christ, or not...*[42] These are not just casual bits of historical information. These are indicators that 30 years after the resurrection of Christ, there are people who believe that John the Baptist is Christ.

---

[38] Luke and Mark both have this weaker form but from context it is an indirect quotation: *I know thee who thou art* (τις ει) *the Holy One of God.*
[39] See Hewett 7.3.1 and 15.6.
[40] *And this is the record* (και αυτη εστιν η μαρτυρια), *that God hath given to us eternal life, and this life is in his Son.*
[41] Matthew 14:2.
[42] Luke 3:15.

καὶ ωμολογησεν
and he confessed

καὶ ουκ ηρνησατο
and did not deny

καὶ ωμολογησεν
but he confessed

οτι ουκ ειμι εγω ο χριστος
that not (I)am I the Christ

ωμολογησεν	This is the aorist of ομολογεω, which means "confess." Its noun equivalent is ομολογια (confession). Here again the signs of the aorist are consistently present – the internal spelling change, the addition of the σ just before the personal endings and, since this verb begins with a vowel, the addition of a helping vowel at the beginning results in a change from ο to ω.

Exegetical Considerations: In our present-day language, "to confess" carries only the connotation of a criminal confession, though it once more broadly included a public acknowledgement of what we say we believe. Christ is said (by Paul) to have given a "good confession" (την καλην ομολογιαν) before Pilate, yet all the Synoptics agree that Jesus made no answer to Pilate when asked if he were king of the Jews. John agrees that Jesus was *essentially* silent about this, yet he did say *something*.

In John, Jesus said to Pilate that 'his kingdom was not of this world, because if it were, his servants would fight.' It is only *after* Pilate has gone beyond the point of no return with the public that John brings in Jesus' dialogue: *Thou couldest have no power at all against me, except it were given thee from above: therefore he that delivered me unto thee hath the greater sin.* John makes it perfectly clear that Pilate <u>would have</u> let Jesus go free, if he had not been beaten at his own political game by those representing the institution of Judaism. For they had played trump upon Pilate's cowardice before he fully realizes his mistake: *If thou let this man go, thou art not Caesar's friend: whosoever maketh himself a king speaketh against Caesar.* Though the Synoptics all make indirect reference to what was said on the placard which was placed above the cross, only John explains the essential mystery of who wrote it - and that it represents Pilate's half-hearted confession – "Jesus of Nazareth the King of the Jews."

Jesus was fully aware of the timing that would have spared him the cross. Only John explains what was said. Only John explains this timing. This is what Paul is talking about. It is not only what is *said* that is a public confession. It is also what is *not* said – that could have spared a personal crucifixion - that this silence is also a public confession.

ηρνησατο   This is αρνεομαι. There are just a half-dozen infrequently used verbs in our literature that begin with an η; therefore we may immediately suspect that the initial η is the result of the addition of a helping vowel. We will see this again and again. If a verb begins with a consonant, we move the verb into the past tense by adding an ε. But when the verb *already* begins with a vowel, the addition of the ε *lengthens* the vowel; i.e., if the vowel is an α or already is an ε, the vowel lengthens to an η (which we see in our sample). When the verb begins with an o as in the above example (ομολογεω), the vowel lengthens to ω.

     We may also assume that there have been internal spelling changes. And if we have noticed in the patterns in Hewett (312), ατο only occurs as the third person singular in the aorist *middle*, indicating not only the aorist tense, but that the verb is probably already a "deponent" verb in its natural state.

     Our deductions have been correct, the verb is αρνεομαι. It means "deny." We see from context that John has set this verb in antonymical relation to ομολογεω. We have already seen in our preliminary discussions of belief (πιστις) that its antonym is not "doubt" - but "unbelief" (απιστια), therefore this is an important distinction which will shed even more light on the meaning of "confession."

Exegetical Considerations: Our response to Christ is to believe or to not believe; to confess him or to deny him. But the one is inward; the other outward. The one concerns the inward man, the other the outward, social man. Therefore we have Paul saying: *For with the heart man* <u>*believeth*</u> *unto righteousness; and with the mouth* <u>*confession*</u> *is made unto salvation.*[43] Only Paul and John combine these two verbs. But John's purpose in combining them is to show that a disconnect can, and does, occur between the two: *Nevertheless among the chief rulers also many believed on him; but because of the Pharisees they did not confess him, lest they should be put out of the synagogue.*[44]

---

[43] Romans 10:10.
[44] John 12:42.

164

James says merely that a 'double-souled' (δίψυχος) or "double-minded" man is unstable in all his ways, implying that this kind of psychology is a freak of nature. Paul, too, seems to allow only a fundamentalistic view of the psychology of belief: *They profess that they know God; but in works they deny him.*[45] But when we consider the *object* of our belief, we know that it is not so simple as all of that. We are not asked to choose some neutral world-view as opposed to some other, relatively neutral world-view. We are asked to deny ourselves and confess the scandal of Christ. This is hard. It is as hard as a camel passing through the eye of a needle.

If there is any good news in the Gospels, it is this: each one of them spends considerable time and effort in setting up the context for Peter's typological denial of Christ. For each of the Gospel writers portrays a complex, multi-stage psychology of belief – of fear, of amazement, of resistance, of belief, then confession, obedience and endurance. It is hard to understand the essentially bi-modal Pauline aesthetic psychology that 'glories in tribulation,' but it is easy to understand the psychology of fear, cowardice, and adulterous appetite we see in the incomprehension, unbelief and denial of the apostles portrayed in the Gospels.

Paul is continually incredulous about this complexity: *How shall we, that are dead to sin, live any longer therein?*[46] If we bring naïveté to the Gospel material we will never understand how Peter's betrayal of Christ is categorically different from Judas' betrayal of Christ. We will never understand the lengthy, progressive conversion of Peter that may be deduced from the historical drama that is presented in the New Testament materials. We will not understand the man who buried his talent, or the virgins who took no auxiliary oil for their lamps, or how Ananias and Sapphira were choked by the deceitfulness of riches. And we will not understand Mark's pastoral brilliance in portraying this psychosis of the soul: "Lord, I believe, help mine unbelief!" But then, Paul did not understand the collapse of his own missionary entourage – Demas, Crescens and Titus having deserted him for the love of this present world.[47]

Paul's purpose was to take a fledgling church through the waters of death to a spiritual rebirth upon another shore. But the Gospels elaborate the confusion which ensues once that other shore is reached. *Hebrews* pushes the audience still further. Assuming an impossible law of Pauline righteousness, the author of *Hebrews* mercifully explains the *priestly* office of Christ, about which Paul is completely silent. Only Hebrews explains why we are in such need of endurance.[48] Only endurance will make the εισοδυς (entrance) into the promised land of Pauline glory, honor and immortality. But only the *enduring* soul will need a very high-powered priestly

---

[45] Titus 1:16.
[46] Romans 6:2.
[47] 2nd Timothy 4:10.
[48] Hebrews 10:36.

system to continually reconsecrate the soul, which is continually falling under the burden of sin which so easily besets her.[49]

και ωμολογησεν και ουκ ηρνησατο και ωμολογησεν

> This clause illustrates how και is sometimes used to conjoin ideas in more unusual ways than simply "and." και, normally translated "and" must also be translated as "but", "also", "even", "indeed" as context requires. This context clearly implies that John is repeating και for <u>emphasis</u> – an emphasis that pushes the third και into the stronger conjunctive role of "but."

<u>Exegetical Considerations</u>: To say that John did not deny an assertion that he was not the Christ is simply too complicated with double negatives to exclude the possibility that he was. By contrasting a positive "confess" with a negative "deny" John is emphasizing that John the Baptist *specifically* said of himself that he was not the Christ. Remember Luke's account. Here we have an extended prologue which seems to do nothing more than to historically relate and distinguish Jesus from John the Baptist.

We already know from Matthew that Herod[50] and many others[51] believed that Jesus was John the Baptist risen from the dead. But even with clear markers in the Synoptic template that Jesus was not John, the cult of John the Baptist flourished. Unless it could be definitively proven that John the Baptist specifically <u>said</u> that 'he was not the Christ', the cult of John the Baptist would linger on indefinitely. The historical witness to a positive confession that John the Baptist said that he was not the Christ would be its death blow. John is here providing that historical witness. John says that John the Baptist *himself* spoke definitively about this. He did not neglect the acclamations of his Messiahship. Any other prophet would have thought: 'perhaps I *am* the Messiah' and would have allowed his followers to nurture the idea. But John the Baptist was no ordinary prophet.

From the Synoptic template we know that when John the Baptist got up every morning he began preaching a repentance and a baptism for the remission of sins.[52] We also know that the people thought of Jesus as a great prophet from Nazareth. It was not unusual among the Jews to have a prophet from the north and one in the south whose prophetic careers ran concurrently. Nevertheless, seen from the perspective of the Synoptic author, the significance of John lay almost exclusively in what he thought of his northern colleague. According to the Synoptic template, John

---

[49] Hebrews 12:1.
[50] Matthew 14:2.
[51] Matthew 16:14.
[52] Mark 1:4 *John did baptize in the wilderness, and preach the baptism of repentance for the remission of sins.*

the Baptist thought that Jesus was a much greater prophet with a much greater ministry. Therefore we have a split between the day to day ministry of John the Baptist and the *theological significance* of his ministry – especially as it is related to Christ.

John is extracting from the well-established prophetic career of John the Baptist, the relatively brief and few events and words of John the Baptist which have only to do with the significance of his ministry as it was related to Christ. But we must understand that the cult of John the Baptist flourished for three reasons. First - the ministry of John the Baptist stood by itself. Listen to his father's prophecy:

And thou, child, shalt be called the prophet of the Highest: for thou shalt go before the face of the Lord to prepare his ways; To give knowledge of salvation unto his people by the remission of their sins, Through the tender mercy of our God; whereby the dayspring from on high hath visited us, To give light to them that sit in darkness and in the shadow of death, to guide our feet into the way of peace.[53]

There is nothing in this prophecy, necessarily, about heralding a Messiah. Secondly, many people never heard John's Messianic theology. If they were not present at Jesus' baptism or at any of John's pointed soliloquies about the significance of Jesus, there could only be hearsay on this subject. All we hear from the Synoptic template is about the intersection of John and Jesus. But the people of that time, to which John the Baptist ministered, heard only the general characteristics of his day to day ministry, which was *to turn the hearts of the fathers to the children, and the disobedient to the wisdom of the just; to make ready a people prepared for the Lord.*[54]

Thirdly, in many ways, the character of the ministry of John and the character of the ministry of Jesus looks very much the same. Both preached themes of repentance and righteousness. Although Jesus performed many miracles and John did not,[55] many of Jesus' public miracles were healing miracles. But faith-healers have never been convincing. At the beginning and the end they merely taunt Jesus about this: *Physician, heal thyself*[56] - and - *He saved others; himself he cannot save.*[57]

Jesus was known primarily as a teacher, not as a miracle worker. Many of the interpretive miracles we see were for private, apostolic consumption. Because of Jesus' constantly veiling his Messiahship through secrecy, even some of his more dramatic public miracles must have been confusing and enigmatic from the

---

[53] Luke 1:76-79.
[54] Luke 1:17.
[55] John 10:41.
[56] Luke 4:23.
[57] Matthew 27:42.

perspective of the crowds which witnessed them.[58] They both operated on the outskirts of Judaism, John even more than Jesus. Both were considered "marginal Jews" by the establishment. Both died a prophet's death. Even if we are considering the words that people heard from Jesus himself, it was hard to distinguish the two. Though the apostles allege that John believed that Jesus was greater, *from the perspective of the crowds*, it would have been difficult to see this, especially in view of the fact that Jesus apparently said the same thing about John: *Among them that are born of women there hath not risen a greater than John the Baptist.*[59] As far as the people were concerned, Many believed that John was holier, for Jesus was a 'gluttonous winebibber,' 'a friend of publicans and sinners.'[60] At least, that was the rumor.

When we read John, we are reading a hybrid Genre which addresses a perceived "weakness" of the Synoptic template; it does not aggressively specify who Jesus is or the nature of his messianic role. In John, Judas is merely a thief,[61] but in the Synoptic template, he is a much more complicated character. And we are thus able to infer from Peter's betrayal and Judas' betrayal, the incomprehension of Jesus' messianic role. John is impatient with mere inference. He will tell you who Jesus is. And he will tell you who John the Baptist is. And he will tell you much, much more about Jesus' messianic character.

οτι	ουκ ειμι εγω	ο	χριστος
that	not (I)am I	the	Christ

χριστος is the only new word here, and of course, it is the Greek rendition of "Messiah." Since it is a referent joined by a linking verb to the subject, χριστος is in the nominative case.

ειμι is the first person singular of the verb "to be." It is rendered "I am" 43 times and has no need of another εγω. Yet for emphasis, another εγω, the primary pronoun for "I," is added. This in itself does not make

[58] For example, the epileptic boy or Jairus' daughter. Think of the feeding of the 5000. You are in the crowds. There are no televisions which can bring you into the heart of every action for a birds-eye view. You have no idea of where all the food is coming from. Even if someone where to tell you that the disciples started only with a few fish and a few loaves of bread, it was from their hands, that the people received it. For all the people knew, it was the *disciples* who were performing, or at least facilitating the miracle, as they had so often done when the 70 were sent out to preach the Gospel without Jesus being present. Even for us the picture is enigmatic. If the "brute fact" of the healing of Lazarus so unequivocally demonstrates the Messiahship of Jesus, why didn't anyone else record it? For that matter, why does John agree with the Synoptic miracles only at the feeding of the 5000, which was confusing, the walking on the water and the resurrection, both of which were not public?
[59] Matthew 11:11.
[60] Matthew 11:19.
[61] John 12:6.

for a word play that hints at the "I am-ness" of God. It is the *order* that does this. For example, ειμι εγω occurs 11 times, and though John accounts for over 70% of these constructions, it means little more than "I *myself* am." For example, Paul says: χριστος ιησους ηλθεν εις τον κοσμον αμαρτωλους σωσαι ων πρωτος <u>ειμι εγω</u>. (Christ Jesus came into the world to save sinners, of whom I *myself* am first.) Yet more often (48 times) the order is reversed. Similarly, John accounts for the majority 65%. It is safe to conclude *from these* that John uses this construction as a word play that puts "I am" in the mouth of Jesus. But remember, a word play is precisely this – play. John is playing with the words to hint at Christ's deity. We know this partly from frequency, partly from context, and partly from coincidence. But we also know this from John's prologue. He wasn't playing then.

εγω amplifies ειμι, and for John, εγω ειμι itself amplifies the logos Christology. Yet εγω ειμι does not *automatically* invoke the import of this word play. For example, in the dialogue concerning the man born blind who was healed (John 9), the man says: ελεγεν οτι εγω ειμι ("he said: (that) I am (he)." Clearly there is no inference of deity here. John will again repeat the substance of this sentence in John the Baptist's subsequent soliloquy about himself and Christ (3:22-36): οτι ειπον ουκ ειμι εγω ο χριστος (I said that I am {myself} not the Christ).

Paul effectively asks the Ephesian Church: "was John the Baptist crucified for you?" The apostle John appears to be answering Paul from the choir stall: no!!!! John will again have John the Baptist repeat: "I am not the Christ."[62] This unusual phrase occurs only once elsewhere. Paul is preaching a sermon and he comes to the identity and purpose of John the Baptist: *And as John fulfilled his course, he said, Whom think ye that I am? I am not he* (ουκ ειμι εγω).[63]

---

[62] 3:28.
[63] Acts 13:25.

και ηρωτησαν αυτον
and they asked   him

τι   ουν ηλιας ει συ
what then, Elijah are you?

και λεγει   ουκ ειμι
and he says not I am

ο προφητης ει συ
the prophet   are you?

και   απεκριθη   ου
and (he) answered no

ηρωτησαν   We have just seen this verb, "ask," (ερωταω) in rare configuration two
sentences ago - in the aorist subjunctive. Here it is in the aorist, with its
typical landmarks: the internal spelling changes, the beginning,
helping vowel lengthening the ε to an η and the presence of the σ
coupler just before the personal ending of αν.

There are *two* modes for the aorist – we have already encountered a
second mode in verbs such as λαμβανω (ελαβον, third person plural)
in the 12th sentence; here is the 1st aorist. This verb has the 1st aorist, 3rd
person plural ending attached (αν). The patterns represented in
Hewett, seem confusing, but remember: these patterns are presented
systematically from a <u>grammarian's</u> point of view. Just as the
systematic notes on the page of music are presented from a
musicologist's point of view. You may study the page of music for a
long time, but unless you *are* a musician, you will hear nothing.

Do not try to understand which verbs present themselves in the first
mode or the second mode. Just learn them as they are presented in a
real piece of literature. And you will see that they are much easier to
recognize and to understand. Take ερχομαι for example. Although it
occurs 35 times in John's Gospel, you will never see any personal
ending except for ηλθεν or ηλθον. As in music, it is much easier to
learn how to play an E^b than it is to first memorize the different key
signatures in which it occurs.

ουν | ουν means "therefore" or "then," but should be put with τι here in order to get the sense in which it is being used. Anyone hearing "τι ουν" would be hearing a very common phrase (10x) which Paul uses to introduce a rhetorical question in his first block of epistles: "what then?" It *could* be translated "why then" as it is in Matthew 17:10b *Why then* (τι ουν) *say the scribes that Elias must first come?* Then the sentence would be 'why then are you Elijah?', which doesn't make sense. Contextually, it must therefore be "what then?" The presence of the interrogative, of course, is the sign of a coming question, but, as you can see, you must determine from context things about the nature of the question. The Priests and Levites are coming from Jerusalem not so much to listen to John's message about repentance and true faith, but to find out what John believes about himself.

ηλιας ει συ | We do not know what idiomatic linguistic convention John is using to frame his question.[64] All we know is that from context it *is* a question[65] (Elijah are you?). It is a question like the two Pilate asks of Jesus in John: βασιλευς ει συ (King, are you?) and ποθεν ει συ (whence are you?). Yet syntax requires context to make it a question. The woman at the well says (not asks): κυριε θεωρω οτι προφητης ει συ (Lord, I see that {a} prophet are you).

Exegetical Considerations: If we know the genre of literature, then certain hermeneutical[66] parameters are automatically set which help our exegesis. For

---

[64] It does not occur elsewhere in our literature except in John's Gospel.

[65] And that it sounds like "Yoda-speak." We would ask, why is John doing this? But translators 1000 years hence will ask why we consistently cast the Koine in the formal and stiff style of the KJV for hundreds of years when the original language was informal and common. Even the NKJV is too formal for the commonness Koine. Yet the question remains. Why did we do this? Perhaps John is attempting to convey an atmosphere of formality in the tone of the address between the priests and Levites from Jerusalem and John.

[66] Hermeneutics is the discipline of understanding the proper literary sense of the text. Exegesis, is the proper extraction of that proper, literary sense, once the hermeneutical boundaries have been set. Genre is an hermeneutical boundary. The perspective of the author is another. Hermeneutics are the "rules of engagement" we bring to the text. Exegesis is the technical act of applying those rules. What makes the Gospel/Acts sometimes so delicate to translate is that it is dialogue. Likewise, Paul's style is not that of a systematic theologian, coolly assembling a theological abstraction – it is really an extended dialogue with the reader – hence the rhetorical questions and the idiomatic interjections: like μη γενοιτο (*may it not be!*) which Paul uses 10 times in Romans. Therefore, it is an unrealistic expectation to "read" much of the New Testament as if it were Virgil or a Latin discourse upon the Trinity from one of the Church divines. Years will pass. And every time you translate the same passage, you will notice new colors and smells of pathos intrinsic to this kind of literature. Do not be discouraged. Notice foreign students of English. They were fluent in our written literature long before they became comfortable with interpreting our dialogue. No matter how many years one has

example, it is now clear that John is a kind of hybrid genre, which combines literary features from the Synoptic format with the theological argumentation found in Paul's epistles. We will therefore not be surprised to find that in some cases, like the soliloquies of John the Baptist, it will not be clear where John the Baptist's dialogue ends and John the Apostle's editorial commentary begins. If we know that John is primarily using seven interpretive soliloquies to present Jesus' teaching to the outside world, we will have just such an hermeneutical parameter which will guide our translation and exegesis of the text within each soliloquy unit.

ο προφητης	Here is an unusual "first declension" noun that seems to mix and match feminine and masculine characteristics.[67] Except for the masculine looking genitive singular, the personal endings for προφητης (prophet) are all feminine, yet this word takes the masculine article. Thus you will find in John 6:45 the dative construction εν τοις προφηταις (in the prophets) – αις is a feminine ending; τοις a masculine article.

Exegetical Commentary: προφητης and χριστος are not mutually exclusive terms. Was Jesus a prophet? According to the Apostles - yes, but much more of a prophet.[68] Yet it will be difficult to deduce this. All four Gospels carry Jesus' statement that a prophet is not without honor except in his own fatherland (πατριδι). Luke adds more verbiage that Jesus implied that he and Elijah were in the same class. (Luke 4:25-27) Matthew and Luke record that Jesus said: *The men of Nineveh shall rise in judgment with this generation, and shall condemn it: because they repented at the preaching of Jonas; and, behold, a greater than Jonas is here.*[69] This implies that Jesus has put himself, conditionally, in the same class as Jonah the prophet.[70] In Luke 13:33 we see Jesus explicitly assume the role of prophet: *Nevertheless I must walk to day, and to morrow, and the day following: for it cannot be that a prophet perish out of Jerusalem.* In the Gospels, there are many neutral confessions that Jesus is a prophet, but there is no very positive affirmation, either editorially, or from Christ. Yet in John, the blind

---

studied English, you will always be doing him a service if you slow down your speech. You must also drop as many of your sophisticated colloquialisms as you can and speak in a direct, simple style. This is exactly what is happening in the "Koine conversation." These authors have slowed down their speech in the straightforward lingua franca of Koine. John, especially, gives plenty of contextual clues as to what he is talking about. Slow down. Look. Listen.

[67] It would be helpful to browse the conventional grammarian theory about the "first declension" which begins in Hewett, 6.2. Again, observe, but do not memorize. See especially Hewett, 6.3.

[68] Jesus says this same thing regarding John the Baptist: ναι λεγω υμιν και περισσοτερον προφητου (*yes, I say to you, but much more of a prophet*).

[69] Matthew 12:41.

[70] Likewise, Jesus statement that 'no sign shall be given except the sign of Jonah' (Matthew 12: 39) also puts him in the class of Jonah the prophet.

man who sees is contrasted with the establishment that does not see. When they ask him for their view of Jesus he says: *He is a prophet.*[71]

It is not until Acts that we get an unequivocal sermon from Peter which identifies Jesus as Prophet: *For Moses truly said unto the fathers, A prophet shall the Lord your God raise up unto you of your brethren, like unto me; him shall ye hear in all things whatsoever he shall say unto you. And it shall come to pass, that every soul, which will not hear that prophet, shall be destroyed from among the people.*[72]

The people, generally, held that both Jesus and John were prophets. The Apostles allege in these ex post facto Gospels that the Scriptures say that Christ must suffer. But how is his suffering of any more significance than the prophecy of Caiaphas - that Jesus must become a sort of "scapegoat" for the stability - if not the very survival - of the nation?[73] The author of Hebrews acknowledges that there have been many prophets which have assumed this messianic role: *By faith Moses, when he was come to years, refused to be called the son of Pharaoh's daughter; Choosing rather to suffer affliction with the people of God, than to enjoy the pleasures of sin for a season; Esteeming the reproach of Christ greater riches than the treasures in Egypt.*[74] *And others had trial of cruel mockings and scourgings, yea, moreover of bonds and imprisonment: They were stoned, they were sawn asunder, were tempted, were slain with the sword: they wandered about in sheepskins and goatskins; being destitute, afflicted, tormented; Of whom the world was not worthy.*[75] What makes the suffering of *this* prophet - the prophet from Nazareth - any different from these?

The Circumcision party, so long entrenched in Jerusalem, would, like Judas, except Jesus as a great prophet after the order of Elijah, but they would not accept his *dominion* as Lord and Savior, the only begotten son, the first born from the dead, the final, High Priest, called after the order of Melchizedek, who would obviate the entire temple establishment and completely change their relationship to the law of Moses. Paul was tolerated, but only as a reed shaken in the winds that bloweth from unknown, Hellenistic quarters. They would not accept the fact that the drama of Paul's life had conformed itself not only to the typology of Moses the lawgiver. Paul's life had conformed itself to the typology of the life of Christ. The inertia here is tremendous. Even after the publication of John and of Hebrews, Peter's first epistle proclaims nothing more than a great prophet after the order of Elijah. If this epistle were stripped of its Pauline and Hebrewine jargonistic importations - if its

---

[71] John 9:17.
[72] Acts 3:22-23 Stephen repeats this same theological point in his sermon (Acts 7:37).
[73] John 11:49-50 *And one of them, named Caiaphas, being the high priest that same year, said unto them, Ye know nothing at all, Nor consider that it is expedient for us, that one man should die for the people, and that the whole nation perish not.*
[74] Hebrews 11:24-26.
[75] Hebrews 11:37-38.

concepts, which seem to elaborate the suffering servant motif of Isaiah 53, are carefully examined, we would end with essentially the same kind of Elijah-like prophet who, as Socrates and so many other prophets of Judaism - for the men of Athens, for the nation of Israel, and for us - died for the sake of truth - the 'just for the unjust.' To the extent that we follow their good example, their blood has (in a figure) *purged* our souls from sin and error to serve the living God of all men.

John is, in large part, a belated attempt to distinguish not only Jesus from John the Baptist, but also to distinguish Jesus from all the other messianic prophets that have ever come before. John is attempting to overcome the inertia which sees the Prophet of Nazareth as nothing more than a favorite servant (παις) of God. It is important to keep this editorial emphasis in mind as we read this sentence. Otherwise we will have John the Baptist in conflict with Christ. Christ says that John the Baptist is both a prophet and that he is the Elijah that is to come. John the Baptist confesses that he is neither prophet nor Elijah. John the Baptist says that he is not the Messiah, though his ministry is Messianic. John is resolving these things.

Christ spoke of the _typology_ of John's ministry. John the Baptist spoke specifically about his own _identity_. He was answering the question of the Priests and Levites. "Who are you?", they asked. 'I am the one spoken of in Isaiah 40:3.' The KJV has the religious establishment ask John: *Art thou Elias? And he saith, I am not. Art thou that prophet?* And again, they translate: *Why baptizest thou then, if thou be not that Christ, nor Elias, neither that prophet?* In both cases a demonstrative "that" is inserted before "prophet," as though referring to a specific prophet. Yet there is only the article **o** preceding "prophet." We have already seen that Koine handles the article differently than English. Koine says:

ουτως γαρ		ηγαπησεν	ο	θεος	τον	κοσμον
so	therefore	loved	the	God	the	world

For us, the article specifies "which one?" so to insert "the" before God is superfluous, but in Koine, as in many other languages, the article specifies grammatical purpose. In this sentence, for example the articles **o** and **τον** specify which is the subject and which is the object. Indeed, God rarely occurs without its accompanying article. In the Koine, there is no indefinite article. If the word is indefinite, it simply occurs without the article: εγενετο ανθρωπος απεσταλμενος παρα θεου (there was **a man** sent from God). The religious establishment is asking: "are you a prophet" or "are you one of the prophets," or even, "are you playing the prophet?" This is a significant question in itself, since the office of the true prophet has essentially gone unfilled since the exile, hundreds of years before, therefore an indefinite construction would already be begging the question. A passage from Mark illustrates how προφητης could occur in the indefinite form without begging the question:

αλλοι	ελεγον	οτι	ηλιας εστιν	αλλοι δε ελεγον	οτι	<u>προφητης</u>
others	answered	that	elias he is;	others but said	that	(a) prophet

εστιν η ως εις	των	προφητων[76]
he is or as one	of (the) prophets	

αποκριθη ου   John uses the aorist passive voice for this verb (αποκρινομαι) with much more frequency than do the Synoptic authors.[77] Often this verb is used in dialogue: Jesus *answered* and said… The Synoptic authors almost always make it a participle; i.e., "Jesus *answering* (αποκριθεις) said…" In a very marked stylistic feature, though the participle, αποκριθεις occurs 109 times in the Synoptic/Acts sequence, John never uses it. He invariably uses the form that we see in our sample: αποκριθη.[78]

                  ου could be "nothing" or "not" but in this case it must be "no" If he had meant "not" or "nothing" the negative would have preceded the word as in Mt 26:62; 27:12; Mk 14:61; 15:5 and Luke 23:9.

---

[76] Mark 6:15.

[77] John uses the aorist passive voice 76 of 78 times when using this verb.

[78] John will use the construction αποκριθη … και ειπεν instead. Of the Synoptic authors, only Luke uses construction – but only twice.

εικον   ουν   αυτω
they said   therefore to him

τις   ει
who are you?

ινα   αποκρισιν δωμεν   τοις   πεμψασιν ημας
in order that an answer   we might give to them sending   us

τι   λεγεις περι   σεαυτου
what (do you) say   concerning   yourself

Since the fourth chapter of this book, we have presented our sample sentences broken up into phrases instead of sentences. And this is because we have moved beyond a word by word approach. A sentence is unintelligible as a mere string of words. Though we know the order of Greek words in a sentence is different than our own, it is not very different within the phrase, and in the arrangements of phrases in the sentence. As you translate, do not attempt to see the entire sentence as a conceptual unit. But *do* look for these phrases. These phrases form the skeletal contours upon which the syntax of the sentence is formed.

In our sample sentence, the first phrase essentially begins (in English) with "therefore" (ουν). Since we are dealing with a lot of dialogue in the Gospels, we will become familiar with these dialogue oriented phrases: *therefore they said to him*. The verb "they said" (ειπον) and the dative construction "(to) him" (αυτω) go together like a bat and a baseball. the presence of ουν distinguishes the <u>*style*</u> of bat and ball, since only John uses this three-word construction. These stylistic features help both our exegesis and our translation. They help our exegesis because they tell us a little bit about the man, John the Apostle. They help our translation because they reinforce that language is not a mathematical formula that must be worked exactly the same way in order to arrive at the correct solution. Style shows us the range of how the same things can be expressed differently by different authors. Genre, author perspective, style, etc. all enter into the translational/exegetical decisions we make.

Continuing our preliminary scan of the sentence, we see that the second phrase is a question, as we have discussed above. And as soon as we see ινα, we know that a new, third phrase has begun. And we know that this conditional phrase is in the subjunctive mood because of the presence of the ω in the personal ending[79] Though

---

[79] Remember what we said above: "Whenever we see an ω appear in the personal ending, we know that the verb has moved out of the normal indicative mood. And since there is the conditional ινα

we do not yet recognize what is going on in the fourth phrase, we strongly suspect that "τι" introduces it.

ειπον[80] ουν αυτω[81]

> "They said therefore to him…" The odd thing about this first phrase is that it is introducing a question. "They therefore said to him" is normally employed to introduce dialogue in the *indicative* mood, not in the interrogative mood. We would say 'They therefore asked him…' The other Synoptic authors generally[82] agree. Unlike John, they never say: ειπον ουν αυτω. John repeats it eight times. Typically, the Synoptic author will use the verb επερωταω (ask). Yet John uses this verb only twice (in the 18th chapter when he is much more closely following the Synoptic template).[83]

τις ει

> Syntactically, this would be "who you are" since the second person singular is indicated in the verb ειμι. But since the interrogative comes first, it changes the phrase to a question: "who are you?" If it were ει τις, it would become, essentially, an expression; i.e., "who

---

lurking in close proximity, we can be sure that this is the subjunctive mood." It doesn't matter that we may not know what δωμεν means. We are looking for the skeletal contours of the sentence.

[80] We have already seen this word before. We will not always refer back to previous discussions of words. In the event that you have difficulty remembering a word – look it up. The best place to begin is in the Greek New Testament. It is very user friendly in this regard, since in the case of ειπον, unlike an ordinary lexicon, you will find an entry. This entry is a "stub" which will redirect you to the primary entry of the verb. For ειπον you will find: "aor. of λεγω." This is very helpful if we do not remember or know the "lemma" of a word – the base word that you would look up in a lexicon.

[81] Note the absence of the preposition. Again, this is very common. Since grammatical function is apparent in the endings, the preposition "to" is unnecessary.

[82] Occasionally they will introduce an interrogative with ειπον…αυτω.

[83] This is an indication of the importation of a stylistic element of another author. Occasionally, the style of an author changes so radically, it helps to demonstrate that there has been a change of author – sometimes for good; sometimes for ill. For example, using the stylistic features of vocabulary alone, Mark 16: 9-20 clearly looks like an imposition of another author. Whereas, the woman taken in adultery in John – while it looks like an insertion of somewhat foreign content – the passage proves to be Johannine. Many stylistic features of 2nd Corinthians change so radically from a "typical" Pauline letter, that it must be assumed that it is, at least in part, heavily influenced by another author. Furthermore, there is a tremendous change of style between 1st Peter and 2nd Peter. So much so that many textual critics assert that they are written by two different authors. This, in part, is due to the fact that Peter *himself* is writing his second epistle, without the editorial finesse of Silvanus (who is, in turn, heavily influenced by the theology of Paul, due to his long association with him). But a vocabulary analysis alone strongly indicates that both letters were written by Peter. Why the change, then? Theological content and *sitz im leben* strongly suggests that Peter may have had a spiritual awakening between these two letters. When this kind of linguistic evidence coincides with other literary elements – for example, the *manuscript* evidence - the circumstantial evidence for pseudonymical activity can be conclusive (for example, Mark 16:9-20). This is the kind of literary evidence which conclusively proved that the Donation of Constantine was a forgery.

ever" or, as the KJV often translates: "if[84] any man." For example the KJV rendition of Mark's ... ει τις εχει ωτα ακουειν ακουετω is: *if any man has ears to hear let him hear*.

αποκρισιν — Although the verbal form αποκρινομαι is often used, its noun form, αποκρισις, a third declension feminine noun, here shown in the dative, is only used four times – twice by Luke, twice by John.

δωμεν τοις πεμψασιν ημας

δωμεν is the aorist subjunctive of a highly irregular verb, διδωμι. (Note the presence of the ω, a strong indicator of the subjunctive, in the personal ending.) This word means "give." Scanning this conditional "ινα" phrase, we expect, and do see the indirect object of the verb "give." First comes the accompanying dative (plural) article τοις. But then comes what looks like a verb – πεμπω, which means "send." Clear evidence of the aorist is reflected in the spelling change.[85] Yet it has no helping vowel at the beginning and it looks like the dative personal ending (3rd plural) for a noun has been attached to the ending. Yes, this is a participle. Most of the time we will encounter participles as defining something about the subject of the sentence. But here is a rare case in which the participle tells us something about the *indirect object* of a sentence.

Exegetical Considerations: You may be wondering why you have not encountered any complex charts about how to form participles in the various tenses. There is a good reason for this. We are learning how to translate John. John uses only the present, the aorist and the perfect participles with any frequency. And even then, John's frequency of use represents a 10th of all the occurrences in the Biblical materials. And in many cases, the use of a participle form for a verb concerns just a few verbs. And the problem with participle formation charts is that they are very complex.

One of the biggest reasons for this is that participle charts treat all the possible variants of participle formation as essentially equal. But they are not all equal. Many of them are quite rare. Many are infrequent. And many of the rare and infrequent participles come from the pen of one man – Luke – not only in books that were written directly by him (Luke and Acts) but also in books which bear his secretarial

---

[84] ει is a homonym meaning both "if" and "you are"

[85] And this is a particular *kind* of spelling change that is a sure sign of adding a ς before the personal ending. Since the verb stem ends in a consonant that would go awkwardly with the ς, in this case it combines to form a ψ. You can read more about this in Hewett, 4.2 and 15.4.1.

hand.[86] So it is better to treat the participle sequentially; that is, as we find it. When the grammarians come upon a grammatical phenomenon of sufficient irregularity, they eventually give up their charts and advise us to "memorize" the individual phenomena. The myriad forms of participle distribution occur with such an irregular distribution frequency that we must learn and remember these participle phenomena on a case by case basis. If we do this, the increased frequency of present, aorist, and perfect use in John and in the New Testament as a whole, will passively suggest its own memory patterns in our minds. If you use the charts, you may never achieve a lasting, working knowledge of participles. Below is the approximate distribution of participles in the New Testament; then, John.

Present	2549/**151**[87]
Present Middle Deponent	31/0
Present Middle	105/4
Present Passive	358/17[88]
Present Passive/Middle	544/**38**[89]
Present Passive Deponent	2/0
Future	11/2
Future Middle Deponent[90]	3/0
Future Passive	1/0
Aorist	714/**70**[91]
2nd Aorist	889/70
Aorist Middle	61/2
2nd Aorist Middle	19/0
Aorist Passive	215/3
2nd Aorist Passive	32[92]/2
Aorist Middle Deponent	88/4[93]

---

[86] Which includes all of Paul's epistles, Hebrews and 2nd Peter. And Luke's literary abilities appear to have had a very strong influence on the vocabularies of both Mark *and* John.

[87] Added to this are occurrences, 191/25, mostly of ειμι.

[88] All but 4 of these have to do with λεγομαι (called).

[89] Half of these are ερχομαι variants; half of the rest have to do with the action of sitting or lying down.

[90] Strong's #5697.

[91] In John, 60% of these cluster around the verbs "sent," "heard," and "made."

[92] This verb form is mostly associated with variants of στρεφω (turn) and found only in the Gospel/Acts sequence.

[93] These all concern θεαομαι (which means: "see," "behold").

2nd Aorist Middle Deponent	137/2[94]
Aorist Passive Deponent	164[95]/0
2nd Aorist Deponent	19[96]/0
Perfect	193/**33**
2nd Perfect	43/1
Perfect Passive	463/**42**
2nd Perfect Passive	0/1
Perfect Middle	5[97]/0
Perfect Middle/Passive Dep.	4/0

The reason that Greek uses participles with so much greater frequency than English is that they are so often used in an *adjectival* sense; that is, they define a noun. We define things in terms of the senses – what color, what shape, what form a thing has. But in this literature, particularly the narrative pieces, it is the *verbal* action of, or upon a thing that helps to define that thing. And most of the time, that thing is the subject.[98] Therefore, verbs are very often turned into adjectives and then they are declined to agree with the nouns they modify. This is a great benefit to us in that it is much easier to understand what adjective goes with what noun. In English, you must depend almost entirely on word order and context. Hence, in English, you often encounter the problem of the "ambiguous modifier." Not so much in Greek.

τι λεγεις[99] περι[100] σεαυτου

> τι, the neuter version of τις, introduces the fourth phrase of this sentence. τι asks about things; τις asks about people. About half the time, the interrogative pronoun is used in this sense of "what?" Therefore it will be in the nominative case (i.e., τι). About a quarter of the time it is used in the sense of "who" or "whom" (τις or τινα,

---

[94] This form occurs mostly in the Synoptic/Acts sequence (115/134), and is most associated with the verbs and verb variants of γινομαι and λαμβανομαι. The variants are used almost exclusively by Luke.

[95] 75% of these are "answer."

[96] Except for one occurrence in a Matthew/Mark synchronicity, this is primarily used by Luke in the Synoptic/Acts sequence and in books which he helped to write.

[97] All of these have to do with the verb ενδυοω ("clothe").

[98] Which is yet another reason for not learning participle paradigms which imply that all possible configurations are equal.

[99] "say" (present active indicative, 2nd person singular). We first encountered this verb, λεγω, as a participle in John 1:15.

[100] "concerning" See John 1:7.

respectively). As we saw on the chart above concerning τι/τις and all its forms, John uses the interrogative pronoun in the ordinary sense; that is, 80% of the time it is simply the ordinary, nominative question, using τις or τι, asking who? why? or what?

σεαυτου — This is a reflexive pronoun meaning, in this case, "yourself." Read (but do not memorize) Hewett's discussion about reflexive pronouns (8.3). John uses σεαυτ- only eight times in his Gospel, and each time it means "yourself."[101] John uses "myself" (εμαυτ-) with considerably more frequency than the Synoptic authors – all of them in the mouth of Jesus. Most of all,[102] you will see variants of εαυτ- which will cover the rest of the reflexives.

Exegetical Considerations: If we are right about John's very strong editorial motive here - that he is elaborating the categorical difference between John the Baptist and Christ, in order to resolve the persistent error of the cult of John the Baptist represented by that which Paul found in Ephesus – then we also have in hand an explanation of the intrusiveness of v 18 *No man hath seen God at any time; the only begotten Son, which is in the bosom of the Father, he hath declared him.* John is saying that Christ declares God; John the Baptist declares Christ. It is one thing to *assert* that John is not the Christ. The clinching testimony is to put John *himself* on the witness stand. What did John <u>himself</u> say when cross-examined? We shall shortly see.

εφη
Said he:

εγω   φωνη   βοωντος
I (am) (a/the) voice   crying

εν τη ερημω
in the desert

ευθυνατε   την οδον κυριου
make straight the   way (of the) Lord

καθως ειπεν ησαιας   ο προφητης
just as   said   Isaiah   the prophet

---

[101] 5x in the accusative (σεαυτον), twice in the genitive σεαυτου (both are constructed with περι - as in our sample sentence) and once in the dative (σεαυτω).
[102] 339x.

φεμι   Just as there are many closely related words for "say," "speak," "tell," mention, exclaim, declare, announce, etc. in English, so there are many Greek verbs: επω, ερεω, ρεω, προερεω, λεγω, λαλεω, αποφθεγγομαι, to describe the act of speaking. And as in English, many of them seem to be used interchangeably and the nuances of the words which distinguish them are lost and are conjectural at best, even from context. We would certainly be hard-pressed to sort out the nuances of *English* connotations. φεμι, a **μι** verb, means more than "say," but less than "exclaim."

Though φεμι appears disproportionately more in the Gospel/Acts sequence, John uses φεμι just twice in his Gospel. Elsewhere it invariably appears to introduce dialogue. For example, consider the sentence: Cornelius said four days ago I was fasting until this hour. Where do you put the quotation marks? Did he say what he said four days ago, or is this part of what he said? The appearance of φεμι indicates that dialogue immediately follows; i.e., 'Cornelius said (φεμι) "four days ago I was fasting until this hour,"' not: 'Cornelius said four days ago: "I was fasting until this hour."'

And in Luke's more literary *Acts*, it seems to introduce somewhat more momentous dialogue, which would explain its sometime appearance introducing Scriptural quotations, as it does in our sentence (Isaiah 40:3). φεμι therefore, introduces dialogue with a formality and intensity beyond merely "say."

εγω   As we have said, εγω is the personal pronoun meaning "I." The Synoptics all use slightly different techniques to make the momentous assertion that Isaiah 40:3 is a prophecy of the ministry of John the Baptist. The problem with Isaiah 40:3 is that there is no referent for who it is that is crying. In the Septuagint (from which the Synoptics quote) it merely says: "the voice of one crying in the wilderness: prepare the way of the Lord…" In English, this is a fragment sentence because there is only a participle, no subject, no verb. The Apostle John has John the Baptist *himself* supply the missing subject – "I," and by convention, the reader may supply the linking verb "am" (this is why the translators of the KJV put the "am" in italics, because it is not, strictly speaking, *there* in the Greek).

Exegetical Considerations: John is about to assert, by the mouth of John the Baptist, that the Baptist is the one that Isaiah is talking about. Yet the Apostle John makes a significant departure from what Isaiah has said. All three Synoptics follow the

Septuagint closely[103] and say: φωνη βοωντος εν τη ερημω ετοιμασατε την οδον κυριου ευθειας ποιειτε τας τριβους αυτου ("the voice crying in the wilderness: prepare the way of the Lord, make strait his paths.")

John does not say "*prepare* the way of the Lord." He says "ευθυνατε την οδον κυριου" ("<u>make straight</u> the way of the Lord") and leaves out the phrase about the paths (τριβους). It seems that the "way" of the Lord is something that pertains to the Lord himself; the "paths," the physical way that is prepared for him. That is, a straight red carpet could have been thrown out before him leading to the heart of Jerusalem, or a path of detours which would make him pass by his intended destination, as Peter did when he attempted to persuade Christ to make a detour around the cross.

As the Psalmist has it: the <u>way</u> is doctrinal; the <u>path</u> is existential: *Teach me thy way, O LORD, and lead me in a plain path…*[104] Proverbs categorizes evil men similarly: *Whose ways are crooked, and froward in their paths.*[105] Indeed, in his next sentence Isaiah makes the same parallel: *the crooked shall be made straight, and the rough places plain.*[106] Micah also illustrates the difference between the "way" and the "path": *he will teach us of his ways, and we will walk in his paths.*[107] The way is taught; the path is walked.

It is easy to see how physical stumblingblocks and detours are placed in the path of Christ, but how can his very own ways be bent? Outside of the Synoptic quotation of Isaiah, "the way of the Lord" is found twice in Acts; in one, the way was insufficiently informed: Apollos knew the way of the Lord, but only up to the point of the Baptism of John;[108] in the second, the way had been made crooked by the false prophet, Elymas, the Jewish Sorcerer.[109]

In our literature, to sort out who Christ was, John or Jesus, and to withstand the Jewish false prophets, were of doctrinal concern only to Paul. The evidence of the Apostle John's mindfullness of Paul's ministry and work is beginning to grow. We may thus say that there is circumstantial evidence that John's mindfulness of Paul's need to distinguish Christ from John the Baptist is, quite possibly, the reason that he has modified this quote away from the Septuagint and the Synoptics.

---

[103] The Septuagint says at the end: "make strait the paths 'of our God.'"
[104] Psalm 27:11.
[105] Proverbs 2:15.
[106] Isaiah 40:4b.
[107] Micah 4:2.
[108] Acts 18:24-26.
[109] Acts 13:6-12.

φωνη   φωνη means "voice," and is used often by John, especially in the Revelation. It is a feminine noun, here used as the subject, so in the nominative case. Occasionally, the KJV will translate "sound" in the case of what we call "inanimate" objects. But remember: "inanimate" is a modern word which is used to divide the world into dualistic categories of life and non-life. But in the Greek (and Hebrew) mind, <u>all things</u> possess life (*seeing he giveth to all life, and breath, and all things*[110]), but some things do not possess <u>souls</u>: *And even things without life giving sound...* The word used for "without life" is αψυχος – ψυχη, meaning soul.

The heavens declare the glory of God,[111] the deep calls to the deep.[112] The Psalmist adjures: *Praise ye him, sun and moon: praise him, all ye stars of light* - and this occurs in a list of "animate" things.[113] These are not "dead" metaphors - because for these authors, the whole world of things lives unto God. Therefore John will say: *The wind bloweth where it listeth, and thou hearest the sound thereof...*[114] and the word John uses here for sound is φωνη.

βοωντος   βοαω, here, is in the form of the present passive participle and means to "cry out." κραυγαζω and κραζω also mean to cry out, but βοαω has a more plaintive connotation than both - as when Mark 15:34 says: *And at the ninth hour Jesus <u>cried</u> with a loud voice, saying, Eloi, Eloi, lama sabachthani.* It is in the genitive because a voice *belongs* to someone. But the sentence was originally designed (by Isaiah), to be vague about *whose* voice. You could translate "the voice crying. "Yet John is clearing up who it is that is crying by prefacing it with "I (am)." John the Baptist is not the voice, but the *possessor* of the voice. He is the one to whom Isaiah refers and to whom the voice belongs. This helps explain why βοωντος, which is a <u>*masculine*</u> genitive ending, does not agree with "voice," a feminine noun. The masculine noun which goes with βοωντος is not voice, but the unspoken possessor of the voice - John the Baptist, a masculine entity.

εν τη ερημω   "in the desert." τη is the feminine article, and although ερημω looks masculine, it belongs to a special category of the "second declension" words that have masculine looking endings and yet are feminine

---

110 Acts 17:25.
111 Psalm 19:1.
112 Psalm 42:7.
113 Psalm 148.
114 John 3:8.

184

nouns.[115] ερημω is, of course, in the dative, which the preposition εν requires.

ευθυνατε | As we have seen, the Synoptics all use ευθειας ποιειτε τας τριβους (make straight the paths). It is not that John is not familiar with the word, ευθειας. He uses it three times, but in all three cases he employs the connotation, "without delay," which pertains to this adjective, but not to the verbal action of ευθυνατε. John says: *But one of the soldiers with a spear pierced his side, and forthwith (ευθυς) came there out blood and water.*[116] John has probably moved ευθυνω to modify "way" because of its singular meaning of straight – as opposed to crooked.

την οδον | Here is "way" (οδον) with its accompanying article (την) in the accusative case, since it is the direct object of the verb ευθυνατε. We have belabored the difference between "way" and "path" because there is a difference in the Greek. οδος is a much more flexible word. It can certainly stand in for τριβους, but it also can be generalized and pressed into the service of metaphor much more easily than τριβους, which is a technical word referring specifically to the worn nature of paths. This limitation may easily account for the fact that τριβους is not used in our literature *except* in this quotation from Isaiah. When John says: *Jesus saith unto him, I am the <u>way</u>, the truth, and the life: no man cometh unto the Father, but by me*[117] he uses <u>οδον</u>.

κυριου | "Lord" is used 748 times in our literature. Unlike θεος, it may also simply be a formal term of respect. For example, John has the woman at the well consistently refer to Christ as "Lord," but she cannot know who he is at this point and so the KJV translators nicely translate merely "sir." When the Greeks come to Philip wanting a private meeting with Jesus they address Phillip as κυριε which the KJV also translates "sir." In the Greek, therefore, there is no prohibition against using "Lord" to refer to a mere man, just as it is used in England.

Since κυριου is used so many times in our literature, and since it is just an ordinary 2nd declension, masculine noun, it would be good to review all of its forms. (See chart next page. Bolded forms appear in John's Gospel; unbolded in Revelation and light grey elsewhere in the New Testament).

---

[115] See Hewett, 6.5.
[116] John 19:34.
[117] John 14:6.

	Singular		*Plural*
N	κυριος		κυριοι[118]
G	κυριου		-
D	κυριω[119]		κυριοις[120]
A	κυριον		-
V	κυριε[121]		-

This chart adds the <u>vocative</u> case (κυριε). This ending is used to designate direct address, as in John 9:38 *And he said, "Lord, (κυριε) I believe!"*

καθως — This is an adverb that is formed by combining the preposition κατα ("according to") with the common adverb ως ("as"). ως draws a parallel between one action and another. For example, Matthew says: And forgive us our debts, as (<u>ως</u>) we forgive our debtors. καθως draws a closer, more important parallel and, often, gives the source of the example - either what has been already said, generally, or what has been said, specifically, in Scripture.[122] The most important thing about both these words, especially in the mouth of Jesus, is that they draw a parallel.[123] Since Jesus always taught in parables, this word is a signpost for an explanation.[124] The parable often begins: "the Kingdom of Heaven is like…" John the Baptist is saying: 'you know this passage in Isaiah – I am fulfilling it, even as we speak.'

John uses this word more than twice as many times as the Synoptics combined; two thirds of his uses occur in John's unique, extended, explanatory "table talk" section with Christ (chapters 13-16). And this follows from the fact that John is much more eager and direct about explaining who Jesus is. In contrast to the Synoptics, John is full of editorial dialogue between himself and the reader.[125] John is saturated with interpretive speeches by Christ - in public and in private.

---

[118] Colossians 4:1 *Masters,* (κυριοι) *give unto your servants that which is just and equal.*

[119] As in Revelation 14:13 *And I heard a voice from heaven saying unto me, Write, Blessed are the dead which die in the Lord* (κυριω) *from henceforth.* The dative goes with the preposition εν. See also 19:1.

[120] As in Matthew 6:24 *No man can serve two masters* (κυριοις).

[121] Of his 51 uses of this word, John uses the vocative form 33 times.

[122] For example: John 3:14 *And <u>as</u> Moses lifted up the serpent in the wilderness, even so must the Son of man be lifted up.*

[123] John 5:23 *That all men should honour the Son, <u>even as</u> they honour the Father.*

[124] John 14:31 *But that the world may know that I love the Father; and <u>as</u> the Father gave me commandment, even so I do.*

[125] For example, see: 2:21-25, 5:18, 6:6, 7:39, 12:16 etc.

The Synoptic Gospel claims that only *one* sign will be given - the sign of Jonas the prophet - specifically, his three-day ordeal in the belly of a fish. John is full of "signs." The Synoptics bring misunderstanding into sharp relief. But John is reluctant to allow misunderstanding to develop. *Then said the Jews, Forty and six years was this temple in building, and will you rear it up in three days? But he spoke of the temple of his body.*[126] *When therefore the Lord knew how the Pharisees had heard that Jesus made and baptized more disciples than John - though Jesus himself baptized not, but his disciples.*[127]

ειπεν

ειπεν, again, is the aorist (3rd person singular) of λεγω, which means "say," is one of the speaking verbs we discussed above in John 1:15. This aorist form is preferred in the narrative genre. Indeed, it is rarely used in the epistolary material, making 96% of its appearances in the Gospel/Acts sequence. For that matter, it occurs, specifically, as ειπεν (he said) 70% of the time. A common construction in John is απεκριθη … και ειπεν: "he answered and said." Often, all three of these speaking words occur together in dialogue: Jesus answered (απεκριθη) them and said (ειπεν), Verily, verily, I say (λεγω) unto you…[128]

ησαιας ο προφητης

Just as we have transliterated the Hebrew into "Isaiah," so the Greek transliteration comes out as ησαιας.

Exegetical Considerations: Isaiah is the first prophet we encounter in the Gospels. In Matthew, the Angel begins with an allusion to Isaiah 7:14, and Matthew, interprets what the angel says to Mary by quoting him directly: *Now all this was done, that it might be fulfilled which was spoken of the Lord by the prophet, saying, Behold, a virgin shall be with child, and shall bring forth a son, and they shall call his name Emmanuel, which being interpreted is, God with us.*[129]

---

[126] John 2:20-21.
[127] John 4:1-2 But sometimes John subtly allows the reader to work things out independently. *Many of the people therefore, when they heard this saying, said, Of a truth this is the Prophet. Others said, This is the Christ. But some said, Shall Christ come out of Galilee? Hath not the scripture said, That Christ cometh of the seed of David, and out of the town of Bethlehem, where David was?* (7:40-42).
[128] John 6:26.
[129] Matthew 1:22-23.

All four Gospels quote (or paraphrase) Isaiah 40:3: *The voice of him that crieth in the wilderness, Prepare ye the way of the LORD, make straight in the desert a highway for our God.* Matthew and Luke both quote Isaiah 9:2: *The people that walked in darkness have seen a great light: they that dwell in the land of the shadow of death, upon them hath the light shined.* John thematically alludes to it: *Then spake Jesus again unto them, saying, I am the light of the world: he that followeth me shall not walk in darkness, but shall have the light of life.*[130] In his Ephesian letter, Paul alludes to it: *But all things that are reproved are made manifest by the light: for whatsoever doth make manifest is light. Wherefore he saith, Awake thou that sleepest, and arise from the dead, and Christ shall give thee light.*[131] Matthew 8:17 quotes Isaiah 53:4 in order to set the stage for a continuing argument about why Christ had to die: *Himself took our infirmities, and bare our sicknesses.* Matthew quotes[132] Isaiah 42:1-4 in order to support the argument that Christ's ministry is truly universal in import: *Behold my servant, whom I uphold; mine elect, in whom my soul delighteth; I have put my spirit upon him: he shall bring forth judgment to the Gentiles. He shall not cry, nor lift up, nor cause his voice to be heard in the street. A bruised reed shall he not break, and the smoking flax shall he not quench: he shall bring forth judgment unto truth. He shall not fail nor be discouraged, till he have set judgment in the earth: and the isles shall wait for his law.*

More practically, Matthew quotes[133] Isaiah 6:9-10 to explain why Jesus uses parables: *And he said, Go, and tell this people, Hear ye indeed, but understand not; and see ye indeed, but perceive not. Make the heart of this people fat, and make their ears heavy, and shut their eyes; lest they see with their eyes, and hear with their ears, and understand with their heart, and convert, and be healed.* Matthew makes a composite quote from Isaiah and Jeremiah to explain why Jesus is cleansing the temple: *It is written, My house shall be called the house of prayer; but ye have made it a den of thieves.*[134]

---

[130] John 8:12.
[131] Ephesians 5:13-14.
[132] 12:18-21.
[133] 13:14-15.
[134] Matthew 21:13 – Isaiah 56:7c; Jeremiah 7:11.

Outside of the Psalms and the Pentateuch itself, Matthew draws most heavily upon Isaiah (Figure 4 below):

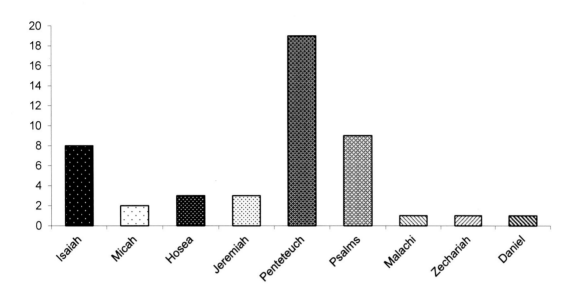

Figure 4. Matthew's Reliance on the Old Testament

Though John is sparse in quoting the OT, his overall reliance is proportionately similar to Matthew's. John has many fewer references to the Pentateuch because he lacks Matthew's sermon on the mount and similar sermons, which make extensive reference to the law. The important thing to remember about John is that though he is sometimes strangely dissimilar to the Synoptic Gospel, this strangeness can only be understood in the context of the many similarities between them. This is one of them.

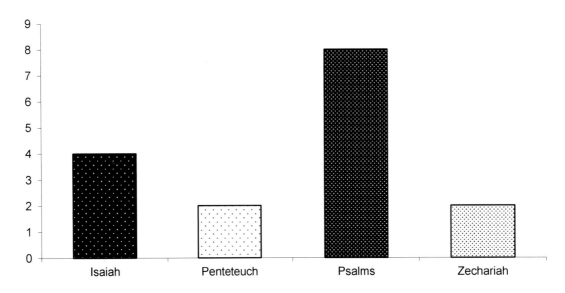

Figure 5. John's Reliance on the Old Testament

προφητης   We discussed this unusual "first declension" noun, which seems to mix and match feminine and masculine characteristics. Here are all its forms. Here again, bold means that John uses this a few times but only in his Gospel. Grey means that John does not use it at all.

	Singular		*Plural*
N	**προφητης**		προφηται
G	προφητου		προφητων
D	-		προφηταις
A	προφητην		προφητας
V	-		-

<u>Exegetical Considerations</u>: We are nearing the end of a major editorial purpose of John: to distinguish Christ from John the Baptist. Note the progression of ideas. First there is an enormous Christology. Second, there is the Apostle John's belabored act to distinguish Christ from John the Baptist. Thirdly, there will be the wedding at Cana, which clearly intimates that that Christ is here to prepare for a wedding, for which John the Baptist will soon identify himself as the bridegroom - just after Jesus concludes a soliloquy with Nicodemus about the children he expects to produce from this marriage.

We have seen what John denies – he is not Christ, nor Elijah. He doesn't even see himself as one of the prophets, although Jesus himself affirms that he is. Now we have seen what John affirms: <u>he</u> is the voice crying in the desert to which Isaiah refers. What is it that this voice cries?

In his Gospel, Matthew reckons three, fourteen generational blocks 1) Abraham to David 2) David to the Captivity (in Babylon) and 3) the Captivity to Christ. That is, Christ has come to deliver his people from captivity. Luke's prologue is also very strongly setting the record straight, showing the inferiority of John the Baptist compared to Christ. And he says that when John the Baptist's Father's tongue was loosed, he prophesied about this very thing – God has visited and redeemed his people. The horn of salvation has sounded. That which has been repeated by the prophets since the world began is now upon us. Now we will be delivered from the hands of those who hold us captive (even if they be, in part, our own) and from all those who hate us (even if they be, in part, our own selves), that we might serve God in holiness and righteousness without fear for the rest of our lives ... and that John the Baptist, Zacharias' own son, will be called *the prophet of the Highest: for thou shalt go before the face of the Lord to prepare his ways; To give knowledge of salvation unto his people by the remission of their sins, Through the tender mercy of our God; whereby the dayspring from on high hath visited us, To give light to them that sit in darkness and in the shadow of death, to guide our feet into the way of peace.*[135]

<u>This</u> is what the voice of Isaiah was crying. Listen to how it resonates with what Zacharias said in Luke:

Comfort ye, comfort ye my people, saith your God. Speak ye comfortably to Jerusalem, and cry unto her, that her warfare is accomplished, that her iniquity is pardoned: for she hath received of the LORD'S hand double for all her sins. The voice of him that crieth in the wilderness, Prepare ye the way of the LORD, make straight in the desert a highway for our God. Every valley shall be exalted, and every mountain and hill shall be made low: and the crooked shall be made straight, and the rough places plain: And the glory of the LORD shall be revealed, and all flesh shall see it together: for the mouth of the LORD hath spoken it. The

---

[135] Luke 1:67-79.

voice said, Cry. And he said, What shall I cry? All flesh is grass, and all the goodliness thereof is as the flower of the field: The grass withereth, the flower fadeth: because the spirit of the LORD bloweth upon it: surely the people is grass. The grass withereth, the flower fadeth: but the word of our God shall stand for ever. O Zion, that bringest good tidings, get thee up into the high mountain; O Jerusalem, that bringest good tidings, lift up thy voice with strength; lift it up, be not afraid; say unto the cities of Judah, Behold your God! Behold, the Lord GOD will come with strong hand, and his arm shall rule for him: behold, his reward is with him, and his work before him. He shall feed his flock like a shepherd: he shall gather the lambs with his arm, and carry them in his bosom, and shall gently lead those that are with young.[136]

και οι   απεσταλμενοι ησαν εκ των φαρισαιων
And those being sent   were of the   Pharisees

απεσταλμενοι

> We have already encountered this perfect passive participle (having been sent) of this word in John's 6th sentence: *there was a man having been sent from God*...(απεσταλμενος). There it was in the nominative singular ending with ος. Here it is in the nominative plural, functioning similarly as the subject of the sentence, ending with οι.

ησαν We have already reviewed the *present* tense forms of the state of being verb ειμι (Hewett, 5.8).

Singular		Plural	
ειμι	*I am*	εσμεν	*we are*
ει	*you are*	εστε	*you are*
εστι(ν)	*he, she, it is*	εισι(ν)	*they are*

Here are the imperfect tense forms which occur in our literature. All but ην occur just a handful of times.

Singular		Plural	
ημην	*I was*[137]	ημεν	*we were*[138]
ης	*you were*	ητε	*you were*
ην	*he, she, it was*	ησαν	*they were*

---

[136] Isaiah 40:1-11.

[137] This occurs only three times in John. For example: *And I am glad for your sakes that I was* (ημην) *not there*...(11:15).

[138] Used very infrequently in the NT, for example: *Even so we, when we were* (ημεν) *children, were in bondage under the elements of the world* (Galatians 4:3).

εκ των φαρισαιων

This phrase, "of the Pharisees," is distinctly Johannine, occurring five time in his Gospel. Indeed, John uses the genitive construction εκ των 33 times, whereas all three Synoptics use it but 19 times. Likewise John uses the genitive singular construction εκ του 47 times, 13 times as εκ του ουρανου[139] ("of" or "from heaven"[140]).

---

[139] εκ των ουρανων (out of the heavens) does occur 3 times, but not in John.
[140] He will use this phrase another 18 times in Revelation, making it primarily a Johannine construction.

και ηρωτησαν αυτον
and they asked   him

και   ειπον αυτω
and (they) said   to him

τι   ουν   βαπτιζεις
why then   do you baptize

ει συ ουκ ει ο χριστος
if you not are the Christ

ουτε   ηλιας
neither Elias

ουτε   ο προφητης
neither the prophet

και ηρωτησαν αυτον

> The verb ερωταω (ask) has already been use once by John in the 19th
> sentence - ερωτησωσιν, in the aorist subjunctive. Here it is in the aorist
> indicative. It is simply: "and they asked him..."

και ειπον αυτω

> "and said to him" is somewhat redundant. Yet it follows the
> convention of the Synoptic template. Very often Matthew will use
> some variant of ο δε αποκριθεις ειπεν ("but he answering, said:") John
> will also use this variant, yet he also uses this preferential phrase (και
> ειπον αυτω) 11 of 13 times. Notice that the verb "say" takes an object in
> the dative case: αυτω, whereas ερωταω above, takes an object in the
> accusative case (αυτον).

τι ουν βαπτιζεις

> This phrase begins with the interrogative, τι. In most cases τι ουν
> means "what then?" Here, context demands a translation of "why
> then?" as in Matthew 17:10b: *Why then* (τι ουν) *say the scribes that Elias
> must first come?*

ει συ ουκ ει ο χριστος

In this phrase, the conditional particle ει ("if") occurs with a homonym ει, the second person singular of the verb "to be" which we have already looked at a few times. This occurs 15 times in the Gospel/Acts sequence – all of which have to do with Christ, but never with the negative, except here. John is still working the argument that John is not to be compared to Christ; as if to say: if John the Baptist is not the Christ, who <u>is</u> he? And this line of argumentation betrays the fact that many thought that John the Baptist was Christ, yet John never directly acknowledges, editorially, that this misconception was so widespread. As we mentioned, Luke, on the other hand, does: *And as the people were in expectation, and all men mused in their hearts of John, whether he were the Christ, or not…*[141]

ουτε ηλιας   ουτε is not declined, that is, it always occurs in this form. Since it means "neither" or "nor," it will, like the English, have another negative (like "no," "not," or even another "neither") close by. The Synoptics all sort out who Elias is in the pericope of Peter's confession and in the pericope of the Transfiguration.

ουτε ο προφητης

But the question is: who is *the* prophet. In sentence 21, the religious establishment grills John the Baptist: Are you the Christ? Are you Elijah? Are you the prophet? We have discussed the significance of this before. The presence of the article does not necessarily mean "the" prophet. But we do find out in Peter's sermon in Acts and in Stephen's sermon in Acts that Jesus Christ is <u>the</u> prophet which Moses foretold would come and be especially like himself. Well into his ministry, Jesus is to tell the people: *what went ye out for to see? A prophet? yea, I say unto you, and more than a prophet. For this is he, of whom it is written, Behold, I send my messenger before thy face, which shall prepare thy way before thee. Verily I say unto you, Among them that are born of women there hath not risen a greater than John the Baptist.* And yet Jesus and all the apostles maintain that Jesus is indeed greater than John the Baptist.

---

[141] Luke 3:15.

απεκριθη   αυτοις   ο ιωαννης λεγων
answered   them   - John   saying

εγω βαπτιζω εν υδατι
I   baptize   in water[142]

μεσος[143]   δε   υμων   εστηκεν[144]
in the middle   but (of) you has stood

ον[145]   υμεις[146] ουκ   οιδατε[147]
(one) whom you   (do) not   know[148]

---

[142] Always means "water" but sometimes used figuratively. It is important to see how John uses figures. (*Jesus answered and said unto her, If thou knewest the gift of God, and who it is that saith to thee, Give me to drink; thou wouldest have asked of him, and he would have given thee living water* John 4:10 Also John 4:14 *But whosoever drinketh of the water that I shall give him shall never thirst; but the water that I shall give him shall be in him a well of water springing up into everlasting life.* Also John 7:38 *He that believeth on me, as the scripture hath said, out of his belly shall flow rivers of living water.* This could be contrasted with out of the mouth: *And the serpent cast out of his mouth water as a flood after the woman, that he might cause her to be carried away of the flood.* (Revelation 12:15) Also John 19:34 *But one of the soldiers with a spear pierced his side, and forthwith came there out blood and water*).

Also this can be contrasted with being baptized in the Holy Ghost. Just as there are two baptisms, there are two births: Jesus answered, *Verily, verily, I say unto thee, Except a man be __born__ of water and of the Spirit* (John 3:5). The word is only used once in the Pauline corpus and that figuratively: That he might sanctify and cleanse it with the washing of water __in__ the word (Ephesians 5:26) Because God did not send Paul to baptize, (Paul says) but to preach the gospel (1st Corinthians 1:17).

For Paul, baptism represented death. Moses was the type for this: 1st Corinthians 10:2 *And were all baptized unto Moses in the cloud and in the sea...* Likewise: *we are buried with him by baptism into death: that like as Christ was raised up from the dead by the glory of the Father, even so we also should walk in newness of life.* (Romans 6:4) But in the end, water represents life: *And he shewed me a pure river of water of life, clear as crystal, proceeding out of the throne of God and of the Lamb... And the Spirit and the bride say, Come. And let him that heareth say, Come. And let him that is athirst come. And whosoever will, let him take the water of life freely.* Revelation 22:1; 17

[143] Here is the adjective which means "in the middle" in the nominative case modifying the verb "stand."

[144] Perfect tense.

[145] Here is the relative pronoun (accusative masculine singular) part of a phrase which defines who is standing. Within that phrase this pronoun stands for the one whom is not known; thus, as the object of verb know, is in the accusative case.

[146] This is the first occurrence of the nominative plural personal pronoun. John uses it almost twice as much as the Synoptics combined.

[147] Only John uses this phrase "you do not know" (six times).

[148] In five more sentences, John will say twice that __he__ did not know him. What could this mean? His limited knowledge of Jesus continues into the present. Both Matthew and Luke record that John is later to send disciples to Jesus from prison, asking him: *Art thou he that should come, or do we look for another?* At this point in the text, it is not clear what John the Baptist knows about Christ except that he knows that he is his younger cousin, but he also knows that he is not worthy to unloose his sandal

αυτος εστιν ο   οπισω μου ερχομενος
this   is   the (one)   behind   me   coming

ος   εμπροσθεν μου   γεγονεν[149]
who   before   me   had become

ου[150]   εγω ουκ ειμι αξιος[151]
of whom   I   not   am   worthy

ινα λυσω[152]   αυτου   τον ιμαντα[153] του υποδηματος[154]
that I might loosen[155]   (of) his -   the   thong   (of) shoe

---

strap. It may be assumed from this that John the Baptist knows some important things about Jesus the Christ. But there are other things about his person and work of which he is completely ignorant.

[149] Except for the relative pronoun ος, (which) we have already seen this sentence fragment in the 15th sentence.

[150] Without markings this might be taken as "not" but there is soon an ουκ that performs this function, thus this must be the relative pronoun again, this time in the *genitive* masculine singular.

[151] This is the first time that we have seen this word – "worthy." This is the only time that John uses this word in his Gospel. Strangely, the other Synoptic writers use ικανος which refers to *quantity* of worth, whereas αξιος is the more familiar – "worthy" as in: Lu 15:21 *And the son said unto him, Father, I have sinned against heaven, and in thy sight, and am no more **worthy** to be called thy son.*

[152] Aorist subjunctive.

[153] Masculine singular accusative (3rd declension).

[154] Luke and Mark both say something similar: οπισω μου ου ουκ ειμι ικανος κυψας λυσαι τον ιμαντα των υποδηματων αυτου.

[155] This is the first time that we have seen this word in John. It means "to free." Sometimes that is a good thing; sometimes bad. **Loose** [Lazarus], *and let him go* - is good. **Destroy** *this temple, and in three days I will raise it up* - is bad. The connecting idea is *undoing*, as in *breaking* commandments, *loosing* colts, *freeing* from an infirmity, *escaping* the pains of death, *freeing* a prisoner, *destroying* the works of the devil…

Summary

John has a single focus in his Gospel: to tell us who Jesus is and to encourage us to believe this. John's opening argument defines Christ as the very logos of God. This grammar has been written so that you might become more fully equipped to understand what John has written and that you might believe him.

Appendix 1: Hewett Grammar Review

Below is a table of most of the main elements of Hewett's grammar that we have mentioned and a recommendation in the "remarks" column about how closely you should study these elements. Our methodology has been to eschew, generally, memorization. But sometimes memorization can be very helpful.

Element	Page	Item #	Remarks
Pronouns	3-4	1.2.1	Know these pronoun categories
The Verbal System	4-5	1.2.2	Read and remember; include participles
Phrases	9-10	1.3	Read and remember
Clauses	10	1.4	Read and remember
Verb Formation	28	4.2	Read
Active and Future	29-30	4.3.1	Memorize present and future forms and endings
Parsing	30-31	4.4	Read
Verbal Aspect	31	4.5.1	Read
2nd Declension Nouns	35-36	5.1	Read
2nd Declension Endings	37	5.3.1	Memorize
Neuter 2nd Declension	38	5.3.3	Memorize
Cases	39-42	5.5	Know these cases
Masc. and Neuter Article	42	5.6.1	Memorize
The Verb "to be"	44	5.8	Memorize
1st Declension	47-52	6.1-6	Read and remember
Personal Pronouns	56-58	7.2	Memorize forms
Relative Pronouns	60-61	7.3.1	Memorize
Demonstrative Pronouns	65	8.1.1; 2.1	Memorize
Prepositions	71	9.1.1	Memorize
Adverbs	79	10.1.1	Memorize
Prepositions (2 Cases)	80	10.1.4	Memorize
Imperfect of "to be"	84	10.4	Memorize
Aorist	92-93	11.4.1-2	Read and remember
Perfect	103-104	12.2.2	Read and remember
Middle and Passive	111-115	13.3-4	Read and remember
Future of "to be"	116-117	13.5	Read
3rd Declension Nouns	140	16.4	Know these noun types
μι verbs	160-4	18.3	Know the conjugation of these verbs
Participle Formation	170-6	19.3	Know these forms
Translating Participles	184	20.2	Read and remember
Terms + Subjunctive	204	22.13	Know these words
Formation of Subjunctive	204-207	22.2-4.4	Read and remember
Infinitive	221	23.2-4	Read and remember
Common Irregular Verbs	274-76	Table 12	Study and remember
Common Verbs	309-10	Apx 5	Study and remember (meanings in Apx 3, pg. 277ff)
Regular Conjugation	311-12	Apx 6	Study and remember

Appendix 2: Steps of Translation:

Step one: clear your mind of noise and fears and expectations. You are entering into another dimension, where the vicissitudes of this life must be left at the gate. You are entering more intentionally into the presence of the Holy Spirit. So offer a short prayer of supplication for the spirit of a patient and obedient learner. And, of course, rejoice for the chance of such an adventure.

Step two: check the GNT for any textual issues.

Step three: do a longitudinal word or phrase study of the key words and phrases and their cognates (noun form, verb form, and any other compound made up with the word).

Step four: do a translational consistency check (if the translators are inconsistent, there might be additional problems with the word or phrase, especially in rendering it into our culture). Look for recurring phrases that use this word.

Step Five: look for antonymical sentences in which opposite words are coupled together (e.g., light and dark). A list of similar words is itself a longitudinal study.

Step Six: look for sentences that list similar words together or conjoin two close connotations (ex: joy and gladness).

Step Seven: start backing out of the passage into the larger literary unit. What function does this passage play in the larger flow of the literary unit (i.e., Gospel, epistle, historical narrative)? What is the author trying to say? How is what he is saying related to his entire corpus? What is the setting (sitz im leben) of the sentence, the larger unit, the corpus?

Remember: as servants of the word, we begin by listening, not by talking. A Biblical passage is not a piece of modeling clay that we immediately begin fiddling with to see what kind of clever piece of existentialism we can make from it. Let the passage make us. Have no agenda. Let it be His agenda. If we are truly in the presence of the Holy Spirit, then we must let our minds be populated by his building blocks. He will arrange them. And he will lead us to understand this arrangement with the rational apparatus of "poetic diction" that he has been creating in us for eons. And what you find at the end of such a passive exploration will be the word of life – for yourself and for the Church of Christ.

Appendix 3: Ten Reasons Why the New Testament is Not Presenting Myth

The Standard Model of Biblical criticism utterly fails to explain why we must exchange a stereoscopic Apostolic Christ for a modern zoo of psychologically determined christs. The Standard Model insists that the Apostolic Christ is nothing but a psychological projection and that the *real*, historical jesus has simply dropped out of historical view. It insists that all that is left to the historian is the certain knowledge that Jesus <u>cannot</u> be the *Apostolic* Christ. This is a very suspicious historical perspective.[1]

Liberalism has wearied the world with who Jesus cannot be. What the world needs now is a convincing idea of who Jesus is. One thing is for certain: whatever sort of ordinary historical jesus we assume as the starting point of our modern theory, we must also end with an ordinary psychological and literary theory of how the Apostles all evolved such an extraordinarily unified, "non-historical" jesus.

At first, the Standard Model seems to work pretty well. The idea that the gospellers projected their *own* personalities and religious "holy man" ideals upon Christ, such that we have a Matthean Christ and a Johannine Christ, could account for the distinctive differences in perspectives of each Gospel. The problem comes in when the Standard Model fails to extract a lowest common denominator jesus from these four psychological projections - despite the fact that we live in a literary age in which men pride themselves on their ability to make critical psychological evaluations. These evaluations should yield comprehensive insights on what motivated individual Gospellers and their formative communities. But so far, we have nothing - except a statement of denial: 'we have not found the historical Jesus. We know not from whence he is.'[2]

The Standard Model assumes a theological evolution which has been projected upon the memory of the historical Christ. This projection is alleged to have begun with the Gospels and elaborately continued by the Apostle Paul. But this model has produced no comprehensive and credible theory about where such a theology could have come from, nor has it been able to extract a credible "historical" Jesus from this process of projection and elaboration. How could Paul have invented a complex, lawless religion in the face of his Pharisaical training? There are no circumstantial motives present in the text. What happened to Paul does not look like a theological

---

[1] When one begins looking into such claims, one is immediately confronted with a profound skepticism about <u>all</u> of history, and not just about the historical Christ.
[2] John 9:29b.

evolution. One day he is killing Christians. The next he is arguing in the Synagogues that Jesus is the Christ. It will not do to say that he had an epiphany about a lawless religion on the one hand and then to accuse him of an excessively legalistic Christianity on the other. And if Paul *did* dream up this vast theological system in the depths of his own, tortured psychology, how did he single-handedly win over Peter, Matthew and Mark, proud, but bigoted Jews - and so many of the other Apostles?

Nevertheless, let us ignore for the moment that the Standard Model does not know what the true historical jesus looks like. Let us assume, for the moment, that the jesus of history is some variant of the "good liberal," preaching some variant of modern existentialism far ahead of his time. The question now is: how did such an ordinary religious existentialist of history become the miracle working, only-begotten son of God in the minds of the Apostles? If the Apostolic accounts cannot be taken at face value as historically true, surely they can be taken at face value as historically false. And if they are historically false, then it should be relatively easy to prove this.

And this is the fatal flaw of the Standard Model - if we would only carefully examine the problem at this level we would find that it is not at all easy to prove that the Apostolic account is historically false. Thus we would immediately find, for example, that the Standard Model is very narrowly limited to the following two alternatives in explaining such a disjuncture; that is, again: how did such an ordinary religious existentialist of history become the miracle working, only-begotten son of God in the minds of the Apostles? Where did the Apostles get such a comprehensive and completed disjointed myth to project upon Jesus of Nazareth?

The Apostles foisted a community myth upon the data: that is, everyone knew that Christ's body was eaten by dogs (for example), but that the "spiritual" Christ was raised in some metaphysically parallel universe. Even though the accounts all seem to say, in the most restrictive and ordinary sense, that Jesus fed 5000 men, what *really* happened was that his teaching that "man does not live by bread alone" so suddenly became so metaphysically real to this very large assembly, that these people began to realize, en masse, that it was *as if* they had all eaten, become full and had twelve baskets of fragments left over.

This hypothesis encounters the following difficulties:

1) Roman and Greek myths come from the upper class. Literalism comes from fishermen, tax collectors, prostitutes and religious legalists. Folk culture does not originate legend and myth – it can only *perpetuate* it.

There is no coherent evidence that the Apostolic Christ has any direct linkage to a parent, established myth. It is *like* the "corn-god" myths. It is *like* Isis and Osiris. But there is no religious mentality pregnant to deliver such a myth into the lower class of Palestine of that time.

2) <u>It projects a Cartesian worldview of dualism upon the apostolic mind.</u> This phenomenon is described as *logomorphism*, which is the tendency to project modern ways of thinking back into a logical age.[3] For example, the religious existentialism of the modern age, with its two-tiered conception of truth[4] appears to be completely unknown to the Apostolic community of the first century. This is everywhere present in the way that the authors of the New testament materials are completely aware of the parabolic nature of language itself; i.e., they do not childishly play with language - they are conscious of all the rhetorical categories - of myth and parable, figures and types, discursively logical and poetically metaphorical. And the major players of the stories are ordinary people - who knew the difference between normal and abnormal - who knew that virgins don't get pregnant.

There is no blurring in the Apostolic narratives between fantasy and reality of the kind which exists in the <u>modern</u> mind. There are no unimaginably unintuitive quantum theories of parallel universes in the Apostolic mind. Either a cat is dead or it is not dead - not dead and alive at the same time - as in some modern ideas of physics. There are no "virtual realities" in which history itself is a shadowy abstraction. There is no "paranormal." There is no reheated Persian pantheism which says that the world is all an illusion or a dream of God. The world of the Apostles was hard and real - just as it was to Aristotle. Yes, it was populated with a pantheon of spirits. But these spirits were as real as rocks. There is no word for "real" in the Greek. The Apostolic world simply did not conceive of a metaphysical, modern world of unprovable parallel "dark" universes, dark energy and dark matter which comes popping in and out of existence. The alleged myth-making of the Apostles looks very much like the projected face of the superstitions of the modern mind.[5]

---

[3] Owen Barfield, *Poetic Diction*. Wesleyan University Press. 1973. Pg. 90 (c 1928 Faber and Gwyer, Ltd.)

[4] This phenomenon was explored at great length and with considerable precision in Francis A. Schaeffer's thesis in *The God Who is There* and *Escape From Reason*. (c 1968, IVP)

[5] It may be suspected that the true modern, psychological motive force behind this blind projection is the unwavering commitment to a pantheistic universe - that Jesus *could* not have been representative of any other reality. That Jesus could have *only* been teaching that his two "worlds " were the worlds of deceptive sense and the incomprehensible "other" wherein all things are god. But the other world of Jesus is a very busy place. It is populated with the same sorts of concrete particulars that inhabit *this* world – angels, for example, and the souls of just men made perfect, who have each been given a "white stone" individuality" that no man can know save himself and God. The suspicion rests on the common unreality of the sensible world between "modern" science and pantheism. And there is a common reductionism at work in both this "eastern" religious ethos and the new "western" scientific

3) <u>It contradicts the expressly stated purpose and reporting methodology of the Apostolic community</u>. All the Apostles are quite aware that there was an "invisible" world everywhere interpenetrating the visible world, but in their witness to the events concerning Christ, it is made perfectly clear that there is no attempt to confuse the two - there is no confounding of "spiritual sight" with physical sight: *That which was from the beginning, which we have heard, which we have seen with our eyes, which we have looked upon, and our hands have handled, of the Word of life.*[6] And this is precisely the reporting methodology which the Apostles say that Christ commanded: *Then Jesus answering said unto them, Go your way, and tell John what things ye have seen and heard; how that the blind see, the lame walk, the lepers are cleansed, the deaf hear, the dead are raised, to the poor the gospel is preached.*[7] It is the same method assumed when Christ chides Nicodemus: *If I have told you earthly things, and ye believe not, how shall ye believe, if I tell you of heavenly things?*[8] And this method is assumed when Christ condemns the self-inflicted blindness of the religious establishment of the day: *You hypocrites, you can discern the face of the sky and of the earth; but how is it that you do not discern this time?*[9]

4) <u>The Apostles could not have been using "myth" as an argument to prove that the supernatural did exist, because in the first century, the existence of the "supernatural" was a universal assumption.</u> The *modern* presumption that the supernatural cannot exist does not fit with the climate of the time. The significance of miracles in the Gospel stories was not that they "really" occurred as opposed to only seeming[10] to occur. The emphasis was on the nature, magnitude and coherence of the miracles. For example, Herod surmised that Jesus might be John the Baptist returning from the dead. This was a superstitious world. It is illogical to suppose that the Apostles felt compelled to "prove" a supernatural one.

5) <u>The Apostles were psychologically incapable of producing a myth of such intensity, creativity and durability.</u> Modern theories place the apostolic myth in conflict with the "historical Christ." But if the Apostles did not get the myth from the historical Christ, where *did* they get it? From some clever, gnostic Essene-like secret cult? Then why do the makers of a very clever and consistent myth portray themselves as unenlightened fools? Whether the Apostolic Christ be right or wrong,

---

epistemology. Higher level structures are dismissed in search of a singular and more elementary (reductionist) *real* force back of all things.

[6] 1st John 1:1.
[7] Luke 7:22.
[8] John 3:12.
[9] Luke 12:56.
[10] This subsequently became relevant to some extent with the Docetists and the Gnostics who believed that the establishment had confused appearance with reality.

the fact remains that the Apostles have created a religion that far, far surpasses any of the tepid "historical jesuses" which have been recently "discovered."

6) <u>The Gospels do not *look* like the Greek, Roman or Pseudo-Gospel myth.</u> The pseudo-canonical writings illustrate this. There, the miracles are the main attraction. They are fantastic, unrelated and almost certainly false. With the New Testament writers, everything is different. One gets the sense that if they all had to choose between presenting the historical Christ-event or relating the miracle accounts, they would have unhesitatingly dropped the miracles. This also explains the inattention to major details, the cavalier attitude about "accuracy", the incidental stuff still embedded in the pericopes (like bending down to draw in the sand, or the young man that fled away naked in the garden) and the unflinching, almost uncaring inclusion of the utter foolishness of the apostles themselves.

The poetically unrelated fantastical flights of fancy (for example, Heracles) are missing in the Gospels. The significant thing is not that documents like The *Infancy Gospel of Thomas* exist; the significant thing is that similar undisciplined literary excursions are rigidly excluded from the four Gospels. There is a distinct genre difference. The earliest observable phenomena of canon formation betrays the fact that others saw this genre difference too. When authorship could not be fixed by reliable testimony as having originated within the Apostolic cadre, this genre criterion was always valid in helping to determine authorship. In such cases it is reasonable to assume that apocryphal writings were rejected by the post-apostolic community not primarily because of their fantastical, mythical content as such, but because it was believed that such content could not have come from an Apostolic hand.[11]

7) <u>There was insufficient time for a myth-making community racked by the Jew/Gentile controversy and the Paul/James theological dispute to generate a mythical overlay of such uniformity.</u> This community did not exhibit the characteristics of "group-think." The Synoptics, for example, all take casual liberty paraphrasing factual details of what happened. One writer softens this; another hardens that, but the uniformity is undeniable and inexplicable. There was insufficient time for a "faith community" to arise that could account for this uniformity. Additionally, there are no visible "mind-guards" to prevent the kind of diversity that we do see and to prevent the presentation of other internal community conflicts and embarrassments such as Paul's censure of Peter, Paul's dispute with Mark, the early unrest in an apartheid Jerusalem Church between Jew and Gentile, and Peter's betrayal of Christ.

---

[11] This helps explain why Revelation was among the disputed books for a time.

Paul's justification by faith is unceremoniously juxtapositioned with James' justification by works. No intermediate argument exists in the New testament materials attempting to reconcile these two positions - which would immediately suggest a revision or "norming" of the facts by a "faith community." Internal to the documents, there is witness to such an authoritative community, but there is insufficient time to account for this authoritative community apart from the mechanism which the documents themselves affirm. If the Apostolic community was not constituted by the historical, Apostolic figure of Christ – where did it come from? And it is not only that a relatively uniform, authoritative set of beliefs about Jesus has to be achieved in a few ticks of the sociological clock. If the genre of the Gospel is myth, we must also account for a *multi*-tiered uniformity. First there must have been a theological consensus (the "good liberal", the "apocalyptic radical", "the lamb of God" etc.). Then there must also be the uniformity of the mythological overlay that was projected upon this consensus.

8) <u>The Apostolic community had no official community theological *system* to "protect."</u> In the case of the evolving community that we see in the Luke / Acts sequence, whether one starts with Mary's hymn of praise, or Paul's warnings about worldly wisdom in Corinthians and Colossians, there is a very clear sense that sophisticated and elite theological systems are things to be very strongly wary of. This was a community that did not embrace a theological system so much as it embraced an unsystematized cluster of beliefs. Their primitive creeds are lists of beliefs which mixed items of historical fact with theological idea: *For I delivered unto you first of all that which I also received, how that Christ died for our sins according to the scriptures; And that he was buried, and that he rose again the third day according to the scriptures: And that he was seen of Cephas, then of the twelve: After that, he was seen of above five hundred brethren at once; of whom the greater part remain unto this present, but some are fallen asleep.*[12] But the fundamentalism of this community is nevertheless severe. Regarding the core of what *was* taught - there is nothing but intolerance for dissent. By contrast, the oracles and visions behind the classical myths were only *partly* believed by the Greeks and Romans, and so their writers felt free to aggressively manipulate even the core facts of their myths in order to preserve and protect their theory of history from political sabotage.[13]

9) <u>There are no linguistic hints in the primary materials that the New Testament Documents are mythological abstractions of perfectly normal sensory events.</u> In a myth, the author is invisible. But in the Gospel materials, we find the author having a dialogue with the reader because the author was a *participant* in the very story that he is telling. The myth, once it has been created, reads like a nursery story - full of one-dimensional flat facts - like an old wives' tale. But in the New Testament

---

[12] 1st Corinthians 15:3-6.

[13] Just as today we use "idealized" history to accomplish the same thing.

literature, there is a rich variety of multi-layered "poetic diction," that is, ordinary figures of speech, which betrays its non-mythical character. In myth, there is very little psychologizing because mythical heroes are not men of flesh and blood. But in Acts, the sophisticated subtleties of interpersonal machination is clearly evident, especially as Luke accurately portrays how Paul is delivered up the chain of command to Caesar through Lysius, Festus, and Agrippa.

10) <u>That Christianity soon found itself in a titanic struggle with Docetism and Gnosticism shows that it was a cluster of historically rooted beliefs that was absolutely intolerant of a mythical reinterpretation.</u>

The Apostles did not embrace myth or religious abstraction. They vehemently fought against it. At every point of contact, the second and third generation Church violently opposed the mythical systems of Docetism specifically, and Gnosticism generally, on the grounds that the historical facts about Christ, as well as the authority and succession of his Bishops, could be established and authenticated on ordinary, rational grounds. Succeeding Bishops were soon to argue that if the Apostles secretly embraced a mythological docetism,[14] then they utterly failed to pass it on to their immediate successors. One can see a battle against these mythical interpretations in the very text of 1st John: *That which was from the beginning, which we have heard, which we have seen with our eyes, which we have looked upon, and our hands have handled, of the Word of life.*[15] One can also see a rigid intolerance against religious abstraction in Paul early in his preaching: *Now if Christ be preached that he rose from the dead, how say some among you that there is no resurrection of the dead? But if there be no resurrection of the dead, then is Christ not risen: And if Christ be not risen, then is our preaching vain, and your faith is also vain...And if Christ be not raised, your faith is vain; ye are yet in your sins.*[16] Surely, if the Apostles were consciously projecting a mythological, theological abstraction upon a perfectly ordinary stream of historical events, despite these statements, they would have been guilty of a conspiratorial hypocrisy of unimaginable proportions.

---

[14] Elsewhere called the "Apostolic Secret."

[15] 1st John 1:1.

[16] 1st Corinthians 15:12-14,17 And Paul reiterates this censure against religious abstraction in his last letter to Timothy: *But shun profane and vain babblings: for they will increase unto more ungodliness. And their word will eat as doth a canker: of whom is Hymenaeus and Philetus; Who concerning the truth have erred, saying that the resurrection is past already; and overthrow the faith of some.* (2nd Tim 2:16-18).

The Apostles were lying.

This hypothesis encounters the following difficulties:

1) <u>The Apostles were incapable of the moral turpitude required to falsely claim literality for a wholly untrue abstraction.</u> There is insufficient motive. One can imagine an investigator falsifying evidence in the name of justice, or a politician bearing false witness against his opponent for the good of the people. But the massive duplicity required in this case could not have arisen from a band of fishermen that went back to their fishing profession immediately after the crucifixion, who, when they finally *did* tell the story, uniformly portrayed themselves as morally defective fools.

2) <u>Men do not give their lives for a lie or a myth.</u> One figurehead man may die for a lie if he is crazy, but not a significant percentage of the leadership. A modern American Liberal, who has completely mythologized the cluster of Apostolic beliefs, would have no difficulty in denying the "literal" divinity of Christ (the virgin birth, etc.), and no difficulty in affirming the "functional" divinity of Caesar (since "we are all God's children") - if *he* had been faced by Roman persecution. Yet the early martyrs did not escape death in this way. They doggedly clung to ordinary propositional creedal statements when a simple admission that these statements were mythical or metaphorical in character would have saved them.

Conclusion: The New Testament accounts are not mythical in nature because the Apostolic community:

1.   had no coherent social linkages with a parent myth.

2.   did not have the necessary Cartesian worldview.

3.   expressly stated that its message was not mythical in nature.

4.   had no necessity to "prove" the existence of something (the supernatural) which was universally assumed.

5.   was incapable of producing a more "interesting" Christ than any of the sub-historical jesuses produced by modern research.

6.   failed to produce documents which conform to the classical genre of myth (for example: no fantastical flights of poetic fancy).

7.   did not have time to eliminate its own internal struggles, let alone create a seamless, multi-tiered, uniform, mythological "Christ of Faith" which seven ecumenical councils of world-wise men and eighteen hundred years of Christendom mistook as fact.

8.   had no theological system to "protect" from revisionism, especially in view of the fact that the struggle to understand what had happen is still going on within the documents themselves.

9.   employed a full range of poetic diction without any linguistic trace of a two-tiered, rigidly compartmentalized, gnostic use of language – and found itself *immediately* embroiled with the myth-oriented systems of Docetism and Gnosticism.

10. did not embrace myth or religious abstraction. They vehemently fought against it. And so did the religious leaders of successive centuries.

Appendix 4: Myth, Language and Parable in the NT

When we say that two things are "like" each other, we also imply that they are dissimilar. We move around the object in question, whether it be a mathematical object or a sensory object, observing its characteristics, making semantic catalogs of similarities between the object and other objects. When the catalog has become sufficiently extensive, we attempt to achieve various subgroupings within those catalogs, to bring concision and precision to our description. For example, in attempting to describe the system whereby the body wards off disease, we first begin to describe what we see by employing the language of mail distribution or traffic flow along city streets, which two things have no necessarily overarching logical patterns. But when we do see a larger pattern emerge, we employ the more restrictively definitive language of a more sophisticated system - like an infantry unit, which does have overarching logical patterns due to its imbedded strategic rationale. After our catalogs have become sufficiently expansive and have achieved a reasonable level of hierarchical simplification, we name the entire catalog with a one-word (or phrase) label. The rationale of choosing a label is very similar to the rationale of how many cultures chose personal names. When once a major characteristic of a person becomes known, a semantic piece of the name of the characteristic is chosen as the "formal" name of the person. Thereby is the relational matrix of all things built up into one whole within our minds.

Intentional failure to shift gears to the next logical level of hierarchical organization, even when virtually everyone sees that it can and must be done, can produce some striking humor. Consider, for example, Andy Griffith's comic routine describing the game of football. It is funny because he places all who know football above him while he apes the ignorance of a child's attempt to comprehend it. This procedure occasionally touches a nerve (regarding the irrational importance which has become attached to every facet of the game) with the innocent, blind wisdom of a child, thereby enabling us to laugh at ourselves in a benign, safe environment. Such a procedure, of stepping back from a "formally" designated phenomenon to a more fundamental stage of catalog building is usually the serious attempt to do "science." This is true since so much of our environment has been provisionally labeled with catalogs which have very few parabolic entries or arrangement in them - many of which are illusory or otherwise mistaken. In this case, the adoption of simpler language is characteristic of men of science who are attempting to avoid the defective labeling systems imbedded in the surrounding culture.

Similarly, if we are teaching at the level of "parable" we are teaching at a very low level of individual phenomena catalog building. Christ did this for many reasons. Firstly, the entire, traditional structure of the establishment religion had become so extensively corrupted with false ideas, that much of it had to be scrapped. Many of the conceptual catalog labels could no longer be employed by Christ without necessarily invoking huge tracts of conceptual corruption. The issue of "Corban" illustrates this. Here was a one-word semantic tool which could invoke an entire mindset regarding giving and responsibility which had effectively repudiated part of the original intent of the fifth commandment itself. So Christ dropped back to more fundamental language[1] in order to rebuild a matrix of semantic catalogs which more "scientifically" described the "Kingdom of God."

This retrograde teaching procedure allowed Christ to say strange things about why he taught in parables: "so that speaking…they would not hear." Nathan the prophet employed this same principle in confronting King David with his adulterous and murderous behavior. If he had simply approached the King with these "labels" he would have been rejected. So he approached the King with an extended, third-party, parabolic analogy which would allow David's mind to wander very deeply into the very catalogs of adultery and murder without knowing where Nathan was placing him on the moral landscape. After Nathan had extracted a self-incriminating judgment from David, he presented David, not with the labels, but with the fact that the metaphorical third-person object of David's contempt was indistinguishable from himself. This can be compared to the parable of the husbandmen who beat and killed the envoys of the absentee landlord. Christ asks the religious leaders to judge the religious establishment under the guise of this parable. After they have rendered it, Christ cinches the noose: "Therefore say I unto you, The kingdom of God shall be taken from you, and given to a nation bringing forth the fruits thereof." (Matthew 21:43)

Paraphrastic Latitude

Before the semantic gnosticism of the modern age, Christians would have explained their confidence in the Judeo-Christian "writings" such that they εκκρεμαμαι "hang on every" word, as implicit in a relationship with God the communicator. This would not be about literalism, per se. These documents are *his* mouthpieces. In considering these words, Christians would have said that they were not considering what others think what God thinks - a thinking of endless regress. They would have claimed to be considering - in the most primary sense possible - what *God* thinks. What *he* has spoken. This is quite independent of any idea of a doctrine of *infallibility*. It has everything to do with an idea of the *nature of inspiration*. In the conventional view, inspiration is a function of *degree of communication* and of *object*. In the Biblical view, inspiration is a function of _kind of communication_ and of _subject._[2] In the speech of nature and of history, God speaks parabolically - and we must infer

---

[1] This is one reason why the New Testament language about the Kingdom of God is easy enough for a child to understand.

[2] Only this could explain why Socrates viewed the utterances of the Delphic Oracles as *categorically different* then the inspiration of the poets or even of his own inner illumination. Obedience to one prophecy of Delphi irrevocably changed his life.

216

his meaning. But in these writings, we have God speaking to us plainly (παρρησια).[3] Though his speech to us is mediated, or brokered, by other men, this does not alter that fact. For God uses the weaknesses of our ordinariness in order to achieve extraordinary precision of expression of his word. God says precisely what he intends through our imprecision.

That is why the Gospellers feel the liberty to *paraphrase* our Lord's words. Because they know that the *intent* (spirit) of those words does not lie in the *technical* arrangement of them, but in the *artistic* arrangement of them. Since any technical grammatical construction (text) cannot convey a static algorithmic solution of fixed factness apart from the *con*text in which it is expressed. Though God's Word is unchanging and eternal, the context in which it is spoken is functionally relative for two reasons: 1) context is defined as the infinite number of *relations* between all his words and 2) God never stops speaking. Which is to say that God is eternally communicating. Which is to say that God is eternally loving. His love is eternal and unchanging. Yet he is eternally creating something out of nothing - that is, new, without changing himself. All the verb tenses have come down into the finitude of our being not as individually inferior shadows of God's "I am" but as a living matrix of a divine logos that is both the Alpha and Omega, the beginning and the ending, which is, and which was, and which is to come. (Revelation 1:8) - the One who makes all things new. (Revelation 21:5)

Each Gospeller is fully aware that though he could, through accurate research, ascertain the exact words of Christ, such exactitude would have little utility towards the project of *re-iterating* them since some provisional and partial replication of the context in which they were spoken must accompany them. We can take any given grammatical formula of words, and by altering the context - even just a little, the solution to the formula changes radically. One element of context which cannot be conveyed textually is the original *intonation* of the words. This is yet another reason to paraphrase the original grammatical algorithm. Then too the individual Gospellers are conscious of the finitude of their own speech - and that we, as their readers, will also be conscious of that speech, so they attempt to make provision for the fact that their own mental furniture - in which that speech must be constricted - has become a crucial part of the context. And that to give a precise replication of what they saw and heard must necessarily be assembled with fragments of their own linguistic equipment.

What is the point then in attempting to reconstruct the exact algorithm of Christ's words, when that algorithm is insoluble without the contexts which will be necessarily stripped away in such a process? What will be left is the same dead letter which the law itself had become. In the giving of the law, no context was given;

_____

[3] Hebrews 1:2.

hence it logically spawned volumes of commentary. It also spawned volumes of human behavior which attempted to conform itself to the letters of those commentaries, while escaping the more demanding spiritual intent which actualized them.

In considering the imprecision of multiple accounts of the same dialogues in the Synoptic tradition, it is an inescapable conclusion that these authors were approximating and interpolating Christ's words. The ultra-literalism of Liberalism sees this as a "corruption" imposed on the "actual" words of Christ. But God would say: "ye hypocrites, you say that you will not obey my words till you find or reconstruct them with the exactitude of a verbal photograph, yet you will not lift one finger in an attempt to obey their approximations. I gave my prophets *license* to do this with my words, and yet you do not hear them. How much less would you have heard my Son?"

The giving of this license is reasonable. Since a photograph means nothing without an explanation of the environment in which it was taken. Likewise, the historically literal words of Christ are often meaningless until they are given a context. Since the context is the infinite matrix of historical events which converge at a particular point, and since it is impossible to relate an infinite matrix, the Gospellers, each in their own way, construct a *representative* historical matrix in which to place Christ words. As the historical matrix is representative, so his words are also representative. They *must* be. Because the *meaning does not reside in the replication of the exact sequence of phonemes which issued from his mouth - the meaning resides in the intent of that sequence.* Since the historical matrix is impossible to reproduce with *any* linguistic model, it is to be expected that the Gospellers will rarely present a "phoneme formula" to us.[4]

We allow as much to disciples of other teachers. It is no breach of truth to move from: "he would have said in this context" to "he *did* say in that context." This is not just literary license. This should be the *expectation* of both the teacher and the disciples of his disciples - that his disciples will teach the meaning of his words and not engage in some superstitious project to acquire their very *physicality* - as if they were the literal relics of the teacher himself. One part of the historical matrix in which Christ's phoneme formulas occurred which cannot be reproduced (again, without the tediousness of the modern historical genre[5]) was the body language and inflections which must have accompanied them. To strip out these inflections and

---

[4] A possible exception to this rule are the one line conclusions to many of the parables, which retain *intrinsic* meaning even while placed in the context of a different pericope. Compare Matthew 19:30/20:16

[5] Which, as all writers know, is itself perishable, since however meticulous it is in recording the historical landscape, every word employed in the attempt to recreate that *landscape* is itself encumbered with perishable idioms.

body language and leave the skeleton of phonemes is surely <u>not</u> historical. But if the body language and inflections are not going to be described by the author in a special editorial narrator/reader dialogue overlay, then the phonemes *must* be changed in order to achieve the same relative meaning within a changed contextual matrix. This change is a change in the direction towards the light, not away.

What good would it do to actually succeed in exhuming the phoneme formula abstracted from the historical matrix which animated it? Wouldn't it be as purposeless as finding a brilliantly executed sketch of Christ by Peter, faithfully but secretly preserved in the Vatican archives? What good is a sketch when Mary saw him face to face and did not recognize him, Cleopas did not recognize him - Peter himself did not recognize him? The project of exhuming the phoneme formula of Christ is as hopeless and physically impossible as exhuming his animal body. The body is not there. It has changed and moved to a different place. Likewise, the words are not there. They have changed and moved to a different place. The letters are different. The spirit of them is eternally the same.

The historical-critical scholars accuse the Apostolic writers of stealing away the body of Christ words and hiding it in a projected mythologization in order to serve their own supposed political or religious ends. Perhaps the man on the street is not so conspiratorial. Perhaps he thinks that the "gardener" of ordinary historical processes has forever removed them, we know not why or how, and that is now pointless to look for him. But Christ has not been kidnapped by the Apostles or accidentally removed by the gardener. It is no wonder that the Gospellers make a close approach to the demanded historical methodology at precisely this point: they do not tell us about the resurrection itself. They tell us about the *absence* of the body and the re-appearance of Christ in the same yet altered form. Unless our "mythologization" exceeds that of Bultmann and Chardin, we will not see the Kingdom of God. Sail out onto the sea of mythologization and we will encircle the whole truth of God, and end our voyage in the same country of ordinary *literality* from which we departed.

Some have asked: 'why would Mark write after Matthew, when 90% of the material in Mark is already contained in Matthew?' But why does an artist paint a landscape that has already been painted by a hundred other artists? Still more distracting is it to suggest that a photograph captures the essence of the landscape better than a painting. For one thing, a photograph only records one slice of the data spectrum, whereas the human sensory apparatus includes a much wider swath. Also, just as in music, an instantaneous reproduction of what is happening in the orchestra (tonally) will not give the slightest hint of where the piece has been or where it is going. The human sensory apparatus - coupled with its time-lapse memory - will capture *movement* in color and tonal relationships. A really good artist can create the "effects" of this wider swath and tonal movement by departing from the parochial idiom of the photograph in unconventional ways. Likewise, poetic diction "deforms" language, as ordinarily employed, to capture the wider, essential, existential swath of life which is not captured by restrictive ("literal") discursive speech - as full as it is with jargon, colloquialisms, dead metaphors and other forms of meaningless - or near meaningless, "verbal behavior." We have already discovered what Mark is doing with his artwork: he has laid down a significant layer of new colors and new detail. His landscape has become more immediately alive. It achieves more gloom, more fear, more astonishment, more joy, and more pathos. It draws the reader further into a canvas which seems electric with the power of Christ.

What would revisionists do with a verbal photograph once they unearthed it? In an age of propaganda - when crafting the environment in accordance with presuppositions can make history mean anything, it really doesn't matter what the main character says - whether it is FDR or Elizabeth I. Even when the verbal photographs *are* in hand there will always be "heated controversy" surrounding the context which gives them meaning. Revisionism wants to "reconstruct" the verbal photographs because they have *already* reconstructed a history along deterministic lines in which to place them. Since the project is intrinsically hopeless, it is no wonder that a plethora of historical jesuses have emerged. The revisionists feel that if the verbal photograph of Christ could be unearthed it could surely be proved that Jesus was a "reed shaken in the wind," that he was demon possessed, or that he was a glutton for power, or that he was a deceiver of the people. That project in a continual state of failure, the Apostles have borne the accusation that they were lying, mythological projectionists, deceiving themselves and the people - presumably because they could not face the world "as it is."

A parable is like a piece of music. The parables and the repetitively episodic ministry have already been "given" by Christ. The Synoptics follow an unmistakable lyric line. Their only latitude is in arrangement. The modern problem comes down to this: revisionists believe that the Christ-event is just a meaningless string of strange happenings. And the Synoptic authors all took pen in hand and said: 'let me compose a literary melody which makes sense of these existential fragments.' And out come three scores that are amazingly similar, even to the employment of various musical clichés. It is therefore concluded that someone must have *plagiarized.*

But anyone who hears Beethoven's famous four notes in his Fifth symphony can no longer see them as meaningless. Hearing those four notes invoke the entire symphony. But give a man some staff paper - even a musical man - and tell him to write the score down, and what he'll reproduce will be too simplistic for even a high-school band. Now give that sheet to a professional musician who has been touring for the last twenty-five years playing nothing but that one piece of music. Now give it to a man who, of those first three years toured with the composer *himself...* He will no doubt be able to reproduce the main line and approximate supporting score - as would two other of his musical colleagues. How dissimilar the dynamics would these reproduced scores *be* - even if one was 2nd chair and the 3rd in a different section altogether?

The intent of this musical parable is not to dance around legitimate, concrete objections - it is to give concrete articulation to a phenomenon that these objections show little evidence of comprehension. And though all the Apostles know how to tell a story - some better than others - they were *not* professional storytellers. The modern project of revisionism first objects that none of these scores is a photographic reproduction of Beethoven's Fifth. That in fact, a completely different score - representing the folksy tunes of the day, has almost completely "washed out" Beethoven's original score. That the famous four notes were not the intention of the original Beethoven - that they were folksy embellishments produced a score of a completely different musical character and genre! This is why a parable is so stunningly precise and forceful in communicating a supernatural catastrophe - better than all of John's "books of the whole world." A parable comes with its own *limits* of interpretation.

How shall we then understand the New Testament? Should we take it "literally"? It is certainly not easy to find an equivalent for "literal" in the Greek lexicon. The word most often invokes an entire matrix of views about language and meaning which can only be understood within the framework of Modern Linguistic Analysis, Docetism or Buddhism or Quantum Physics - in which the sensory world, for one reason or another, is an illusion; i.e., things are not what they *seem* (δοκεω) to be. The problem, in our culture, is not that we cannot parse the various literary modes in the New Testament. It is that what is really buried in these questions is a skepticism so profound that parsing the literary modes of the New Testament is beside the point. As we mentioned at the beginning, it is not so much that we live in a "post-Christian" culture as that we live in a "post-language" culture. And there is simply no point in asking how we should parse the literary modes of a piece of religious literature, when we have already been immunized against the classical, philological basis of Western language as it has been handed down to us from the Greco-Roman world with very strong inoculations of modern views of communication which see language as nothing more than Wittgenstein's language game or a Skinnerian exercise of "verbal behavior."

And even if we were operating under the rules of classical language and logic, the question is not only an oversimplification; it is a species of the "excluded middle." One can think of any number of similar "excluded middle" kinds of question: "Do you believe in freedom?" But the context of this question is that it is asked within a milieu in which it is believed that there are two and only two extremes: hedonistic chaos or tyrannous conformity. In such a dualistic context, the words "For he that is called in the Lord, being a servant, is the Lord's freeman" would be meaningless.

One needs only to read a few pages of any serious, classical work on "Figures of Speech" to sense the underlying oversimplification of this question. The New Testament is to be accorded the same sort of empirical respect as any other literary phenomena. If we do not do this, we will be forced to consign the entire western literary project of discursively capturing the essence of objective reality into the dustbin. If we prejudge the New Testament as an essentially meaningless, non-discursive religious allegory, then it is simply a logical corollary to agree with the Buddhist, who views *all* Western discursive literature as the falsest sort of religious allegory, whether it be an *Elegy written in a Country Churchyard*, *Origin of Species* or *The Declaration of Independence*.

Bullinger says: "It would be safer to say that there are no allegories in Scripture than to follow one's own judgment as to what is allegory."[6] As Bullinger points out, the only express use of allegory in the New Testament is Galatians 4:24: "Which things are an allegory (αλληγορεω): for these are the two covenants; the one from the mount Sinai, which gendereth to bondage, which is Agar." Bullinger continues by making a crucial distinction: "The modern and common usage of the word *allegoria* is thus quite different from this Scriptural definition. According to the modern sense it is taken to mean a fictitious narrative which has another and deeper meaning then that which is expressed."[7]

One should not lightly dismiss the entire phenomena of the New Testament documents by means of philosophical presuppositions uncritically held by one's own culture. Because the general schemata of the New Testament literature, and the pointed statements of its authors are that we are here not dealing with religious allegory. Nor are we dealing with metaphor. In order for the metaphor to work properly, one thing is said to *be* another thing. For this literary trope to work properly, the two nouns must be mentioned and must be taken in their ordinary sense. The simile says for example, all flesh is *as* grass (1st Peter 1:24). The metaphor carries the figure across at once and says, "all flesh *is* grass." (Isaiah 40:6)[8] The surprise is in the suddenness of the copulative *is*. But it forces the reader to look for the points of comparison and discard the rest as beside the point. It is left to the ordinary reader what is to be retained and what is to be discarded. A lion is used of Christ *and* the devil.[9] Thieves will not inherit the kingdom of God, yet the coming of Christ is *as* a thief in the night.

What we are dealing with in the Gospels is openly stated by various editorial comments and explicit in their individual redactional emphasis. The genre is *parable*.

---

[6] *Figures of Speech Used in the Bible* Bullinger (Baker Book House), 749.
[7] Ibid.
[8] Ibid.
[9] Revelation 5:5 and 1st Peter 5:8, respectively.

The corresponding literary trope is a continued *simile*. Each of the Synoptics lacks a conclusion. This was so unnerving to early scribes that one was forcefully added to Mark. This is because each of the Synoptic authors is conforming to its genre: "no sign shall be give this generation except the sign of Jonas the Prophet." The book of Jonah ends with questions. So do the Synoptics.

The New Testament material is stated to be ordinary discourse which any *gnosis* discipline might use. Peter sums up this conviction in 2nd Peter 1:16 "For we have not followed cunningly devised fables, when we made known unto you the power and coming of our Lord Jesus Christ, but were eyewitnesses of his majesty." This sums up where parable leaves off and normal, empirical discourse begins. Though the feeding of the 5000 *was* parabolic of Christ as manna in the wilderness of Church formation, the disciples recorded as sensory data that 5000 *were* fed. To ensure that there is no possibility in missing this "literalism", it is added: *and they took up of the fragments that remained twelve baskets full*. The Gospel writers are unequivocal about the straightforward eyewitness character of the deeds and words of Christ. In terms of the parabolic content of Christ's teachings, the Gospel authors rivet our hermeneutics to the limitations of *simile*. That is, the parable of the sower is to be taken as "literally" *representational* of how God will judge the world as two similar triangles are to be taken in a geometric proof.

Beyond this, the ordinary rules of classical language apply. When we take an oath, we say that we have no mental reservations - that is, we are not harboring any philosophical allegories in our head which would allow us to ethically subscribe to our idiosyncratic representations of the oath against the commonly excepted representation of the official who administers it to us. This is what Christ accused the religious establishment of Israel. He claimed that their rationalistic interpretive allegories (paradosis) had *set aside* the ordinary, *literal* meaning of God's commandments and had substituted man-made ideas in their place.

The Epistle writers saw themselves as explicating the Christ-Parable of the Synoptic *Jonas-Genre*. And just as Christ explained his parables to the disciples privately, so we see the Pauline tradition explaining the purpose of Christ's death. And Paul would brook no deviation from this explanation. *But though we, or an angel from heaven, preach any other gospel unto you than that which we have preached unto you, let him be accursed. As we said before, so say I now again, If any man preach any other gospel unto you than that ye have received, let him be accursed.*[10]

It is perfectly normal to see Paul's *experience with Christ* as relative. It is simply a matter of fact that others had other interpretations of the facts. One can think of the Judas Experience or the Sanhedrin Experience or the Herodian experience. But to

---

[10] Galatians 1:8-9.

223

assert that Paul believed himself to be humbly offering his own religiously, existentially, unsubstantiated conjecture is simply bad history and bad literary criticism. Paul believed his interpretation and his divinely appointed authority as an apostle of this interpretation was <u>non-negotiable</u>. And his interpretation was as rigidly exclusivist as any of Christ's parabolic interpretations. Paul claimed that Christ's death was the means whereby a righteous God could be self-consistent and still justify those who were moral lawbreakers. He claimed that Christ's sacrificial blood "justified" us before God. And that if we relied on any other means of reconciliation with God - whether it be a fundamentalistic legalism or a vaguely sentimental religious existentialism, we are "fallen from grace" and the "wrath of God rests upon us." The author of Hebrews is equally uncompromising: "Of how much sorer punishment, suppose ye, shall he be thought worthy, who hath trodden under foot the Son of God, and hath counted the blood of the covenant, wherewith he was sanctified, an unholy thing, and hath done despite unto the Spirit of grace?" Peter too agrees: *But there were false prophets also among the people, even as there shall be false teachers among you, who privily shall bring in damnable heresies, even denying the Lord that bought them, and bring upon themselves swift destruction.*[11]

The modern religious existentialist has, in fact, generated an entirely new kind of interpretive schemata for understanding the "literal" world around him. It is a genus which removes us from the classical world of "literary" meaning altogether. Beyond simile. Beyond metaphor. Beyond allegory. He sees the world as an art critic would see an abstract painting. In this case, the critic may speak in some limited sense regarding the technical methods employed in the creation of the *physical* work of art, but is almost entirely limited in interpreting the poetic content or *meaning* of what the artwork might say. The real question that is being asked then is this: "Can there be any epistemological approach to sensory data which is not a complete abstraction of its objective essence? A "yes" answer is simply no longer permitted to this question. A "yes" argument is no longer permitted for this question. Imagine the shock and resentment that would ensue if a modern art professor, standing before an abstraction, then turning to his audience of art loving students and said: "this, now, is the *literal* meaning of this work of art. It is what the author *intended* to say by creating it. And you had better remember what I say to you now because if you do not reproduce this interpretation on the examination, you will receive an automatic failure." For the modern world, all reality has become a hopeless abstraction. Meaning must therefore be invented in the soul as personal myth. To suggest, in a post-language culture, that there is any objective meaning which transcends all personal myths, is psychopathic.

Myth was never intended to *give* meaning to that which is intrinsically meaningless. Myth was devised as a conceptual placeholder for *pre-existing meaning* when only

---

[11] 2nd Peter 2:1

partial data was available. For example, the Greek myths preserved the personhood and plurality and righteousness of the Godhead but did not know many things about how these ideas fit together. Consequently, we see that many of the mythical particulars could be altered or disbelieved, but if the entire mythical system were rejected, then a serious charge of atheism was forthcoming - punishable by death. We see Socrates brought up on charges of atheism for creating a general *atmosphere* of disbelief in the State gods even though the particulars of the myth were aggressively manipulated by other poets with impunity.

In early Christian attempts at corporate orthodoxy we see the reverse phenomena. The New Testament writers, for example, *specifically* say that if any one of a number of *fundamentals* is denied then the entire faith is denied. One can see Paul employ this principle regarding circumcision (Galatians 5:3-4) and the physicality of the resurrection (1st Corinthians 15:17) and serious breeches of moral behavior (1st Timothy 5:8). Modern theologians say that the New Testament authors used myth to embody truth. But this, again, is diametrically opposed to what Peter (2nd Peter 1:16) and Paul (2nd Timothy 4:4) *do* say: *For we have not followed cunningly devised myths, when we made known unto you the power and coming of our Lord Jesus Christ, but were eyewitnesses of his majesty* and: *they shall turn away their ears from the truth, and shall be turned to myth* (μυθος). The Apostles emphatically did not use "myth" - even as a place holding device in theological areas which remained dark even after the "dayspring on high" had lit up the world with the light of that which has been kept secret before the foundation of the world. The conceptual placeholder that *was* used when only partial revelational data was available - was ***mystery*** (μυστηριον).

"Mystery" is only used once in each Synoptic Gospel in this synchronous passage: "Unto you it is given to know the mystery of the kingdom of God: but unto them that are without, all these things are done in parables." It is used elsewhere in reference to the resurrection (1st Corinthians 15), the blindness of Israel (Romans 11), the marriage estate (Ephesians 5) and of iniquity in the world (2nd Thessalonians 2:7). But the entire project of the Gospel is everywhere assumed to be a project of brokering a mystery which had been kept secret for generations and generations (Colossians 1:26) and not *erecting* one by projecting a mythological overlay onto perfectly ordinary events.

The Gospel writers say that Christ gave the secret of the Kingdom to them and they have given it to us. The early Gnostics claimed that Christ did not give the Apostles the *full* secret but an *abstraction* of that secret. They further claimed that Christ gave the *actual* secret to the Gnostics. The modern Liberal Gnostics say that Christ probably *did* give the Apostles the full secret but because they could not fully comprehend it or did not want to fully comprehend it, they gave *us* an abstraction of the secret. Either way, the Christian rank and file is short-sheeted with an impenetrable theological abstraction which he must make the best of. The modern

Liberal Gnostic claims that through turning certain keys of physical and philosophical "gnosis," they can sweat out the full secret from the abstraction that has come down to us as the New Testament documents. The actual documents that we see before us show writers of integrity, creativity and intelligence - who had a clear sense of the limitations of human language[12] and a clear sense of its *power*.[13] Their view of language was the classical view, and their language is filled with an impressive index of terms which belong to the lexicon of figurative diction. There is absolutely no hint in the *language* employed in the New Testament Documents that indicates that any of its narrative, parabolic or theological literary genres were anything other than what they claimed to be: a plain statement of what was "seen and heard" within the ordinary sense and strictures of those genres.

The Apostles had a clear sense of the ordinary and the extraordinary. Matthew records: "And when the disciples saw him walking on the sea, they were troubled, saying, It is a spirit; and they cried out for fear." (14:26) And when Peter was delivered from his prison as a result of prayer, we do not hear the disciples calmly say "why, yes of course, that's the way things *are* now." No. We hear the story of ordinary men confronted by extraordinary phenomena. *And as Peter knocked at the door of the gate, a damsel came to hearken, named Rhoda. And when she knew Peter's voice, she opened not the gate for gladness, but ran in, and told how Peter stood before the gate. And they said unto her, Thou art mad. But she constantly affirmed that it was even so. Then said they, It is his angel. But Peter continued knocking: and when they had opened the door, and saw him, they were astonished.* (Acts 12:13-16) Mark has expanded the walking on the water pericope which has enabled us to see that the apostles had a clear sense of the apparent and the real. "But when they saw him walking upon the sea, they supposed (dokeo) it had been a spirit (phantasma) and cried out..." (Mark 6:49) The combination of dokeo and phantasma are intentionally chosen to ensure that the reader knows that this is a real appearance of Christ.

The Apostolic lexicon of poetic diction terms is impressive and indicative of the classical view of language

1504 εικων eikon "image"

Hebrews 10:1 *For the law having a shadow of good things to come, and not the very image of the things, can never with those sacrifices which they offered year by year continually make the comers thereunto perfect.*[14]

---

[12] Romans 6:1 *I am speaking in human terms because of the weakness of your flesh.* (ανθρωπινον λεγω)

[13] Especially as it was employed by God himself: Psalms 12:6 *The words of the LORD are pure words: as silver tried in a furnace of earth, purified seven times.*

[14] Here "shadow" is specifically contrasted with "icon." For moderns, "icon" is itself contrasted with the unknown other. And this is the difference: For the Apostles, there is a cognitive relationship between the shadow and that which casts it; but there is no intrinsic relationship between the icon

5123 τουτεστι "That is to say"

Hebrews 10:20 *By a new and living way, which he hath consecrated for us, through the veil, that is to say his flesh…*

3667 ομοιωμα homoioma "likeness"

Romans 6:5 *For if we have been planted together in the likeness of his death, we shall be also in the likeness of his resurrection…*

3665 ομοιοτης homoiotes "similitude"

Hebrews 7:15 *And it is yet far more evident: for that after the similitude of Melchizedek there ariseth another priest…*

3666 ομοιοω homoioo "to be made like"

Matthew 13:24 *Another parable put he forth unto them, saying, The kingdom of heaven is likened unto a man which sowed good seed in his field…*

Hebrews 2:17 *Wherefore in all things it behooved him to be made like unto his brethren, that he might be a merciful and faithful high priest in things pertaining to God, to make reconciliation for the sins of the people.*

5481 χαρακτηρ charakter (the instrument used for engraving or carving)

Hebrews 1:3 *Who being the brightness of his glory, and the express image of his person, and upholding all things by the word of his power, when he had by himself purged our sins, sat down on the right hand of the Majesty on high…*

871 αφομοιοω aphomoioo "made like"

Hebrews 7:3 *Without father, without mother, without descent, having neither beginning of days, nor end of life; but made like unto the Son of God; abideth a priest continually…*

2059 ερμηνευω hermeneuo "interpreted"

John 1:42 *And he brought him to Jesus. And when Jesus beheld him, he said, Thou art Simon the son of Jona: thou shalt be called Cephas, which is by interpretation, a stone.*

---

and the "unknown god" of modernity except one of irrational contact. For moderns, God is infinite regression from the Hegelian synthesis by which we attempt to approach him. For the apostles, God has approached as closely as possible without killing us by means of his own icon - the Son.

3954 παρρησια parrhesia "plainly"

John 11:14 *Then said Jesus unto them plainly, Lazarus is dead.*
John 10:24 *Then came the Jews round about him, and said unto him, How long dost thou make us to doubt? If thou be the Christ, tell us plainly.*

3946 παρομοιος paromoios "like things"

Mark 7:13 *Making the word of God of none effect through your tradition, which ye have delivered: and many such like things do ye…*

4592 σημειον semeion "sign" (many connotations)

Matthew 12:39 *But he answered and said unto them, An evil and adulterous generation seeketh after a sign; and there shall no sign be given to it, but the sign of the prophet Jonas.*

Matthew 16:3 *And in the morning, It will be foul weather to day: for the sky is red and lowring. O ye hypocrites, ye can discern the face of the sky; but can ye not discern the signs of the times.*

John 2:11 *This beginning of miracles did Jesus in Cana of Galilee, and manifested forth his glory; and his disciples believed on him.*

Romans 4:11 *And he received the sign of circumcision, a seal of the righteousness of the faith which he had yet being uncircumcised…*

2nd Thessalonians 3:17 *The salutation of Paul with mine own hand, which is the token in every epistle: so I write…*

3850 παραβολη parabole "a placing of one thing by the side of another, juxtapositioned, as of ships in battle"; "parable"

Luke 8:11 *Now the parable is this: The seed is the word of God…*

3942 παροιμια "a saying out of the usual course or deviating from the usual manner of speaking"; "proverb"; "parable"

John 16:29 *His disciples said unto him, Lo, now speakest thou plainly, and speakest no proverb.*

3945 παρομοιαζω paromoiazo "like"

Matthew 23:27 *Woe unto you, scribes and Pharisees, hypocrites! For ye are <u>like</u> unto whited sepulchres, which indeed appear beautiful outward, but are within full of dead men's bones, and of all uncleanness.*

3954 παρρησια parrhesia "plainly"

John 11:14 *Then said Jesus unto them <u>plainly</u>: Lazarus is dead.*

1718 εμφανιζω emphanizo "manifest"

Hebrews 11:14 *For they that say such things <u>declare plainly</u> that they seek a country…*

5179 τυπος tupos "imprint"

Romans 5:14 *Nevertheless death reigned from Adam to Moses, even over them that had not sinned after the similitude of Adam's transgression, who is the <u>figure</u> of him that was to come.*

Hebrews 8:5 *Who serve unto the example and shadow of heavenly things, as Moses was admonished of God when he was about to make the tabernacle: for, See, saith he, that thou make all things according to the <u>pattern</u> shewed to thee in the mount.*

499 αντιτυπος antitupos "figure"

Hebrews 9:24 *For Christ is not entered into the holy places made with hands, which are the <u>figures</u> of the true; but into heaven itself, now to appear in the presence of God for us…*

3345 μετασχηματιζω metaschematizo "transform"

1st Corinthians 4:6 *And these things, brethren, I have in a figure <u>transferred</u> to myself and to Apollos for your sakes.*

3454 μυθος muthos "myth"

1st Timothy 4:7 *But refuse profane and old wives' <u>fables</u>*

3466 μυστηριον musterion "mystery"

Matthew 13:11 *He answered and said unto them, Because it is given unto you to know the mysteries of the kingdom of heaven, but to them it is not given*

5158 τροπος tropos "even as"

Matthew 23:37 *O Jerusalem, Jerusalem, thou that killest the prophets, and stonest them which are sent unto thee, how often would I have gathered thy children together, even as a hen gathereth her chickens under her wings, and ye would not!*

4639 σκια "shadow"

Colossians 2:17 *Which are a shadow of things to come...*

5262 υποδειγμα hupodeigma "example"

Hebrews 9:23 *It was therefore necessary that the patterns of things in the heavens should be purified with these; but the heavenly things themselves with better sacrifices than these.*

3026 ληρος leros "idle tales"

Luke 24:11 *And their words seemed to them as idle tales and they believed them not.*

Modern religious existentialism, nevertheless, insists that there is a vast conspiratorial "Apostolic Secret" in the telling of the musterion (mystery) of Christ. And that secret is that the entire evangelical project - the entire pragmatum of the good news - was a complete fabrication of religious existentialism - a unified *myth* which brokers every statement and every sentiment and every sensory experience of every purveyor of this religious abstraction. The uncanny thing about this "Apostolic secret" is that it uniformly tracks through several different genres - through the Synoptic template, the Lukan narrative called Acts, through the theological epistles and even through the Apocalypse, which necessarily *shares* many conventions characteristic of mythical literature. It is a *total* secret. The lexicon above shows that the New Testament writers had at their disposal a powerful range of words in which to make a clear distinction between what was a mythologization and what was a demythologization, but this conversation is everywhere absent in the New Testament. In *actual* myth, while many of the illiterate may naively demand consistency and certainty in areas that have not been illuminated, there is always a priestly intelligentsia freely acknowledging that the myth is only "something like the truth" For example, after a long "mythical" Dantesque dissertation about the disposition of the souls of the damned, Socrates concludes with this statement:

230

Of course no reasonable man ought to insist that the facts are exactly as I have described them. But either this or something very like it is a true account of our souls and their future habitations - since we have clear evidence that the soul is immortal - this, I think, is both a reasonable contention and a belief worth risking, for the risk is a noble one. - Phaedo

In the New Testament Documents, there is no trace of such a discussion. Its fundamentalism is total in that which is revealed and its intolerance diminishes proportionally as the revelation of the musterion recedes into the twilight of that which has not yet been revealed. For example, regarding the pragma that *was* taught, there is nothing but intolerance for dissent. We have John saying: *For many deceivers are entered into the world, who confess not that Jesus Christ is come in the flesh. This is a deceiver and an antichrist* (2nd John 1:7).

But in regard to what we do *not* know, we have him saying: *Beloved, now are we the sons of God, and it doth not yet appear what we shall be: but we know that, when he shall appear, we shall be like him; for we shall see him as he is.* (1st John 3:2). Likewise Paul: *But though we, or an angel from heaven, preach any other gospel unto you than that which we have preached unto you, let him be accursed.* (Galatians 1:8) But then he says: *as it is written, Eye hath not seen, nor ear heard, neither have entered into the heart of man, the things which God hath prepared for them that love him* (1st Corinthians 2:9). Ironically, the early "heresies" to this fundamentalism were not fought on the field of fundamentals. They were fought on fields which were knowingly and fearlessly left undefended in the transmission and application of the Greco-Roman myths. They were fought on the level of the theological *system.* The articulation of the fundamentals remained relatively unchanged, but were nevertheless completely redefined by the contexts of the global systems in which they were placed: Gnosticism, Marcionism, Manichaeism, Docetism and all the Christological heresies (especially Arianism) - all fell *outside* the fundamentals as global theological considerations, yet as heretical *systems,* they effected every one of the fundamentals.[15]

These global systems challenged the early church at the very limits of orthodoxy and could not be proof-texted out of existence. Scripture was not quoted except in matters of fact. Global, presuppositional apologetics were developed. The first creeds emerged. The Apostolic succession was codified. And the canon of Scripture

---

[15] Ironically, this was the charge against Socrates. In his own words Socrates explained the principle of how a staunch advocate of the reality of God could be brought up on charges of atheism: because "those who hear [that] …there is a wise man called Socrates who has theories about the heavens and has investigated everything below the earth…suppose that anyone who inquires into such matters must be an atheist." Likewise, the early Christians were also charged with atheism for repudiating State sponsored religious syncretism. In similar fashion, Christians of today are charged with sociopathic behavior in repudiating State sponsored religious syncretism.

was defined. This kind of defensive strategy is indicative of the clash of theological *systems* and not the fundamentals within those systems. Contrary to popular belief, the councils were not political slugfests over fundamentals, such as the date of Easter or the mode of baptism. No. These were titanic struggles over the semantic *fields* in which the fundamental articulations could be placed and still retain the intended Apostolic meaning. This is why the struggle often turned on a single word - because that one word invoked a linguistic paradigm which would empower and interpret all the fundamental articulations under its jurisdiction.

Within the New Testament documents there is also no trace of a two-tiered gnostic view of reality which can be deduced from the forms of poetic diction employed. The rich variety of poetic diction found in the New Testament documents is itself a testament of its non-mythical character. Because one does not find poetic diction *within* a myth that is itself created by poetic diction. The myth, once it has been created, reads like a nursery story - full of one-dimensional flat facts - like an old wives' tale. But in the New Testament literature we have the unlikely appearance of multi-tiered *poetic diction* - much as one would find in the conceptualization of a scientific hypothesis. In the New Testament we see an allegory (Hagar and Sarah) *imbedded* in religious typology (the Old Covenant, visible Church) which is itself imbedded in a parable (the Bride of Christ) which is all analyzed and given eternal significance in ordinary, discursive, propositional, logical language!

If the apostles <u>didn't</u> know that the Gospel was all a gnostic myth, then the "apostolic secret" is a misnomer for a vast *misconception* about the physical world. Surely, preconceptions about physics could generate some distortions - but of this magnitude? What kind of bizarro-world physics could possibly account for the vast scope of how badly the Apostles "unwittingly" mis-interpreted reality? One can understand how a disease can be over-explained as a demon possession, but again, these men knew that virgins don't get pregnant on their own. However bad their mathematics might have been, five loaves of bread and two fish do not feed 5000 men and give twelve baskets of fragments as a remainder. And dead men do not walk out of graves four days after they have been buried. The point of this is that they were either intentionally mythologizing or lying - or they were not. This is why that after initial forays into an attempt to make the apostolic secret *un*intentional, such works collapse in absurdity and always end in making it *intentional*.

Appendix 5: Reading the Bible "Literally"

If any man come to me, and hate not his father, and mother, and wife, and children, and brethren, and sisters, yea, and his own life also, he cannot be my disciple. (Luke 14:26)

In the New Testament, the opposite of love is not indifference; it is hate.[1] When the New Testament says that we must hate our fathers and mothers and wives in order to be Jesus' disciple, this is surely a piece of what Owen Barfield called "poetic diction,"[2] which means that a word is deformed from its ordinary meaning and stretched to suggest another. A higher one. That is, the word or phrase is not to be taken in its ordinary, restrictive sense – it is being used to create a "figure of speech."

Conservatives and Fundamentalists often give the impression that the entire Bible should be taken "literally." And by *literally* they mean that each word should be taken in its most restrictive sense. But the problem with reading the Bible *literally*, (as it has come to be defined), is that such a process is entirely *un*literary. It violates the divine logos.

When we deform language in the process of poetic diction, we *preserve* language from becoming senile - and from eventually dying the ultimate death of every dead metaphor. We've all heard them. A metaphor is used so many times, its original contribution to the birth of a new idea is lost, and the new idea itself becomes a mechanical object that no longer conveys any life or power. If our language is filled with clichés, it is a sure sign that it is in the process of dying. We are no longer using language to convey meaning, but to manipulate our environment. And as everyone knows, there are better ways to manipulate our environment than by words. There are sticks and stones and guns and bombs.

When we deform language in the name of poetic diction, we do not lower language, we raise it. When we say that a thing is not literal, Fundamentalists and Conservatives object on the grounds that we are *distorting* language, perhaps even as Satan distorted language, as he distorted the ideas of language in his conversation with Eve. Though nothing that Satan said was entirely untrue, truth consists in giving the proper sense of a thing in <u>all</u> of its relations. If it is twisted into something that cannot be harmonized with those relations, we say that it is false. For example, the serpent claimed that if Eve ate the fruit, that she would <u>not</u> die. In one sense, the serpent was absolutely correct – when Eve ate the fruit, nothing happened. But there

---

[1] Hebrews 1:9 *Thou hast **loved** righteousness, and **hated** iniquity; therefore God, even thy God, hath anointed thee with the oil of gladness above thy fellows.*

[2] See his book: *Poetic Diction.* Owen Barfield was a good friend of C. S. Lewis. Lewis said of him that 'he read all the right books but got all the wrong things out of them!'

was another sense that Satan failed to mention to Eve – the *primary* sense. And that primary sense was a figure of speech. Eve would die, *spiritually*.

Thus to be literal is to be literary. Every word of Scripture, just like our own words, must be taken in their proper *sense*. Sometime words are used in a very restrictive sense. "Jesus wept", for example. Sometimes, however, words are used in a creative, figurative sense. Jesus says: "Behold, I come as a thief." The clue that some figurative sense is being employed is the word "as" which indicates that this is a particular kind of figure of speech; i.e., a simile. The Lord is not a thief. For we know that a "thief cometh not, but for to steal, and to kill, and to destroy."[3] The Synoptic simile, therefore is using just <u>one</u> of this word's connotations to tell us something about Christ's return. He will come *suddenly*, when we are not looking for him. Thus we hear: "Blessed are those servants, whom the lord when he cometh shall find watching..."[4]

In our Gospel passage, Jesus tells us that in order to be good disciples we must 'hate our fathers and mothers.' And while we are at it, we should also hate our wives, and our children, and our brothers and sisters. And in the end, we must hate ourselves. Now remember that the Father of all lies; that is, Satan, is constantly *deforming* language to conform to his own agenda of self-glorification – not to shed more light and meaning. And this is what makes his kind of literary deformation a lie – and not innocent, poetic diction. For Satan takes that which must be taken restrictively and gives a *figurative* sense to it. And he takes that which is figurative and gives a *restrictive* sense to it. All to mislead us to draw the wrong conclusions about the intent of the author. So we need to take care that the deceitfulness of sin does not persuade us to do the same thing.

Take the case of corban. Corban is a thing that has been dedicated to God. Now what the Pharisees were doing with this idea is creating a "loophole" from which they might escape the weightier sense of the fifth commandment: "love thy father and thy mother." Listen to how Jesus handles this deceit:

And he said unto them, Full well ye reject the commandment of God, that ye may keep your own tradition. For Moses said, Honour thy father and thy mother; and, Whoso curseth father or mother, let him die the death: But ye say, If a man shall say to his father or mother, It is Corban, that is to say, a gift, by whatsoever thou mightest be profited by me; he shall be free. And ye suffer him no more to do ought for his father or his mother; Making the word of God of none effect through your tradition, which ye have delivered: and many such like things do ye.[5]

---

[3] John 10:10.
[4] Luke 12:37a.
[5] Mark 7:9-13

The Pharisees and the Sadducees knew not the proper sense of Scripture nor the power of God, thus their theology and their spirituality was nothing but a humanistic rationalism completely removed from the heart of God.

We must constantly beware that this does not happen to us. There are theologies and spiritualities everywhere we go in the world today – and also in the churches – which come up with all sorts of zany and *unliterary* interpretations which lead the unstable or the unlearned into the way of sin. But 'how do we know the <u>correct</u> interpretation?' – many ask. And we must say that the interpretation of any passage of Scripture is, ultimately, up to you.

The pastor's job - as a shepherd of the flock of Christ - is *not* as interpreter. God doesn't *need* an interpreter. And the more you think about it, the sillier such an idea becomes. God speaks in a universal, common language. The only place an interpreter can go from here is *downward* - into obscurity or deceit. This is how Satan deceived Eve – by *interpreting* that which needed no interpretation.

When the Bible uses the word "interpretation", it is always in the sense of translating Aramaic or Latin words into Greek words. Thus, the Aramaic "Messiah" is Christos, Cephas is Petros and ελωι λαμμα σαβαχθανι, being translated is: ο θεος μου ο θεος μου εις τι με εγκατελιπες. And "Golgotha" is the "place of the skull." And in Latin, that means "Calvary." The only exception to this sense of "interpret" is when someone speaks in a truly *unknown* tongue – like the ecstatic utterances of the Corinthian church – then, someone must *interpret*.

But God does not speak to us in an unknown tongue. And even if he did – with groanings which cannot be uttered, the Spirit *himself* will translate them to us.[6] Thus for as much as we use the word, "interpret" or "interpretation" - the New Testament almost completely ignores it. Yet colleges and seminaries have *departments* of hermeneutics, which is a transliteration of this Greek word for "interpret"- teaching students to interpret the Bible.

If we understand – or rather, if we have been convinced that the Holy Spirit was dynamically present in the creation of the written, Apostolic record, then we must know that God needs no interpreter. God does not have a communication problem. He does not 'lisp in human language' as one great theologian once said. God doesn't want interpreters. He wants leaders and teachers. The pastor's job is to give the proper <u>sense</u> of a passage.

---

[6] Romans 8:26 *Likewise the Spirit also helpeth our infirmities: for we know not what we should pray for as we ought: but the Spirit itself maketh intercession for us with groanings which cannot be uttered.*

If a word or a passage or an idea of a theology is taken out of the Biblical context, he needs to clean up the mess and put the idea back into context. If people come to him with worldly presuppositions in their heads that retard their comprehension of the proper sense of a passage, he needs to fully understand these worldly presuppositions and try to find ways to circumnavigate them. He must be _as_ a divine subversive, just as Jesus is _as_ a thief in the night, sneaking around in men's mental furniture, defusing booby traps designed to go off as soon as truth approaches. He must fish for the man behind his restrictive ideas. He must catch him with guile (as Paul once said) just as he catches fish – all of these, of course, figures of speech - a poetic diction of ideas.

It is by poetic diction that the 'divine thief' steals by our defenses and captures our attention and thrusts bread and meat and milk and everlasting rivers of water before our souls. We try to keep him out with our traps and minefields and walls and moats. But we never succeed. Our puny disobediences and our hardened hearts and our dulled hearing is no match for the overwhelming power of his word and of his spirit and of his love.

Our sinful tendency is to capture God's word and imprison it as a dead metaphor – or at least as a _manageable_ metaphor. We want to _corbanize_ every word of his that threatens our disobedient freedom to be slaves to our appetites. Men have pasteurized his word. They have attempted to sterilize every controversial aspect of biblical theology with their own "systematic theology" which "harmonizes" Gospels and "reconciles" the views of James and Paul concerning justification by faith or works. They have also homogenized his word. Every difference of clarity, every difference of density and every difference in depth has been utterly disguised in glittered gold and literary glue that has cut and pressed each and every word and letter and book into a uniform mold of Evangelical "inspiration." And what is left has been chopped up into a million disassociated pieces and fed to Christian sheep in miniscule, harmless doses.

But nothing will hinder God's word. He will sweep away centuries of bad theology with one poor Augustinian friar. He will chase away a thousand armed men by some Joan de Arc. He will completely overcome a hundred thousand Syrians with 300 Gideons that lap up Scripture like a dog. He said it in the Old Testament: his word will not return to him without having achieved its purpose. Every bit of it.[7] _The word of God is quick, and powerful, and sharper than any twoedged sword, piercing even to the dividing asunder of soul and spirit, and of the joints and marrow, and is a discerner of the thoughts and intents of the heart._[8]

---

7 Isaiah 55:11.
8 Hebrews 4:12.

In what _sense_ then must I 'hate my father and my mother and my wife and my children etc.' – which covers every significant human relation that I could ever have. The Psalmist says: "As far as the east is from the west, so far hath he removed our transgressions from us."[9] How far _is_ the east from the west? Of course it is not a matter of distance. Our sins are _gone_. They are no longer on this playing field. They have been forever buried in the depths of the sea.[10]

There _is_ no Greek word for love that describes the categorical difference between the love of God and the love of some worldly object. It is on a different playing field. Matthew's version reads: "He that loves father or mother more than me is not worthy of me: and he that loves son or daughter more than me is not worthy of me."[11] And that's why Luke's variation is so important; he makes it _absolutely clear_ that the love of God is categorically different than all earthly loves. The word in Matthew is the ordinary φιλεω. There is not one single word for "divine love."

There is _idolatry_. If we love the world with the love that belongs to God, we commit idolatry. If we love God with worldly love, we also commit idolatry. Modern idols are not silver and gold anymore. They are steel and concrete, titanium and plastic. Our _love_ of God must be like our _worship_ of God; it is completely inappropriate to worship any created thing. Because only God is worthy of worship. Only God can receive and return the love that he is asking for. Nothing can compete for it because it is not of this world. The loves of this world are as categorically different from the love of God and things eternal as the east is from the west and love is from hate. And that's why Luke says we must hate our father and mother. Because Christ is God, and our love for him is categorically superior than any human love.

---

9 Psalm 103:12.
10 Micah 7:19.
11 Matthew 10:37.

Epilogue: Corpus Criticism[1]

This book is not really about grammar. If you have followed this grammar and read the appendixes, I think that you must have seen this. It is about *understanding* the apostolic conversation, which happens to be in Koine. In all of the research that I have done over the last eighteen years, I discovered that I could not resolve any of the issues of higher criticism - or of lower theology – or of "Biblical interpretation" - unless I first allowed a comprehensive theory of communication and language and epistemology to be formed in my mind. As soon as I allowed this to happen, the landscape upon which the issues of Biblical criticism and Biblical interpretation are written, suddenly clarified.

If Christ is the word, as John claims, then we cannot study grammar without him. We must study grammar Christologically, and we must translate Christologically and we must do theology Christologically. There is no alternative. If God is speaking to us through ordinary language and ordinary literary conventions in the New Testament materials, we must understand what we mean by language and literature and about the communication mechanics that necessarily exists between God and man. This too is important, because (as we said above) modern language theories tell us what language is not, but they do not tell us what language is. If language is merely verbal behavior, or if it is merely a set of essentially mathematical descriptions, or if it is just a game, then we will have an enormous epistemological problem on our hands. And in the twentieth century, we certainly do. We no longer have any confidence that we can know the world around us. We no longer have any confidence that our senses can connect our world with our mind.

Plato said that the mind starts with innate ideas, but he was not clear where they came from. Thomas Aquinas said that there is nothing in the mind which was not first in the senses, but it is unclear how the senses could give the mind an idea of the senses themselves. On the other hand, the witness of the apostolic community is that Christ is language. *In the beginning was the Word, and the Word was with God, and the Word was God.*[2] He created the senses and the world, and all ideas resolve in him. They tell us that Christ is the universal Son of Man and Son of God, and that we are all particular men who have been given the right and the power to become sons and daughters of God. And they tell us that it is in Christ that "we live and move and have our being." Paul says "in Christ" 72 times in his letters. Though John never

---

[1] A significant amount of material in this section has been imported from other, related discussions about language from two other books by me: *The Jonas Genre*, which attempts to solve the "Synoptic Problem," and *From Exodus to Eisodus*, which attempts to solve the question of who wrote Hebrews.
[2] John 1:1.

uses this phrase, he expresses in his own language the very same thing: *At that day you shall know that I am in my Father, and you in me, and I in you.*[3]

John has clearly said that men have language because Christ gives it to them. John says that Christ does not speak about God. John says that Jesus *is* the speech of God. The apostolic community of authors assert that Christ begins a dialogue with the human soul from the very beginning. Even though we are now children of a terrible moral catastrophe long ago, even while we are yet enemies of God, Christ nevertheless begins this conversation.

Every infant already knows a little history. He cries because he already knows, in part, the tragedy of the fall of man. An infant laughs because he already knows, in part, what is funny. The infant is too young to have been taught these things by human intervention. Yet he must have heard it somewhere before. He knows these things because he is immersed in the amniotic fluid of the ordinary speech of God. God can speak to us in ordinary speech – because the creator of the ordinary worlds became an ordinary man. *And the Word was made flesh, and dwelt among us…*[4]

The difference between man and the animals is not the opposable thumb. Nor is it the extra cranial capacity. What most distinguishes the consciousness of man from the rest of the animals is that Christ is having a higher order conversation with the consciousness of man, thus elevating the consciousness of man to extraordinary levels. Some would say - to the level of the gods themselves. Indeed, conversation begets consciousness; consciousness begets conversation. We observe the same thing in lesser animals. What distinguishes the domesticated dog from the wolf, for example, is that the domesticated dog is constantly interacting in conversation with man; thus his consciousness is developed to a very high level. Indeed, many books have talking animals in them for precisely this reason.

The New Testament materials clearly assert that <u>all</u> man's knowledge must be revealed by God. His epistemology cannot be autonomous on any level. And if all is revealed by the logos of God, then it is also true that the ordinary man understands the weather in the very same way that he understands prophecy: *[Jesus] answered and said to them, When it is evening, you say, it will be fair weather: for the sky is red. And in the morning, it will be foul weather today: for the sky is red and lowring. Hypocrites - you can discern the face of the sky; but to discern the signs of the times you are not able.*[5]

The New Testament materials assert that the ordinary man can understand the world around him because all of his senses have been created by God – created to hear and see and taste and touch the logic of the cosmos or the songs of the stars.

---

[3] John 14:20.
[4] John 1:14a.
[5] Matthew 16:2-3.

Zen Buddhism claims that a "flower does not talk." And that's because there is nothing to say in Zen Buddhism. But this is not the language theory of the Psalmist. He claims that the world is ablaze with communication: *The heavens declare the glory of God; and the firmament shows his handiwork. Day to day utters speech, and night unto night shows knowledge.*[6] And the logic that his senses reveal is more than mere order and stability. The logic that his senses reveal is beautiful.

Mathematics, music, physics - all make the same speech. However plausible a scientific theory, even if it seems to have passed the rigors of the scientific method, if it is not *elegant*, the scientist will immediately know that there is something wrong with it. The New Testament materials tell us that God created the ear and all the other senses, the emotions, the conscience, the memory, and the rational processes of the mind, in order to "hear" that speech. And they tell us that the logic of that speech is elegantly beautiful. Through the senses and the mind we hear and see the beauty of the cosmos – whether it be the smell of black humus or the mathematical proportions of a black hole.

The universe is beautiful because it bears the impress of inexpressible beauty. Our souls must embrace the beautiful because we are hopelessly in love with the beautiful. The New Testament does not coax us to love our own souls. They coax us to love our neighbor's soul. We must love our own souls because they too are beautiful. They are beautiful because they bear the impress of inexpressible beauty. There is no alternative to reason and beauty. The souls of human beings cannot repudiate reason and beauty any more than the fetus can repudiate the womb. The alternative to reason and beauty is not just absurdity and ugliness. The alternative to reason and beauty is a hellish insanity of weeping and gnashing of teeth. That which is beautiful is in the eye of the beholder because it is also everywhere outside the beholder. And that beauty is Christ.

The New Testament claims that Christ is the intersection between God and man, between flesh and spirit, between the infinite and the finite, between the creator and what has been created. John is emphatic about this. He says that when we reach out and touch Christ, we are touching God. John does not say that Christ merely speaks the words of life. John says that Christ *is* the word of life: *That which was from the beginning, which we have heard, which we have seen with our eyes, which we have looked upon, and our hands have handled, of the word of life.*[7]

The reason that a man can know himself is because from the beginning, Christ begins to tell him who he is. The reason that a man can understand the language of another man is because they both are having the same conversation with Christ. The

---

[6] Psalm 19:1-2.
[7] 1st John 1:1.

reason that a man may understand the world around him is that the world is being spoken into existence by the same voice that is speaking a man's soul into existence. The reason that a man may understand the mind of God is because the Son of God tells him what he is thinking. And the reason that a man can understand and know the truth of apostolic preaching is because he has heard what they are saying somewhere before.

Christ makes the very same argument to the religious establishment of the day: *For had you believed Moses, you would have believed me: for he wrote of me.*[8] Christ said that the reason that the religious establishment rejected the gospel of Christ was because they had already rejected the dialogue of God within the soul: *And you have not his word abiding in you: for whom he has sent, him you believe not.*[9] John says that the reason that a man surrenders himself to the gospel conversation of Christ is because he has already surrendered himself to the conversation of Christ in which the soul has been bathed since the moment of its conception.

Jesus characterized his ministry as an act of speech: *The Spirit of the Lord is upon me, because he has anointed me to preach the gospel to the poor...*[10] *For he whom God has sent speaks the words of God...*[11] *For I have given to them the words which you gave me; and they have received them, and have known surely that I came out from you, and they have believed that you sent me.*[12]

Modern language theories say that God's words cannot, ultimately, be put into temporary human languages. Jesus says: 'Yes they can. And furthermore, that's just what I have done.' Jesus says that his words are the intersection of God and humanity. They are the incarnation of spirit and flesh: *It is the spirit that quickens; the flesh profits nothing: the words that I speak unto you, they are spirit, and they are life.*[13] And he told his disciples that their words would also be the incarnation of spirit and flesh: *For it is not you that speak, but the Spirit of your Father which speaks in you.*[14] And that spirit was the Spirit of truth itself: *Howbeit when he, the Spirit of truth, is come...*[15]

As Christ claimed that he was sent to speak the words of his Father, so he sent the disciples to speak his words to the world: *He that hears you hears me; and he that despises you despises me; and he that despises me despises him that sent me.*[16] Therefore,

---

[8] John 5:46.
[9] John 5:38.
[10] Luke 4:18.
[11] John 3:34.
[12] John 17:8.
[13] John 6:63.
[14] Matthew 10:20.
[15] John 16:13a.
[16] Luke 10:16.

after Christ's ascension, the Apostles believed that their ministry was also an act of speech: *For we cannot but speak the things which we have seen and heard."*[17] Paul reiterates this: For Christ sent me not to baptize, but to preach the gospel…[18]

The New Testament materials say that the created order is a standing speech of Christ. They say that Christ created the senses and the mind in order to hear that speech. They say that the content of that speech is beautiful. They say that Jesus had come to the ordinary world from a world beyond the ordinary senses in order to tell us extraordinary things in ordinary language – yet much of what he had to say was so straightforward, a child could understand it. Children do not understand mystical sacraments, systematic theologies, or religious existentialism, but Matthew claims that children did understand who Christ was:

And when the chief priests and scribes saw the wonderful things that he did, and the children crying in the temple, and saying, Hosanna to the Son of David; they were very displeased, And said to him, Do you hear what they are saying? And Jesus said to them, Yes; haven't you read, Out of the mouth of babes and sucklings you have perfected praise?[19] It is no wonder that Jesus prays: *I thank you, O Father, Lord of heaven and earth, because you have hid these things from the wise and prudent, and have revealed them unto babes.*[20]

In this book we have intentionally belabored the question of communication between God and man because much of the modern world believes that there is no possibility that God exists, or if God exists, there is no possibility that God can speak to creatures that he has made, or if he can speak, there is no possibility that he can speak clearly, or if he can speak clearly, there is no possibility that anyone can hear clearly enough to represent his words. If these things are true, then there is no point in attempting to understand the New Testament materials. But if the underlying theological presuppositions of the New Testament materials are true – that Christ is language and that Christ is the very Son of God, then the apostolic literary materials are but one step removed from a cameo appearance of God within his own creation. And it is therefore crucial that we understand the nature of the literature in which he is portrayed.

But it is precisely here that we must come to an important distinction about the divine nature of the New Testament. Although the apostles believed that language is Christ; that is, all language is God-breathed, the apostles consciously knew that they were inspired by the Holy Spirit of God in some special sense, uncommon to man. They all say it. Jesus says to his apostles: *ye shall be brought before governors and kings for my sake, for a testimony against them and the Gentiles. But when they deliver you up,*

---

[17] Acts 4:20.
[18] 1st Corinthians 17a.
[19] Matthew 21:15-16.
[20] Matthew 11:25.

take no thought how or what ye shall speak: for it shall be given you in that same hour what ye shall speak. For it is not ye that speak, but the Spirit of your Father which speaketh in you.[21] These men believed that they were giving legal testimony about what they had seen and heard – and that the Holy Spirit was helping them so to do in some special way.

The Apostle John extends this line of thinking in his Gospel even further as Jesus says: *Howbeit when he, the Spirit of truth, is come, he will guide you into all truth: for he shall not speak of himself; but whatsoever he shall hear, that shall he speak.*[22] And it is here that we get our first glimpse of what would eventually become obvious to the disciples: that the revelation of the Gospel of Jesus Christ was progressive. The revelation of Jesus Christ during his three-year ministry with the apostles was just the beginning. In order to hear the rest, these men must first mature as Christians. The entire community must mature – as a community. Near the close of his physical ministry with the apostolic community, Jesus himself very clearly said: *I have yet many things to say unto you, but ye cannot bear them now.*[23]

What was not so clear to the apostles, at least to judge by their unassuming editorial dialogue with us, is that they seemed to be wholly unconscious of the fact that not only would their individual dialogues – their personal testimonies – be especially inspired and divine – but that taken together, the apostolic community dialogue would also be inspired and divine. And if there is anything of divine significance that the post-apostolic Church has given to the world, it is this: the idea that the New Testament is a literary body. It is not only canon – it is corpus. There is not just the Pauline corpus and the Johannine corpus. There is the New Testament corpus. However unconscious, however clumsy, however accidental or serendipitous, the formation of the canonical corpus occurred. The modern church takes this formation for granted, but no one in the apostolic age did. And surely no individual writer of the New Testament materials did either.

The implications of this are profound. Because without this kind of corpus criticism, biblical "interpretation" is essentially contextless and thus, ultimately, useless. Could we not consider that though the individual writers of the New Testament are wholly conscious in their literary efforts, which precludes any idea of inspiration by "divine dictation" (as many Evangelical Fundamentalists have maintained), they are (as may be expected) wholly unconscious of the existential fact that the divine Spirit of all human communication is behind another, meta-dialogue with the world by means of the community interconnectedness of their individual dialogues? And thus, what the Church has naïvely assumed for centuries is far more profoundly true

---

[21] Matthew 10:18-20.
[22] John 16:13.
[23] John 16:12.

than could have been first imagined: that the New Testament materials – taken together, as a body – are a special incarnation of the Holy Spirit?

Again, the implications of this are profound. If the New Testament materials are a specific, special incarnation of the Holy Spirit - as the human body of Jesus was the incarnation of the Son, then we should expect his revelation to be weak in places and strong in others. This is merely to affirm what the Apostle Paul himself has said about the body itself: *Nay, much more those members of the body, which seem to be more feeble, are necessary.*[24] Nevertheless, in most Evangelical theories regarding Biblical inspiration, these materials have been reduced to an un-systematized, homogeneous, contextless mass of disconnected words and sentences, the logic of which has been pushed up into a gnostic, "upper story" religious dimension which is not accessible to ordinary literary methods.

This conventional Protestant theory of Scriptural inspiration has produced a kind of "paper pope" bible which has in turn produced a host of conflicting theological prejudices, and a flood of complex, systematic theologies which have become less and less convincing as systems. And this is because they are fundamentally disconnected from their presumed, underlying source - the very logos which has orchestrated this corpus, not by any human systematic theology, but by its own divine schema.

Against the Evangelical view of the New Testament materials is a species of Liberal, linguistic docetism, or Gnosticism, which maintains that God cannot truly speak in human language without his truth becoming immediately and necessarily tainted with untruth. In this view, the words of Christ and of his Apostles are entirely provisional - conditional upon the artifacts of this creation. When she passes away, these words will also pass away as subjective, temporary, irrelevant and meaningless. This is flatly contradicted by Christ: *Heaven and earth shall pass away, but my words shall not pass away.*[25]

The Apostles maintain a third alternative. They maintain that their words have the same authority as the words of Christ - and that the words of Christ are the very words of God. This idea first occurs in Exodus 4:15-16: *And thou shalt speak unto him, and put words in his mouth: and I will be with thy mouth, and with his mouth, and will teach you what ye shall do. And he shall be thy spokesman unto the people: and he shall be, even he shall be to thee instead of a mouth, and thou shalt be to him instead of God.* This may be coupled with Deuteronomy 18:18 *I will raise them up a Prophet from among their brethren, like unto thee, and will put my words in his mouth; and he shall speak unto them all that I shall command him.* Jesus claimed that his words had been expressly

---

[24] 1st Corinthians 12:22.
[25] Matthew 24:35.

given to him by his Father: *…whatsoever I speak therefore, even as the Father said unto me, so I speak.*[26] And the Apostles claim that their words had been expressly given by Christ: *For I have given unto them the words which thou gavest me; and they have received them, and have known surely that I came out from thee, and they have believed that thou didst send me.*[27]

Furthermore, the Apostles maintain that the revelation of Christ is indeed a project of the Apostolic community. Again, if the Holy Spirit has incarnated himself into the New Testament materials, we should not be surprised that his body should be found in both the unity and the diversity - the individual and the corporate - of the Apostolic community witness: *For our comely parts have no need: but God hath tempered the body together, having given more abundant honour to that part which lacked: That there should be no schism in the body; but that the members should have the same care one for another.*[28] And just as we should not be surprised to see the New Testament materials grow in wisdom and in stature and in favor with God and man, so also we should not be surprised to see the parts of that Apostolic body growing together, informing each part. For God has so arranged the parts of the body that no part may stand alone. His tempering is such that the theology of one Apostle must be informed by the theology of another, and from that interdependency, the expression of that corpus becomes clear and perfect - and its authority, eternal.

The New Testament materials are a body. But it is not enough to say that some parts of that body are strong, some are weak, some are clear, some are not so clear, some are simple, some are hard to understand - or that the whole body matures in its communication - from milk to meat. There are also dissonances. Yet, just as in music, dissonances do not detract from the whole. They are not mistakes by the composer. They are deliberately put in to the music not only that they might be resolved in a pleasant and fitting way, but they might be resolved in a *particular* way – a way that brings a new level of awareness to the meta-dialogue of the entire composition.

And surely no one would imagine that a credible musicologist would take a piece of music and analyze every instantaneous chord in isolation from the whole piece – as Fundamentalists often do with individual passages. Nor would anyone devise a synthetic categorization system and rearrange chords or melodic lines by some scheme other than that of the composition itself – as systematic theologians do. The music - and every passage in that music - must be judged against the whole. The Epistle of James, for example, provides an underlying dissonance which pushes comprehension of the Pauline melodic line to its furthest limit. And that melodic line – "justification by faith apart from works" - is like the repeating eight measure "gospel" in Bach's Passacaglia and Fugue in C Minor. Everything in the piece

---

[26] John 12:50b.
[27] John 17:8.
[28] 1st Corinthians 12:24-25.

supports and informs that repeating, eight measure stretch. Sometimes the development is so intricately delicate that the listener finds himself mentally supplying that melodic line when it is purposely omitted. The composer intentionally did this. As with the Passacaglia, so with the New Testament; the entire piece grows in maturity - from utter simplicity - to a conclusion of power, meaning and glory.

The New Testament corpus has grown as a body has grown, one part supplying what the other part lacked, and that whole body itself grows to maturity, supping for so long on just milk, and then, suddenly in Hebrews and the Apocalypse - upon the very meat of truth. The men who wrote the New Testament materials are not telling the world about haphazard verbal traditions about how a pre-existing community of faith "feels" about certain data. No. These individual spokesmen are all grappling directly with an object which lies entirely outside themselves – outside of any pre-existing faith community. And the more they grapple with it, the larger it becomes, until the cosmos itself is just a footstool.

These men believe that a fellowship has been begotten by this object. These men believe that they are the "temple of the Holy Spirit of God." These men believe that this koinonia is an entirely new wineskin into which has been poured the very wine of truth. The continued aging of this wine in its own wineskin is a process so dynamic, no pre-existing community of faith could have contained it without bursting - neither Jew nor Greek, Essene or Persian, Barbarian, Scythian, bond or free - not even the empire of Rome.

The New Testament materials are not ad hoc, individualistic productions of first century existentialists, cobbled together by a purely accidental community, driven solely by the winds of ordinary historical forces to a mythological land of religious make-believe - substantially decoupled from the historical phenomenon of Jesus of Nazareth. No. The apostolic community believed itself to be in possession of a unitary, living parable. They believed that as Hosea "acted out" his prophecy, so Jesus acted out his. And it was their responsibility and privilege to broker this parable to the world. But they would not be alone in this effort.

The parable originated in the mind of God and had been spoken into the world by the life of his Son - and it would be brought before the understanding of the disciples by the Spirit of the living God. Just as the logos was united with ordinary flesh, so the logos was united with ordinary historical processes which produced ordinary literary documents, filled with ordinary propositional language, which could be studied using ordinary literary analysis. If we say anything more or less than this, we say that God cannot speak in human language. And like rain in the desert that never touches the ground - it would have been better had he never spoken at all.

The New Testament corpus - if it is truly a unified revelation of God - is therefore not a random gaggle of humanistic religious sentiments that must be systematized by some Protestant philosophical scheme or "authenticated" by modern Liberal existentialism or canonized by any Roman Pope. If we are to fully confront a revelation from God, we must throw out these buffering schemes. We must let the historical documents and the historical setting for those documents speak for themselves - just as Jesus of Nazareth spoke for himself. We must let it be possible that God has not only spoken within each discrete gospel or letter, but that he has also spoken through the very arrangement of those literary instruments within a discernible, historical drama.

And we must allow, too, that the New Testament materials and the historical setting for those materials should not require a special charismatic or mystical experience to comprehend them. Though common sense is sometimes wrong, if the New Testament is a revelation from an omnipotent God, especially when it comes to communicating with his own creatures, we should expect that this revelation requires nothing more than the sense of a child - who intuitively understands that the wood is haunted, that the dog that has bitten him once will probably bite him again, and that the moon follows him wherever he goes.

We must also allow that just as Christ was incarnated into ordinary flesh and ordinary blood, so the Holy Spirit has been incarnated into ordinary flesh and blood. His body is a unitary, living organism - complete with its own logic, the logic of the cosmos - complete with its own authentication, the same authentication which authenticates our own reason – and, of course, any epistemology or language theory that we might make. The word of God incarnated as a literary organism is a sword coming from the mouth of God. It is quick and powerful and so sharp in its precision that we are bleeding before we know that we have been cut by it.

Just as the revelation to the world has been progressive and holistic, so is the revelation to the soul and the process of its salvation progressive and holistic. No one, for example, saw in that Arabian desert the process whereby the Spirit of revelation slowly dismantled the intransigent, rebellious mind-set of Saul - who would be called "Paul" - and replaced it, progressively, with the Christian Gospel. We must not think that it did not happen. If we think otherwise, we must deny the truths of human psychology and of our own consciousness and replace them with a mythical conversion theory that simply will not conform to the circumstantial evidence recorded in Acts. The Gospel of Paul did not fall from the sky - like the goddess Diana of Ephesus. *The Kingdom of God is within you*, Jesus said.[29] The everlasting Gospel works within, through the Holy Spirit, progressively and

---

[29] Luke 17:21b.

subversively casting down imaginations, and every high thing that exalts itself against the knowledge of God, inexorably bringing into captivity every thought to the obedience of Christ.

If we may take Paul's own theological system as autobiographical, we would be safe in assuming that Saul knew God, but he did not glorify him as God, neither was he thankful, at first, for the visitation and salvation of his Christ. As he had absorbed the orthodoxy of his day, he had become vain in his imagination, and his foolish heart had become darkened. Professing himself to be wise, he had become a fool. At some point, which Luke shows as a sudden conversion experience upon the road to Damascus, Paul is dramatically and completely converted. It is a complete catharsis. His letters unfold this complete change of mind – a change of mind so thorough that Paul refers to it as a crucifixion of his soul. He became dead to everything he once knew, and came alive again – in a spiritual resurrection – as a willing prisoner of Jesus Christ – a servant to his righteousness.

Yet however seemingly sudden the rising of the daystar in Paul's darkened consciousness, it was, after all, a progressive, comprehending motion of shadows in the mind - a process which saw a carnal child become a spiritual man. We should therefore expect to see development of ideas within the mind and letters of Paul - ideas which begin as hints, grow tentatively to assertions, then blossom maturely as strong aromatic convictions. We did not blush to watch this physical process at work with the infant Jesus - why should we blush when we see it happen in the spiritual process of the production of the New Testament materials? To say that there is progressive revelation in the pages of the New Testament is to say nothing more radical than that Jesus became a man.

And yet there were limits to Paul's spiritual manhood. He was quick to acknowledge them: *For now we see through a glass, darkly; but then face to face: now I know in part; but then shall I know even as also I am known.*[30] Thus as Paul begins to strain against the limits of his own apocalypse, we should expect to see a transitional, tapering off of clarity and a tendency to supply a human solution to an emergent unprofitability of mere milk. We thus read such things as: "I speak, not the Lord." "What if God?" "I speak as a man." We should therefore not be surprised to see a relatively rapid theological maturation process occur before our very eyes in the growing inter-relationship between Paul and other authors - where milk is gradually replaced with meat, and where the blood of "Christ crucified" matures into the aged wine of a fraternity of flesh with a High Priest after the order of Melchizedek.

---

[30] 1st Corinthians 13:12.

Likewise, if the New Testament corpus is truly the incarnation of the Holy Spirit, progressively revealed and inter-related symphonically, we should also expect to see a progressive, maturation in the very institutionalization of this corpus into human civilization. And we do see writings that were everywhere accepted without question, but also writings that were uncertain, doubtful and disputed. We should even expect to see writings that still cause considerable doubt. No matter, this is God's communication with the world. He neither stutters nor lisps.

Jesus himself needed no earthly interpreter or authentication - he simply said the words that his Father had put into his mouth. The writers of the New Testament materials all claim to be teaching the parable of Jesus to the world as God has commanded and as God has helped them to do. No more; no less. Just as Jesus claimed in John's writings: God is the interpreter of his own words. God is the authenticator of his own words. He needs no systematic theology or religious existentialism or ecclesiastical institution to flatter or defend them - or to reach out and steady them lest they "accidentally" fall upon uncanonical ground.

God is not the disenfranchised, effeminate fool of modern religious existentialism. He is strong and powerful and wise and kind. He does not need our help. If he were in need of our help, he would not tell us. God takes the weak and the broken and he binds them up and makes them strong. And our fiercest rebellion and most desperate limitations always play right into his hand. With merely ordinary human communication, he says precisely what he wills to say. He takes our ordinary words and utters things which have been kept secret before the world began. His words do not create meaning; they *are* meaning. And the word became flesh and dwelt among us.

Made in the USA
Columbia, SC
20 September 2020